MANAGING TERRORISM

New Titles from QUORUM BOOKS

The Uses of Psychiatry in the Law: A Clinical View of Forensic Psychiatry
WALTER BROMBERG

Abuse on Wall Street: Conflicts of Interest in the Securities Markets
THE TWENTIETH CENTURY FUND

The Politics of Taxation
THOMAS J. REESE

Modern Products Liability Law
RICHARD A. EPSTEIN

U.S. Multinationals and Worker Participation in Management: The American
Experience in the European Community
TON DEVOS

Our Stagflation Malaise: Ending Inflation and Unemployment
SIDNEY WEINTRAUB

Employee Stock Ownership and Related Plans: Analysis and Practice
TIMOTHY C. JOCHIM

Psychology and Professional Practice: The Interface of Psychology and the Law
FRANCIS R. J. FIELDS AND RUDY J. HORWITZ, EDITORS

American Court Management: Theories and Practices
DAVID J. SAARI

Budget Reform for Government: A Comprehensive Allocation and
Management System (CAMS)
MICHAEL BABUNAKIS

Railroads: The Free Enterprise Alternative
DANIEL L. OVERBEY

MANAGING TERRORISM

Strategies for the Corporate Executive

EDITED BY PATRICK J. MONTANA
AND
GEORGE S. ROUKIS

QUORUM BOOKS
WESTPORT, CONNECTICUT . LONDON, ENGLAND

Q

Acknowledgment

"Terrorism and the Media: Observations from the American and British Experiences," by Abraham H. Miller was originally published in *Clandestine Tactics and Technology* 8, no. 3 of the International Association of Chiefs of Police, Gaithersburg, Md., and is reprinted by permission.

Library of Congress Cataloging in Publication Data
Main entry under title:

Managing terrorism.

  Bibliography: p.
  Includes index.
  Contents: Growth and prevalence of
terrorism / Edward F. Mickolus — Economic and
political forces affecting terrorism / Phillip
A. Karber & R. W. Mengel — Psychological
forces affecting terrorism / Robert A.
Friedlander — [etc.]
  1. Terrorism—Addresses, essays, lectures.
2. Business enterprises—Security measures—Addresses, essays, lectures. I. Montana,
Patrick J. II. Roukis, George S.

HV6431.M36 1983 658.4'73 82-11224
ISBN 0-89930-013-8 (lib. bdg.)

Library of Congress Catalog Card Number: 82-11224
ISBN: 0-89930-013-8

First published in 1983 by Quorum Books

Greenwood Press
A division of Congressional Information Service, Inc.
88 Post Road West
Westport, Connecticut 06881

Printed in the United States of America

10 9 8 7 6 5 4 3 2 1

Contents

Figures

Tables

Introduction

The growth of international business during the past two decades has been phenomenal. It will continue to grow during the 1980s despite the recessionary conditions in the industrial countries. For American corporations, who will share in this growth, the benefits of expansion and profits will be offset to some degree by the dangers of terrorist activities. In recent years there has been an outpouring of books and articles on terrorism, which has been beneficial to the concerned and educated public, and a prolific group of experts have provided policymakers with the knowledge needed to make intelligent decisions. Their contributions have indeed been invaluable and one might say there is little to add to their prodigious research.

In reviewing the literature on terrorism, however, it became apparent that a book was needed for the business community. The book would have to provide the corporate executive with an in-depth understanding of the terrorist menace and also provide him or her with the practical tools to address its many manifestations. It would be more than a guide or a perfunctory how-to-do-it manual, but it would not be a pedantic treatise. It would serve a pragmatic purpose, namely, helping the corporate executive to assess the potential terrorist threat or crisis, if it should occur. It is for the executive's survival that we prepared this book.

Recognizing that it was important to understand the dimensions of the terrorist danger, we asked Edward F. Mickolus, a noted authority in the field, to develop a chapter on the growth and prevalence of terrorism. His findings indicate an alarming future. Not only is terrorism accelerating worldwide, it is being directed toward Americans with increasing frequency. Latin America, for example, is the most dangerous region for Americans at this time and accounts for most of the kidnapping of corporate executives. The extensive local undergrounds in these countries permit terrorist groups to kidnap foreign personnel, but more alarming is Mickolus's projection that terrorist groups will adapt better to corporate and government antiterrorist measures and he predicts the rise of a new generation of terrorists.

In the Phillip A. Karber and R. William Mengel article dealing with the economic and political forces affecting terrorism, the authors painstakingly develop the relationship between the types of political infrastructures and terrorist incidents and note that terrorism is becoming more discriminate in its targeting of civilians. Interestingly, it appears that once terrorism reaches this stage of violence, the ability of government to combat it is inversely related to the strength of democratic values. While political forces are the most significant factors determining the level and intensity of terrorist violence, Karber and Mengel recognize that economic reasons underlie terrorist attacks and show by example how the Italian Red Brigades target their attacks against corporate executives on behalf of the workers. This meticulous analysis of the salient forces affecting terrorism will assist the business executive in assessing the dangers confronting his or her organization in a foreign country. The Karber-Mengel chapter provides a comprehensible typology for risk analysis and is ably complemented by the excellent article written by Robert A. Friedlander, entitled, "Psychological Forces Affecting Terrorism."

Friedlander avers that politically or ideologically motivated terrorism constitutes the major terrorist threat to liberal, democratic, pluralistic society and identifies two kinds of political terrorists. The terrorist-liberationist or political successionist groups represented by the Palestine Liberation Organization (PLO), Irish Republican Army (IRA), or South-West Africa People's Organization (SWAPO) consider themselves as guerrilla soldiers engaged in military combat, while the nihilistic or anarchist terrorist groups focus their efforts on destroying an entire state structure. The latter type is invariably motivated by a distorted messianic idealism. Anonymity not only is the protective shield of political terrorists, it also characterizes their method of operation. As Friedlander points out, violence is the sine qua non of the terrorist trade, and the media is recognized as a valuable adjunct in conveying their message. His chapter provides the corporate executive with a realistic understanding of the terrorist mind set, which is a necessary prerequisite for effective planning. As we can readily see, naiveté has no place in terrorist assessment.

The chapter written by Charles A. Russell, "Businesses Becoming Increasing Targets," is more pointed. Business is the single largest category of activity targeted by terrorist groups today and the dangers unfortunately will increase. In 1980, 48.7 percent of 1,006 recorded bombings were directed against corporations. During the January 1979-June 1980 period, known losses suffered from bombing attacks totalled $165,013,800 of which more than 60 percent involved business targets. U.S. business losses alone amounted to $45,518,500. Between January 1, 1970 and June 30, 1981, ransom demands for kidnapped victims totalled $405,256,000 and known payments for their release totalled $156,666,400. These figures, however, represent only 32 percent of all recorded abductions. Direct attacks against corporate facilities were more costly. Based on 10 percent of the 2,510 facility attacks reported during 1970-1980, total dollar losses amounted to $224,333,502. In all 2,510 actions, 4,944 persons were killed and 2,911 were injured. These are discouraging statistics and the dangers, as Russell indicates, will not abate. He predicts that business firms will remain high on the priority list of terrorist groups and Latin America will remain the focal point for most attacks. However, more unsettling is the possibility that terrorists will attack electrical power plants, electrical transmission systems, telephone microwave communication systems, water purification facilities and petroleum pipelines, and pumping stations. If these attacks occur, then the power and communication system linking a nation's cities and economic centers will be severed. Russell's chapter is important reading since it provides concrete data on the terrorist threat and permits corporate executives the opportunity to determine potential dangers.

In the chapter by Joseph A. Malley, "Preparing and Protecting Personnel and Property Prior to a Terrorist Attack," the executive is provided a detailed policy framework for implementing a corporate security program. In a chapter divided into four sections, planning, management, personnel security, and property protection, Malley methodically shows how to prevent or deter acts of terrorist aggression, reduce personnel losses, and minimize property damage when an attack takes place and how to return to normalcy or recovery following such an incident. He provides practical how-to-do-it advice, which includes a sophisticated format for conducting a risk assessment analysis, and he identifies the components of a physical security program. A terrorist contingency plan, for example, would include an executive protection plan, a bomb protection plan, a fire plan, a disaster and emergency preparedness plan, and an evacuation plan. Since an executive suffers the risk of being kidnapped at home or while travelling to and from work, Malley develops the ingredients of an effective protection plan. Homes should be equipped with duress, fire, and intrusion detection alarm systems connected to and monitored by local police organizations. Background investigations should be conducted on all domestic help to ensure loyalty, and travel routes should be varied. At the corporate situs, property should be divided into security zones based on the relative importance of the building equipment to the organization's operation, and industrial plants should have back-up emergency power generator systems in the event of a terrorist attack. The importance of preparation cannot be understated and Malley's treatment of this vital subject is excellent and useful. If properly followed, it could save lives and property.

Abraham Miller, who is no stranger to the nation's cadre of terrorist experts, provides an illuminating analysis of terrorism and the media. In his chapter, entitled "Terrorism and the Media: Observations from the American and British Experience," Miller demonstrates that it is important for the media and law enforcement agencies to develop guidelines for handling terrorist incidents. While the media is concerned about getting firsthand, on-the-spot information of a terrorist attack, the police are concerned with containing, controlling, and terminating the terrorist incident. This dichotomy of purpose oftentimes leads to unnecessary conflict and endangers hostages. Drawing upon the British experience, Miller notes that the 1974 Prevention of Terrorist Act, which was directed against the IRA, made it a crime for a person not to come forward when he or she knowingly had information that would prevent an act of terrorism or lead to the arrest of a terrorist. The act, in effect, forced the police to regulate the media, but the commissioners of New Scotland Yard, Sir Robert Mark and his successor, Sir David McNee, followed a policy of cooperating with the media. They negotiated a gentlemen's agreement with the media, which now governs the media's reporting of terrorism, but it was not implemented without difficulty. When the Iranian Embassy was seized on April 30, 1980 and held for six days by seven Iranians, known as the Group of the Martyr, a BBC editor, recognizing a good story, took advantage of the opportunity to interview the main terrorist leader. Not only did he interfere with the negotiating process, and, in effect, endanger the hostages, but his intervention was compounded when British Independent TV aired on television live coverage of the Special Air Services assault on the embassy. The decision to transmit was made at the scene. Fortunately, a BBC journalist who was called to speak to a BBC newsman held hostage at the embassy decided not to publish the captors' demand that Arab ambassadors be called to mediate between the terrorists and the police. The police with the approval of the British prime minister were not inclined to comply with that demand and the journalist respected that decision. While the above incidents indicate that problems will inevitably occur under such circumstances, the British experience still provides a model for the United States to follow. In particular, it is necessary for corporations to join in the dialogue between the media and law enforcement agencies to make certain that a workable understanding is reached that benefits and protects all parties. Corporate executives are increasingly subject to terrorist activities and their input into the policy process should be welcomed. This is especially true when an executive is kidnapped. The efforts of the corporate crisis management team and the police and media should be effectively coordinated to ensure that a terrorist incident is properly managed.

In the chapter by George S. Roukis, "Negotiating with Terrorists," Roukis provides a realistic assessment of the terrorist negotiating drama. His focus is on the hostage, who must adapt, however unpleasantly, with the captive environment. Since the police and government security forces are usually trained to contain and negotiate with terrorists at a barricade location, unprotected kidnapped corporate executives must rely on their own resources to save their lives. Distinguishing hostage negotiations from the institutionalized ritual known as collective bargaining, Roukis emphasizes that the hostage must attempt to cooperate with the captors. This does not mean that the captured executive must identify with the terrorists, but he or she must not become competitive. The evidence shows that cooperative bargaining strategies work best with terrorists, when corporate executives are held hostage. Admittedly, understanding the dynamics of a hostage environment is not enough to allay the emotional distress an executive experiences when kidnapped, but it is possible to simulate this milieu and train high-risk executives how to cope with it.

Similarly, what are the effects of terrorism on business operations? We know that terrorist actions against business will increase during the 1980s and the Malley, Miller, and Roukis chapters provide practical information on how to deal with these contingencies. In a well-written chapter by Eleanor S. Wainstein and Susanna W. Purnell, the authors note that terrorist attacks have their impact on business operations and at times are costly. Several law suits have been filed in U.S. courts against firms which raise the issue of corporate responsibility toward an employee before and during a kidnapping event, but there have been no dispositive rulings thus far. By and large, corporations have accepted responsibility for the safety of their employees, which necessitates organizational changes and costly security measures, but these costs must be balanced against the higher costs of a terrorist incident. For smaller firms, however, the costs of securing their operations from terrorist attacks are prohibitive. For larger firms, which can afford these protective measures, the sudden removal of a highly trained executive or technician because of a probable attack could incur losses. If the local replacement is not fully prepared to assume the vacated position, it could penalize operations. More often the company's handling of a kidnapping crisis might strain relations with the local government. The corporation understandably is willing to negotiate directly with the terrorist group and, pressured by the victim's family, begins back-door negotiations with the captors. Sometimes the firm's direct negotiations with the terrorists reflect a lack of confidence in the ability of the local government to manage the crisis and this leads to exacerbated relations. Family social life is curtailed in high-risk places as there are few safe public places for the family to go. This not only affects the morale and stability of the family, but it could affect the executive's professional performance. The effects of terrorism on business costs and productivity are high and corporations should learn how to minimize and control them.

In the chapter by Patrick J. Montana and Stacey M. Krinsky, we have for the first time a listing of the major organizations serving the executive protection field. The authors provide a detailed justification for the use of security services and delineate the major organizations serving the corporate world. The types of services offered by these firms are carefully reviewed, and the telephone numbers and addresses of their senior officers are made available. We believe this is an important chapter for a book on managing the terrorist threat, since it provides a compendium of sources for the interested corporation to consult. Depending on the company's individual needs, there are specialist organizations to serve them. As the evidence so persuasively shows, terrorism will increase in the 1980s and business will be the priority target. Bombings, kidnappings, and attacks against vital facilities will continue making it difficult to administer our foreign subsidiaries. The tragedy in El Salvador shows us what can happen when terrorism and revolutionary warfare brings an economy to a standstill, and we must be mindful of these consequences. We might not also be able to prevent the hostile takeover of a country friendly to our business interests, but we can reduce the disquiet and insecurity of potential terrorist threats if we know how to manage the problem.

This book was purposely written to serve the corporate executive threatened by terrorist actions, and we are confident that we have provided him or her with the understandings and tools needed to combat this scourge. By carefully preparing for a terrorist incident and developing the myriad of complementary contingency plans, the corporate executive, as is true to this calling, can ably manage the threat. If executives are objective and systematic in protective planning and calculate objectively the management of this phenomena, they can reduce the risks and costs significantly and enhance the benefits required.

MANAGING
TERRORISM

Tracking the Growth and Prevalence of International Terrorism

EDWARD F. MICKOLUS

The scourge of international terrorism has become one of the major policy concerns for governments in recent years. On any given day, the world's newspapers and electronic communications media herald new episodes of the assassination of government leaders, sabotage of critical facilities, bombing of embassies and foreign corporate installations, assaults on military bases, skyjackings, kidnappings of diplomats and business executives, and the takeover of embassies and holding of their staffs for ransoms. Growing global interdependence, sophisticated communications and transportation networks, and facilitation by sympathetic patron states and like-minded organizations have all contributed to the empirical and popularly perceived rise in transnational mugging.

Predicting the likely evolution of this phenomenon and devising adequate countermeasures for potential targets requires an examination of the patterns in terrorist behavior we have seen in the past decade. This study will discuss recent trends in terrorist attacks, selection of victims and sites, and the responses of their chosen adversaries.[1]

The Scope of Inquiry: Definitions and Typologies

That terrorism is in the eye of the beholder has become a truism for students of the subject. "Terrorism" is what someone else does. Incidents considered terrorist by beleagured pariah states are viewed by many radical regimes as the legitimate acts of freedom fighters. Indeed, it has become so hard to satisfy all the governments of the world that in the United Nations one does not officially discuss "international terrorism" but rather Item 92: Measures to Prevent International Terrorism Which Endangers or Takes Innocent Human Lives or Jeopardizes Fundamental Freedoms, and Study of the Underlying Causes of Those Forms of Terrorism and Acts of Violence Which Lie in Misery, Frustration, Grievance and Despair, and Which Cause Some People to Sacrifice Human Lives, Including Their Own, in an Attempt to Effect Radical Changes.

We shall avoid becoming stuck in the value-laden morass of considering motivations in our definition, and instead define international terrorism as the use, or threat of use, of anxiety-inducing extranormal violence for political purposes by any individual or group, whether acting for, or in opposition to, established governmental authority, when such action is intended to influence the attitudes and behavior of a target group wider than the immediate victims and when, through the nationality or foreign ties of its perpetrators, its location, the nature of its institutional or human victims, or the mechanics of its resolution, its ramifications transcend national boundaries. We can further distinguish international terrorism from other forms of violence by noting that *interstate* terrorism is such action (as described above) when carried out by individuals or groups controlled by a sovereign state. Examples include assassinations of exiled Libyan dissidents by Tripoli's hit squads, and the Iranian government's support for the takeover of the U.S. embassy. *International* terrorism is such action when carried out by basically autonomous nonstate actors, whether or not they enjoy some degree of support from sympathetic states. Such acts include the kidnappings of foreign businessmen and diplomats and the hijacking of international flights. *Domestic* terrorism has the aforementioned characteristics of extranormal violence, but does not involve nationals of more than one state. It is the domestic parallel to international terrorism, in that it is carried on by basically autonomous nonstate actors but only affects citizens of one state. Attacks by the IRA upon the civilian population in Northern Ireland fit this category. *State* terrorism is conducted by a national government within the borders of that state and is the domestic parallel of interstate terrorism. Examples include genocide in Nazi Germany and incidents of torture in police states. Our typology is graphically illustrated in Table 1-1. Forms of nonpolitical terrorism, such as criminal and psychopathic acts, will not be covered in our discussion.

TABLE 1-1.
Types of Political Terrorism
Source: Central Intelligence Agency.

		Direct involvement of nationals of more than one state?	
		Yes	No
Government controlled	Yes	Interstate	State
or directed?	No	International	Domestic

International terrorism is often described as violence for effect. Strategically, it differs from conventional war by not intending to secure territory via military engagement. It instead seeks to give the impression that the numerically weak terrorist group can strike anywhere and is, therefore, stronger than the government.

Annual Trends

Terrorist incidents generally take one of two forms: (1) incidents in which the terrorists attempt to injure or kill individuals and/or damage or destroy property, and (2) incidents in which individuals are taken hostage, and destruction of property and injury to the hostages are conditional upon the response of a target group to the demands of the perpetrators. Table 1-2 examines the frequencies of several types of actions in the terrorist repertoire designed to lead to these two effects.

Kidnapping occurs when a diplomat, businessman, or other victim is taken to an underground hideout and held until a monetary ransom is paid, prisoners are released, the group's manifesto is published, or some other demanded action is carried out. Barricade and hostage situations include incidents in which the terrorists seize one or more hostages but make no attempt to leave the original scene of the crime. Negotiations are carried on with the perpetrators themselves effectively being held hostage, unable to leave the scene at their choosing. Such scenarios frequently occur at the end of an incident in which the seizure of hostages was not the terrorists' primary aim, for example, a bank holdup in which the robbers were discovered by the authorities before they were able to escape, with the group seizing any hostages who happened to be handy, or an attack on an airport lounge or residence, in which hostages are seized as pawns to be used to secure free passage away from the site of the murders.

Hijackings involve the alteration of the direction of an airline flight due to actions by the terrorist. We can distinguish between those situations in which the hijacker is merely seeking a means of transportation to a nation giving him or her asylum ("Take this plane to Cuba"); situations in which the hijackers force the pilot to land the plane, release the crew and passengers, and blow up the plane without making any ransom demands (engaged in for the shock value of the action); and incidents in which the hijackers make specific demands upon governments or corporations, threatening the safety of the passengers and crew.[2] Hijackings may involve any form of transportation, including planes, trains, ships, and automotive vehicles.[3]

Bombing involves the attempt, whether successful or unsuccessful, to explode a device that will cause some amount of damage. Timing mechanisms are usually employed, and the incident is not considered part of a general armed assault. Incendiary bombing involves the attempt to set afire a

TABLE 1-2.
International Terrorist Incidents,
1968-1980, by Category of Attack
Source: Central Intelligence Agency.

	1968	1969	1970	1971	1972	1973	1974	1975	1976	1977	1978	1979	1980	Total [a]
Total	**142** (2.1)	**214** (3.2)	**391** (5.8)	**324** (4.8)	**648** (9.7)	**564** (8.4)	**528** (7.9)	**475** (7.1)	**599** (8.9)	**562** (8.4)	**850** (12.7)	**657** (9.8)	**760** (11.3)	**6,714**
Kidnapping	1	6	43	30	16	45	43	57	34	40	39	30	17	**401** (6.0)
Barricade-hostage	1	0	8	1	4	13	13	16	6	11	19	16	31	**139** (2.1)
Letter bombing	3	4	5	1	306	58	18	5	15	17	12	23	3	**470** (7.0)
Incendiary bombing	12	25	56	46	22	47	48	42	119	110	128	53	45	**753** (11.2)
Explosive bombing	79	115	119	129	148	168	274	232	216	210	235	219	227	**2,371** (35.3)
Armed attacks	12	13	8	9	13	16	31	21	21	21	40	22	51	**278** (4.1)
Hijacking [b]	3	12	24	10	16	7	10	5	6	9	6	29	36	**173** (2.6)
Assassination	7	12	22	13	16	25	16	23	53	33	54	61	107	**442** (6.6)
Sabotage	1	2	0	4	4	3	4	1	2	0	0	3	0	**24** (0.4)
Exotic pollution	0	0	0	0	0	1	0	0	0	0	17	3	1	**22** (0.3)
Threat	12	12	61	53	77	132	32	34	81	67	234	96	117	**1,008** (15.0)
Theft, break-in	3	7	22	10	5	3	10	8	6	2	13	4	14	**107** (1.6)
Conspiracy	4	4	7	2	3	21	14	9	7	6	16	13	15	**121** (1.8)
Hoax	0	0	2	1	0	0	0	0	2	0	0	5	48	**58** (0.9)
Other actions	0	0	4	8	8	3	9	10	7	11	17	20	20	**117** (1.7)
Sniping	3	2	7	3	6	4	3	10	18	12	17	44	23	**152** (2.3)
Shootout with police	0	0	1	0	0	2	0	1	3	6	0	0	3	**16** (0.2)
Arms smuggling	1	0	2	4	4	16	3	1	3	7	3	16	2	**62** (0.9)

[a] Figures in parentheses are percentages of the total accounted for by each category of attack.
[b] Includes hijackings by means of air, sea, or land transport.

selected installation. Molotov cocktails and arsons are included in this category rather than in the explosives type. Letter bombs are devices that are sent through the mails and are intended to explode when attempts are made to open the envelope. They range in size from a large parcel to a first-class letter.

Armed attacks involve assaults upon facilities using missiles, hand-held weapons, grenades, thrown bombs, and/or incendiary devices. They range from machine gun and grenade assaults upon airport lounges to storming of an embassy. Assassination involves the attempt to kill a specific individual for political purposes.[4] Sabotage entails the attempted damage of facilities by means other than explosives or incendiary devices. Exotic pollution includes attacks involving nuclear, chemical, or biological agents intended to cause harm or contaminate and make unfit for use. Threats involve warnings to commit any terrorist act, but which for whatever reason is not carried out. Theft or break-in involves the forcible entry of facilities and an illegal attempt to acquire money or documents from the installation. The robbery of individuals by political terrorists is also included here. Conspiracy involves the apparent planning to commit any form of these terrorist acts, but which ultimately does not come to fruition. Sniping involves taking shots at a facility or crowd without the apparent intention of harming any specific individual. Shootouts with police involve only those incidents that occur when a policeman is making an otherwise routine arrest. Gun battles at the end of any other type of terrorist incident are classified according to that type of incident, rather than as a shootout.

During the past thirteen years, kidnapping was easily the most frequent hostage incident, although it is declining after its mid-1970s peak. Barricade-and-hostage operations may have taken their place. Moreover, terrorists have become more adept at successfully seizing a hostage. Hijackings have an inverse relationship to kidnappings. Security improvements made in 1973, as well as the unwillingness of countries to grant asylum to hijackers, made this type of incident a comparative rarity. However, hijackers adapted their tactics (although with a lag time much longer than that recorded for other types of terrorist incidents) to these countermeasures. Pilots tend to give the individual claiming to be armed the benefit of the doubt, despite the elaborate x-ray and body-search precautions taken before boarding. Thus, we have seen a dramatic rise in hijackings in the last two years.

Although the better-known terrorist groups have demonstrated an aptitude for the careful planning and coordination required for spectacular hostage-taking operations, the cost of such endeavors is high. One must be a dedicated full-time terrorist to mount such attacks. The vast majority of those engaging in terrorist incidents could be viewed as delving into a part-time hobby rather than a full-time profession. Hence, low-level attacks constitute the vast majority of reported operations. Particularly noteworthy is the ranking, as well as the rise, in bombings, arson, and murder, which are low-risk, not time-consuming, and do not involve the perpetrators in immediate confrontation with authorities but nonetheless have symbolic effect.

Similarly, terrorists infrequently resort to weapons or tactics involving technological sophistication, despite repeated warnings in the press and popular fiction about the consequences of such potential actions. Rifles, pipe bombs, and Molotov cocktails, easily acquired and handled, will remain far more popular with terrorists than a homemade atomic bomb.

Simple bombings are the most frequent type of destructive acts, constituting a continuing threat to embassies, consulates, and corporation facilities. In recent years, terrorists have become more indiscriminate in the timing and location of their bombings, and many innocent civilians have become victims. Letter bombs peaked in 1972 and 1973 with a wave of bombings by Irish and Palestinian groups, rather than a worldwide phenomenon conducted by many organizations. Most bombs apparently are sent from the same post office on the same day to targets around the world. Because of their general unreliability in successfully harming the chosen victim (many letter bombs are intercepted by police or explode in post offices, injuring innocent workers and leading to negative publicity for the terrorists) as well as the technical sophistication required to make them, other terrorist groups do not use letter bombs.

Armed attacks and assassinations follow a slowly rising cyclical trend—1980 set annual records in both categories. Sabotage and exotic pollution remain comparatively rare.

In general, we experience a two-year cycle of terrorist incidents worldwide, with the total gradually rising. Excluding threats, 1980 was the worst year in history in terms of numbers of international terrorist attacks recorded. This gloomy conclusion is paralleled by statistics on casualties, (Table 1-3 and Figure 1-1), in which 1980 set records for numbers of casualties and of incidents involving casualties. When methods have proven too difficult to engage in or are relatively ineffective, terrorists change their tactics to satisfy their goals. Unfortunately, these methods involve a great probability of injury or death to victims.

Geographic Trends

Conventional wisdom argues that most terrorism occurs in emerging less developed nations.[5] Although this may be true for cases of domestic terrorism, this does not seem to be correct when analyzing international terrorism. Nearly one-half of the incidents reported in the last thirteen years have occurred in Westernized, highly affluent nations (Tables 1-4 and 1-5).[6] The United States alone experiences more international terrorist bombings and hijackings than several continents combined. Discounting the inflationary effects of the letter bomb and threat figures, international terrorism

TABLE 1-3.
Deaths and Injuries Due to International
  Terrorist Attacks, 1968-1980*
Source: Central Intelligence Agency.

	Number Wounded	**Number Killed**
1968	**208**	**35**
1969	**202**	**64**
1970	**212**	**131**
1971	**227**	**36**
1972	**413**	**157**
1973	**551**	**127**
1974	**1,100**	**344**
1975	**748**	**276**
1976	**920**	**415**
1977	**461**	**261**
1978	**690**	**442**
1979	**664**	**738**
1980	**1,078**	**642**

*Casualty figures are particularly susceptible to fluctuations due to inclusion of especially bloody incidents.

FIGURE 1-1.
International Terrorist Incidents That Caused Casualties, 1968-1980
Source: Central Intelligence Agency.

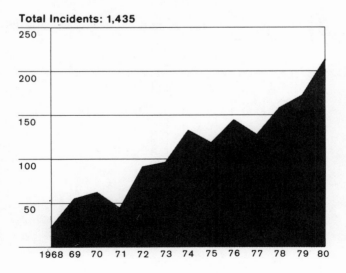

Total Incidents: 1,435

TABLE 1-4.

Geographic Distribution of International Terrorist Incidents, 1968-1980, by Category of Attack

Source: Central Intelligence Agency.

	North America	Latin America	Western Europe	USSR/ Eastern Europe	Sub- Saharan Africa	Middle East/North Africa	Asia	Pacific	Other	Total
Total	**674** **(10.0)**	**1,446** **(21.5)**	**2,206** **(32.9)**	**62** **(0.9)**	**218** **(3.2)**	**1,382** **(20.6)**	**495** **(7.4)**	**56** **(0.8)**	**176** **(2.6)**	**6,714**
Kidnapping	5	203	47	0	61	57	25	1	2	**401**
Barricade-hostage	8	51	38	2	2	33	4	0	1	**139**
Letter bombing	26	17	200	0	15	32	131	0	49	**470**
Incendiary bombing	85	101	390	3	6	113	36	7	12	**753**
Explosive bombing	325	496	859	16	28	489	96	16	46	**2,371**
Armed attack	4	54	52	1	23	122	21	0	1	**278**
Hijacking [a]	29	35	30	3	11	38	21	0	6	**173**
Assassination	29	94	140	2	27	111	34	3	3	**443**
Sabotage	2	3	8	0	2	8	1	0	0	**24**
Exotic pollution	0	0	21	0	0	1	0	0	0	**22**
Threat	99	228	275	29	21	240	78	27	11	**1,008**
Theft, break-in	4	56	19	1	7	17	3	0	0	**107**
Conspiracy	9	17	36	1	4	30	9	1	14	**121**
Hoax	18	10	10	0	1	6	11	0	2	**58**
Other actions	12	10	39	1	5	22	13	0	14	**116**
Sniping	17	63	15	1	3	42	10	1	0	**152**
Shootout with police	0	8	6	0	0	1	0	0	1	**16**
Arms smuggling	2	0	20	2	2	20	2	0	14	**62**

[a] Includes hijackings by means of air, sea, or land transport.

TABLE 1-5.
Geographic Distribution of International
Terrorist Incidents, 1968-1980
Source: Central Intelligence Agency.

	1968	1969	1970	1971	1972	1973	1974	1975	1976	1977	1978	1979	1980	Total [a]
Total	**142** (2.1)	**214** (3.2)	**391** (5.8)	**324** (4.8)	**648** (9.7)	**564** (8.4)	**528** (7.9)	**475** (7.1)	**599** (8.9)	**562** (8.4)	**850** (12.7)	**657** (9.8)	**760** (11.3)	**6,714**
North America	42	10	28	46	19	42	53	83	60	59	78	63	90	**673 (10.0)**
Latin America	47	82	163	102	113	122	140	74	143	73	112	97	178	**1,446 (21.5)**
Western Europe	24	41	86	53	239	243	188	170	252	263	245	198	204	**2,206 (32.9)**
USSR/Eastern Europe	3	1	3	10	2	3	2	3	6	6	10	6	7	**62 (0.9)**
Sub-Saharan Africa	1	9	15	6	6	11	14	27	18	31	27	24	29	**218 (3.2)**
Middle East and North Africa	20	36	61	60	71	89	82	88	92	87	302	199	195	**1,382 (20.6)**
Asia	1	22	28	40	153	30	22	22	23	21	31	56	46	**495 (7.4)**
Pacific	1	6	2	3	3	2	1	4	0	7	21	3	3	**56 (0.8)**
Other	3	7	5	4	42	22	26	4	5	15	24	11	8	**176 (2.6)**

[a] Figures in parentheses are percentages of the totals.

11

is very infrequent in the developing countries of Asia and Africa. Attacks in Eastern Europe are rare. The region experiences only sporadic hijackings by asylum seekers. Latin America ranks ahead of the Middle East in incident frequency. Arab terrorists do not have preferred targets on their home soil — there are no Israeli diplomatic or military installations available — and so do not engage in certain types of incidents to the extent that one would otherwise expect. Rather, they have resorted to overseas operations requiring small teams. Latin groups, on the other hand, use their extensive local undergrounds to engage in elaborate kidnappings of foreign personnel. Hence, logistic constraints can rule out the imitation of tactics of other groups.[7]

Although many nations' citizens suffered in one or two incidents, Westernized, industrialized nations are the most frequent targets of attacks. Citizens of the United States have been the victims in nearly 40 percent of all events, with the British also facing a serious security problem. Asia and Africa remain relatively untouched by international terrorism. East European nations have been relatively safe when one discounts hijackings by domestic dissidents. The immunity of the latter may be due to their verbal and material support of many of the contemporary terrorist groups. In the Middle East, Israeli citizens are the most harassed. The more moderate regimes in the Arab-Israeli conflict also find themselves singled out for attack. Palestinian terrorists are also frequently ambushed.[8] Latin Americans frequently attack non-Latins, particularly those perceived to be rich capitalists. Overall, nationals of the poorer nations who are victimized are most often ambassadors or managers of multinational corporate subsidiaries. Hence, although no one country is perfectly safe from terrorist attack, the problem is primarily one for Westernized, capitalist nations (Figure 1-2).

The U.S. Experience

After a comparative lull in the mid-1970s in attacks on American citizens overseas, anti-U.S. attacks have reached record levels (Table 1-6). Bombings and unfulfilled threats are by far the preferred method of operation for anti-American groups, accounting for more than half of all incidents. Incendiary bombings, principally as a form of nonlethal political graffiti, is also often reported against American official vehicles.

Diplomats and businessmen have traded places over the last thirteen years as the principal U.S. victims of terrorism (Table 1-7), with the former presently in ascendancy. Publicity for the seizure of the U.S. embassy in Tehran, allegations of U.S. complicity in the attack on Mecca, and resort to new tactics may account for this shift.

Unlike the case of international terrorism in general, Latin America has been the most dangerous area for Americans (Table 1-8), with the Middle East and Western Europe virtually tied for second place.

FIGURE 1-2.
Nationality of Victims of International Terrorist Attacks, 1968-1980
Source: Central Intelligence Agency.

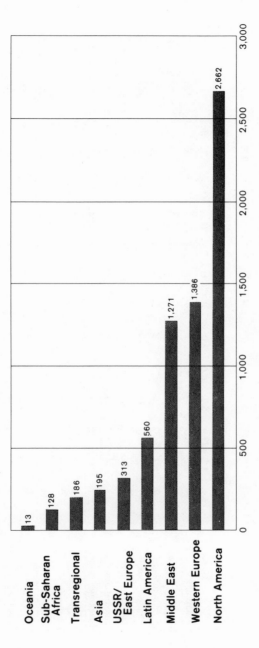

TABLE 1-6.

International Terrorist Attacks on U.S. Citizens or Property, 1968-1980, by Category of Attack

Source: Central Intelligence Agency.

	1968	1969	1970	1971	1972	1973	1974	1975	1976	1977	1978	1979	1980	Total [a]
Total	71 (2.4)	124 (4.2)	266 (9.0)	243 (8.2)	255 (8.6)	237 (8.0)	216 (7.3)	181 (6.1)	231 (7.8)	195 (6.6)	396 (13.4)	256 (8.7)	278 (9.4)	2,949
Kidnapping	1	3	25	19	5	23	14	23	8	7	8	8	10	154 (5.2)
Barricade-hostage	1	0	4	0	1	3	2	1	2	3	0	6	7	30 (1.0)
Letter bombing	2	1	2	0	29	3	1	0	4	7	0	4	2	55 (1.9)
Incendiary bombing	12	21	46	42	18	30	31	17	56	58	80	29	23	463 (15.7)
Explosive bombing	35	71	87	100	97	74	127	95	65	70	95	93	72	1,081 (36.7)
Armed attack	1	4	3	5	10	8	6	7	8	5	12	10	11	90 (3.0)
Hijacking[b]	1	5	12	4	4	0	1	2	5	4	3	15	20	76 (2.5)
Assassination	3	3	10	2	4	4	2	8	15	6	7	10	19	93 (3.2)
Sabotage	0	0	0	3	3	1	0	1	1	0	0	1	0	10 (0.3)
Threat	11	12	51	51	71	77	19	19	53	22	161	47	50	644 (21.8)
Theft, break-in	0	3	15	8	1	3	4	3	1	0	7	4	13	62 (2.1)
Conspiracy	1	0	2	2	1	2	4	3	1	2	4	3	6	31 (1.1)
Hoax	0	0	1	0	0	0	0	0	0	0	0	1	25	27 (0.9)
Other actions	0	0	3	5	7	2	2	1	4	2	11	3	10	50 (1.7)
Sniping	2	1	5	2	3	0	3	1	6	8	7	20	9	67 (2.3)
Shootout with police	0	0	0	0	0	0	0	0	2	1	0	0	1	4 (0.1)
Arms smuggling	1	0	0	0	1	7	0	0	0	0	1	2	0	12 (0.4)

a Figures in parentheses are percentages of the total accounted for by each category.

b Includes hijacking by means of air, sea, or land transport.

14

TABLE 1-7.
International Terrorist Attacks on U.S. Citizens or Property, 1968-1980, by Category of Citizen
Source: Central Intelligence Agency.

	1968	1969	1970	1971	1972	1973	1974	1975	1976	1977	1978	1979	1980	Total [a]
Total	**68** **(2.4)**	**124** **(4.3)**	**262** **(9.1)**	**243** **(8.5)**	**248** **(8.7)**	**225** **(7.9)**	**197** **(6.9)**	**179** **(6.3)**	**227** **(7.9)**	**193** **(6.7)**	**386** **(13.5)**	**241** **(8.4)**	**271** **(9.5)**	2,864
Diplomatic officials or property	21	26	96	97	92	78	27	23	38	42	63	90	112	**805** **(28.1)**
Military officials or property	6	15	44	45	28	29	22	30	63	58	48	38	30	**456** **(15.9)**
Other US Government officials or property	30	37	63	34	43	10	18	20	6	9	23	16	35	**344** **(12.0)**
Business facilities or executives	8	37	38	57	57	89	108	72	90	60	151	68	66	**901** **(31.5)**
Private citizens	3	9	21	10	28	19	22	34	30	24	101	29	27	**357** **(12.5)**

[a] Figures in parentheses are percentages of the total accounted for by each category.

TABLE 1-8.
Locations of Terrorist Attacks on U.S. Citizens or Property, 1968-1980, by Category
Source: Central Intelligence Agency.

	North America	Latin America	Western Europe	USSR/ Eastern Europe	Sub- Saharan Africa	Middle East/North Africa	Asia	Pacific	Other	Total
Total	**282**	**854**	**691**	**29**	**76**	**692**	**245**	**32**	**48**	**2,949**
Kidnapping	2	92	3	0	22	27	7	0	1	**154**
Barricade-hostage	3	10	4	0	0	12	1	0	0	**30**
Letter bombing	13	6	2	0	2	4	26	0	2	**55**
Incendiary bombing	42	78	212	1	3	91	27	6	3	**463**
Explosive bombing	146	334	260	4	8	236	69	4	20	**1,081**
Armed attack	0	32	13	0	8	26	11	0	0	**90**
Hijacking [a]	27	6	14	0	0	6	9	0	4	**66**
Assassination	5	37	6	0	7	26	11	0	1	**93**
Sabotage	0	1	1	0	2	6	0	0	0	**10**
Threat	36	167	139	22	13	194	51	20	2	**644**
Theft, break-in	1	38	6	0	7	9	1	0	0	**62**
Conspiracy	4	8	4	0	0	8	3	1	3	**31**
Hoax	0	5	8	0	0	3	10	0	1	**27**
Other actions	0	6	15	1	1	15	8	0	4	**50**
Sniping	1	29	2	1	0	25	8	1	0	**67**
Shootout with police	0	4	0	0	0	0	0	0	0	**4**
Arms smuggling	0	0	2	0	0	3	0	0	7	**12**

[a] Includes hijackings by means of air or land transport.

External Support for Terrorist Groups

Contacts between terrorist groups and sympathetic governments have in recent years become a major concern of U.S. foreign policy. The Reagan administration considers its eradication a cornerstone of its foreign policy, with the Soviet-terrorist connection of particular concern. The Central Intelligence Agency (CIA) recently concluded that

> The Soviets are deeply engaged in support of revolutionary violence, which is a fundamental element of Leninist ideology. Such violence frequently entails acts of international terrorism. The ostensible position of the Soviets that they oppose terrorism while supporting so-called national liberation movements is further compromised by Moscow's close relationship with and aid to a number of governments and organizations which are direct supporters of purely terrorist groups. In the Middle East, for example, the Soviets sell large quantities of arms to Libya—knowing that Libya is a major supporter of terrorist groups—and they back a number of Palestinian groups that have conducted terrorist operations. In Latin America, Moscow relies heavily on Cuba—which provides guerrilla and terrorist groups with training, arms, sanctuary, and advice—to advance Soviet interests. In other parts of the world, particularly Africa, the Soviets have long supported guerrilla movements and national liberation organizations that occasionally engage in terrorism.[9]

Radical Arab regimes, North Korea, and East European governments have also given forms of aid to international terrorist groups. Some governments may believe that conventional warfare has become too expensive and that hiring mercenary terrorist groups to disrupt enemy societies is far cheaper and permits the government to deny involvement in the terrorist action.[10]

What is far more disturbing to many are the contacts between terrorist groups. Palestinians have apparently trained Latin Americans, members of the Red Army Faction of West Germany, members of the Irish Republican Army, and Japanese anarchists. Latin groups that have acquired fantastic ransoms[11] reportedly have shared their booty with less affluent, but possibly more violent, smaller groups. Such groups have held worldwide meetings, conducted joint operations, and engaged in operations designed to secure the release from prison of members of their own and other organizations. No "Terrorism Incorporated" directs or even coordinates the activities of the world's terrorists—the goals and personalities of terrorists are too diverse. However, if such trends continue, and terrorists can rely upon each other for funding, training, arms, and technical skills, they may develop a greater autonomy from their current nation-state mentors and not be subject to whatever restraints are now placed upon their activities by these nations. More spectacular, grisly incidents (some of which we may already be seeing) may be the result.

Effects of Terrorism

Terrorists have experienced a wide range of success and failure in achieving their myriad short- and long-term goals.

Strategically, some groups aspire to control of the apparatus of the state. Although no campaign of terrorism by itself has ever led to the fall of a government, the independence of Algeria and Israel can be attributed in part to pressure on colonial authorities by the sustained attacks of the Algerian National Liberation Front (FLN) and Irgun, respectively. Other groups seek policy changes, such as greater autonomy for a province of the country or increased wages for workers.

At a tactical level, terrorists have sought changes in sentences, elimination of torture, or the outright release of specified political prisoners, including members of their own bands. Monetary ransoms and extortion payments have also been demanded.

Terrorism has been overwhelmingly effective in securing publicity. Dramatic actions attract sensation-seeking media coverage, giving a false impression of terrorist strength and government impotence. Terrorists aim at embarrassing the government and corporations viewed as exploiters by releasing damaging information secured in interrogation of hostages and by theft of documents, as well as by cleverly maneuvering hostage negotiations. Terrorists also use such media coverage as a forum for expounding their political views, frequently demanding the publication of the group's manifesto as well as granting interviews to press reporters.

The type of terrorist action and the government's response affect the amount and kind of publicity given to the incident. For example, formerly dramatic embassy bombings are now commonplace and are given little attention. In some regions even indiscriminate bombings of civilians have become a tacitly accepted hazard of everyday living. In order to again capture the headlines, groups may feel forced to develop innovative schemes, such as embassy takeovers. However, with the advent of paramilitary rescue squads, even the drama of the barricade scenario may become a passing fad. Terrorists may soon be forced to devise a new incident model to gain attention.

Responding to the Terrorist Threat

Unfortunately, the global response to international attacks has been feeble. The UN General Assembly has been mired in definitional debates, and its conventions grapple with only certain types of incidents. Many states that support terrorist groups have refused to ratify these conventions. Effective sanctions against states who disregard the prosecute-or-extradite clauses of the conventions have not been created. Finally, the conventions deal with response, not prevention.[12]

Like-minded nations have developed bilateral treaties, such as the successful United States-Cuba antihijacking agreement. Extension of such treaties region-wise is hampered by asylum traditions. Government leaders recognize that they may be requesting asylum after the next coup. Hence, proposals to ban the granting of asylum to political offenders (either the terrorists instigating the action or the prisoners whose release is demanded) are resisted.

Unilateral measures have met varying degrees of success in fulfilling the government's task of demonstrating that official duties to society can be carried out in the face of the terrorist threat and decreasing whatever influence the terrorists have. Five strategies, at times employed simultaneously are often seen.

First, the government can work with the press to alter public perceptions of the terrorists. This can range from a complete ban on the reporting of terrorist actions (exemplified by Argentina in 1976), to a ban on the use of the name of the terrorist group (as occurred in Uruguay during the height of the Tupamaros' activities), to more subtle methods. These can include "black propaganda" (placing in the press a story falsely attributed to terrorist authorship, which puts the group in a bad light), or falsely reporting terrorist actions. Such types of responses frequently misfire, leading to greater support for the revolutionaries. Other governments have attempted to work with the press by explaining an incident's unfolding, thereby lessening counterproductive speculation. The government can also caution the press against revealing possible government plans during an event, such as reporting the movement of extra troops to a barricaded area in preparation for a surprise attack.

Second, the government can aim at deterring particular types of incidents. Elaborate preflight searches have eliminated hijacking of El Al flights. Full-scale armed attacks by large groups of terrorists are at times the only way in which a head of state can be assassinated.[13] Such manpower resources are luxuries not available to many violence-prone groups. Those unwilling to risk death will channel their talents into less dangerous operations.

Third, the government can refuse to give in to terrorist demands. This makes the perpetrators appear powerless as time drags on, and the terrorists often surrender without harming their hostages. However, many governments that have taken the no-concessions position have been faced with new incidents.

Fourth, the government may enact emergency measures that severely limit civil liberties in a nationwide antiterrorist crackdown. Indiscriminate, society-wide repression, however, is often precisely what the terrorists seek. If the government mishandles this campaign, it may temporarily cure a symptom at the cost of adding to the causes of terrorism.

Fifth, vigilante squads have mixed effects. On the one hand, they add to the societal demoralization brought on by an increasing disregard for normal, nonviolent legal measures for dealing with political grievances. They are viewed by others, however, as supplementing police efforts in rooting out terrorists, and, as a bonus, common criminals. Such groups, perhaps with the aid of official intelligence organizations, may also conduct overseas attacks. Although this tactic can lead to a temporary increase in security (that is, fewer terrorist attacks) as terrorists burrow even deeper underground, it does not root out terrorism's causes, and often worsens interstate relations.

What Next? A Glimpse into the Future

The trends in terrorist behavior we have just surveyed may give us an indication of near-future terrorism. While prediction of the activities of a specific individual or small band is a hopeless task, we can nonetheless note a few macrolevel phenomena that will continue well into the 1980s.

Terrorists will continue to engage most often in simple forms of attacks, involving little risk to themselves, and entailing few casualties. Multiple-casualty operations, however, will occur from time to time, now that the precedential barriers to such events have been broken repeatedly.

Terrorists will adapt to measures taken by governments, corporations, and other potential victims to keep their activities in check.

Although some bilateral cooperation between terrorist groups will continue, and governments will furnish support to their surrogates despite counterpressures, the widely varying ideological, personality, geographic, and operational characteristics of terrorists will hinder the formation of a "Terror, Incorporated" cartel.

Although new terrorist groups will form to pursue idiosyncratic limited goals, the majority of terrorist attacks will be conducted against symbols of Western wealth and power. A "new generation" of terrorists will rise, with identities, goals, and methods of operation unfamiliar to authorities tasked with responding. The "big name" terrorists of the 1970s—members of the Baader-Meinhof Gang, headline-making Arab guerrilla leaders, and other radicals—are now dead, incarcerated, or too well-known to operate successfully in a clandestine fashion. Their intellectual descendants will begin with the advantage of being unknown.

Ethnic terrorist groups will probably continue with their limited tactical successes. Armenian terrorists were, in terms of numbers of operations, the most active terrorist group of the 1980s, and the new tactic of hunger strikes once again made the IRA a British headache. The ability of terrorism alone to secure the ethnic groups' long-term autonomy goals is open to question, however.

Notes

While this study has been reviewed by the Central Intelligence Agency's Publications Review Board to assist the author in ensuring against the unintentional compromise of classified information, its review and the institutional affiliation of the author, should not be interpreted as necessarily reflecting U.S. government agreement with the views expressed by the author.

1. In the tables and figures, only incidents of international terrorism are included. Events related to the Vietnam conflict are not included, nor are numerous cross-border raids between Arabs and Israelis against military targets. Due to omissions in reporting for some incidents, grand totals for the tables may disagree. Data are taken from unclassified aggregate statistics released by the U.S. Central Intelligence Agency.

For a discussion of how to construct a computer-assisted terrorist event monitoring scheme, consult Edward Mickolus, "An Events Data Base for Studying Transnational Terrorism" in Richards J. Heuer, Jr., ed., *Quantitative Approaches to Political Intelligence: The CIA Experience* (Boulder, Colo.: Westview, 1978), pp. 127-63. Summaries of many of the incidents enumerated herein can be found in Edward Mickolus, *Transnational Terrorism: A Chronology of Events, 1968-1979* (Westport, Conn.: Greenwood, 1980), 967 pp.

2. Hijackings must have the attributes of our definition of international terrorism in order to qualify for inclusion. Incidents that did not involve a crossing of a border (such as events involving the payment of ransom and parachuting of the hijacker from the plane within the territorial confines of the nation of embarkation), domestic attempts to hijack a plane to another country that involved no injuries in the resolution of the apparently nonpolitical incident, and incidents that involved only one nationality of passengers, crew, hijacker, and destination and embarkation point of the flight are thus not included.

3. Although hijackings can become barricade and hostage situations, these incidents are not treated in the barricade-and-hostage category if they occurred in transit. Hence, the multiple hijackings of the Popular Front for the Liberation of Palestine in September 1970 are treated as hijackings, although negotiations were conducted on the ground.

4. A score of definitions have been offered for assassination. Rather than attempt to distinguish between the political murder of a low-level official and a high-level official (if such an arbitrary cut-off point could be established) or to categorize on the basis of the motivations of the killer and other criteria, a general category of political murder and assassination is used. To qualify for inclusion, such acts must satisfy the conditions of the definition of international terrorism.

5. The location of an incident is considered to be the place in which the incident began, while its year is that date on which it became known to individuals other than the terrorists that a terrorist event was taking place. In the case of hijackings, the location is the nation in which the plane had last touched ground before the hijackers made their presence as hijackers known. In cases in which the embarkation point is not known, the location is considered to be that nation in which the plane landed and the negotiations took place, where appropriate. If both of the above do not apply, the nation of registry is used.

6. The location of an incident need not be a nation-state. Protectorates, colonies, and mandated territories may also experience terrorism, and are considered by the government to be different types of security and administrative environments, not comparable to the metropole.

7. For a more extensive treatment of contagion, consult Edward Heyman and Edward Mickolus, "Imitation by Terrorists: Quantitative Approaches to the Study of the Diffusion of Terrorism" in John Gleason and Yonah Alexander, eds., *Behavioral Approaches to the Study of Terrorism* (New York: Pergamon, 1981); Edward Mickolus, "Combatting International Terrorism: A Quantitative Analysis" (Ph.D. diss., Yale University, 1981), 600 pp.; and Edward Heyman and Edward Mickolus, "Observations on 'Why Violence Spreads,'" *International Studies Quarterly* 24, no. 2 (June 1980): 299-305.

8. The Israelis are frequently accused of being behind these attacks. Interfactional battles between Palestinian guerrilla groups, however, may also account for many of these incidents.

9. *Patterns of International Terrorism: 1980* (Washington D.C.: U.S. Central Intelligence Agency, National Foreign Assessment Center, PA 81-10163U, April 1981). For an alternative view, see Claire Sterling, *The Terror Network* (New York: Holt, Rinehart, 1981). Also see Roberta Goren, "Soviet Attitude and Policy to International Terrorism, 1967-1977" (Ph.D. diss., University of London, in preparation). In general, consult the Links and Geographic Areas sections of Edward Mickolus, comp., *The Literature of Terrorism: A Selectively Annotated Bibliography* (Westport, Conn.: Greenwood, 1980).

10. An interesting early discussion of this possibility is found in Brian M. Jenkins, *International Terrorism: A New Mode of Conflict*, Research Paper no. 48, California Seminar on Arms Control and Foreign Policy (Los Angeles: Crescent Publications, 1975).

11. Ransoms in Latin America have ranged from as low as a tractor demanded and received by Bolivian peasants to $60 million in cash, $1.2 million in food for peasants, and the publication of a manifesto in selected foreign newspapers received by the Montoneros from Bunge y Born in 1975.

12. A primer on the international legal regime regarding terrorism is offered by Edward Mickolus, "Multilateral Legal Efforts to Combat Terrorism: Diagnosis and Prognosis," *Ohio Northern University Law Review* 6, no. 1 (1979): 13-51. Consult also the works of Robert A. Friedlander, including "The Origins of International Terrorism: A Micro Legal-Historical Perspective," *Israel Yearbook on Human Rights, 6* (1978); "Coping with Terrorism: What Is to Be Done?" in Yonah Alexander, David Carlton, and Paul Wilkinson, eds., *Terrorism: Theory and Practice* (Boulder, Colo.: Westview, 1979), pp. 231-45; "Terrorism and International Law: What Is Being Done?" *Rutgers-Camden Law Journal* 8 (Spring 1977); 383-92; *Terrorism: Documents of International and Local Control* (Dobbs Ferry, N.Y.: Oceana, 1978), 2 vols.; "Reflections on Terrorist Havens," *Naval War College Review* 32 (March-April 1979): 59-67.

13. Paradoxically, many "lone nuts" find cracks in the armor.

2

Political and Economic Forces Affecting Terrorism

*PHILLIP A. KARBER AND
R. WILLIAM MENGEL*

Throughout the course of the past two decades the world has witnessed an increase in the frequency and intensity of terrorist violence. This escalation has been accompanied by an evolution in the application of the forms of violence. Kidnappings have evolved to focus more on senior government and business leaders. Bomb incidents are more frequently directed toward people, with the traditional target symbolism playing a lesser role. Armed assaults on government officials, businessmen, and ordinary citizens have dramatically increased on a worldwide scale. [1]

The evolution and escalation of terrorism is, undoubtedly, related to a number of factors that are themselves interrelated. Without question, terrorists perceive the need to achieve a level of public attention. The cliché "terrorism is theater" is still appropriate. This need for publicity has been a direct contributing element in the changing face of terrorist acts. Underlying each discrete terrorist attack is the political and economic milieu within which the terrorists survive and exist.

Historically, U.S. diplomats and businessmen have been prime, if infrequent, candidates for terrorists in overseas areas. Symbolic of U.S. presence and dominance, these executives have made readily acceptable targets to the local population. The changing nature of terrorist attacks coupled with the hardening of official U.S. government installations abroad appear to pose new problems and vulnerabilities for U.S. business interests. In all likelihood terrorists will not only continue to target U.S. businessmen, but may begin attacking U.S.-owned facilities without regard for the safety of the indigenous workers, heretofore seldom done.

While it is not plausible for the average executive abroad to develop and maintain current intelligence on terrorist groups that may be a threat, there are a number of general factors that might serve as indicators. Foremost among these are the political and economic forces that affect terrorism. The purpose of this chapter is to examine those forces and present a framework within which events can be evaluated relative to terrorist activity.

An underlying premise of the following discussion is that political forces have by far the most important societal impact on terrorism. Terrorism is by definition political.[2] Perhaps more crucial from an operational point of view, changes sought by terrorists, short of total revolution, must be achieved within a given political context, that is, the government institutes reforms, the government falls, or alternatively, the government represses the terrorists.

While the political contexts within which terrorism occurs are almost as numerous as the terrorist groups themselves, a highly discernible evolution of a terrorist group and its levels of violence is evident. Depicted in Figure 2-1, the starting point for terrorist organizations is generally some form of aboveground movement that operates within the existing political system. The movement would have been formed to articulate some grievance with the government (usually at the national level). Activities of these groups are generally within the accepted norms for that particular political environment.

FIGURE 2-1.
Spectrum of Terrorist Violence

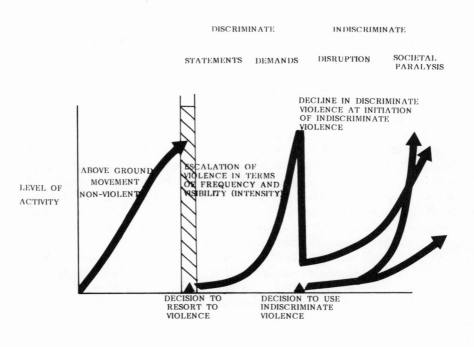

The extent of success achieved by this movement is, in the main, the measure for the likelihood of a splinter element evolving into a terrorist group. The greater the degree of success the less likely members will be inclined to resort to violence. Conversely, as frustration builds because of the lack of success or because of actual repression, the more probable a terrorist group will result.

Formation of a terrorist group is not a matter that can be taken as a given, even in situations where the circumstances appear appropriate. Many aboveground movements continue to operate within the political system irrespective of results. Although extreme frustration with the political system or resentment of either physical or psychological repression may alienate large numbers of people, most individuals eschew violence. Each person, in his or her own mind at least, weighs the relative risk and attractiveness of aboveground movements that spawn violent groups.

Terrorist groups themselves, particularly initially, are extremely small, indicative of a lack of interest in undertaking violent actions on the part of the vast majority of people. For example, the Tupamaros had a core estimated at 50 members five years after their formation; the Italian Red Brigades are believed to have an active core of fewer than 150; the Weather Underground in the United States was never more than 50 strong; and the Puerto Rican Armed Forces of National Liberation (FALN) is estimated to have a core of fewer than 100 members.

At this point it is appropriate to address the political system as a force in the formation of terrorist groups. Regardless of the political system, the potential terrorist must envision some way to achieve success, even if the chances are remote. Thus, the political system must provide the opportunity for a terrorist group to form and operate. Opportunity is measured in terms of the type of government and the established societal infrastructure to support the government.

Figure 2-2 offers a graphic portrayal of the range of political systems and the relative level of terroristic violence that has occurred in each. Countries with a totalitarian government and a supporting infrastructure are relatively free of terrorism, to which Eastern European nations are witness. Only two terrorist incidents since 1970 have been undertaken, both bombings, which killed a total of twelve Chinese. Authoritarian systems are somewhat more susceptible to terrorism because that type system usually permits nominal aboveground interest groups, if not direct political opposition. In nations with a strong infrastructure and tradition of authoritarian rule, terrorism has not become widespread. Brazil, Iran (pre-1978), and Saudi Arabia are examples of this type society.

As the infrastructure supporting the authoritarian government weakens, the incidence of terrorism increases. Two distinct types of nations fall in this category. First, nations with broad economic and social problems across time, such as Argentina, are susceptible to the formation and operation of

FIGURE 2-2.
Types of Political Systems and Terrorist Violence

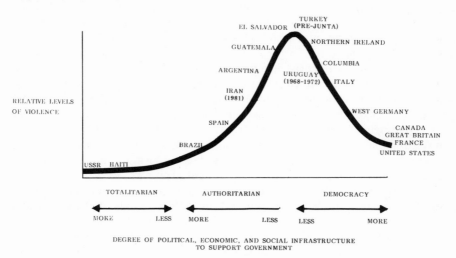

DEGREE OF POLITICAL, ECONOMIC, AND SOCIAL INFRASTRUCTURE
TO SUPPORT GOVERNMENT

terrorism. These long-standing problems weaken the societal infrastructure and the values that previously had deterred terrorist type violence. Often compounding the problem in this type country is a history of coups and military involvement in government.

The second type of nations are those with recent changes in government that drastically alter the political system. In these nations, such as Iran in 1979-1981, the infrastructure to resolve conflicting demands on the political and economic systems has not been developed. Hence, no legitimate avenue of redress is available. For example, in Iran the new religious government restricted dissent, did not offer opposition views a chance to survive, and has clearly indicated that all opposition will be brutally suppressed. The only response to opposition has been jail and hundreds of executions. In turn, during 1981 an extremely violent and successful terrorist campaign was waged, including the assassination of the president and several high-ranking officials as well as the bombing of Parliament in which nearly one hundred deputies were killed or wounded.

A critical influence on the forces affecting terrorism in authoritarian and nominally democratic countries is the pressure placed on the government by outside nations. In recent years the United States and other industrialized nations have attempted to dictate humanitarian standards for many developing countries. The threats of sanctions and actual reduction or withholding of economic aid have been used as leverage to force countries to institute primarily political changes. The focus of these changes has been on human rights.

While improved human rights are an ideal goal to strive for, there has been little recognition of the impact these demands for change have on the poltical system and the stability of the country. With respect to terrorism, these changes further weaken the political infrastructure, often leaving a void where the government previously had a means of response to terrorist violence. This serves as a force that encourages the formation of terrorist groups and enhances their ability to survive and grow. Excellent examples of this situation are Nicaragua, El Salvador, Guatemala, Turkey, Iran, and to a lesser degree the Philippines.

The last major category on the spectrum of political systems is democracy. In countries with a weak democratic infrastructure, the political system is ineffective in resolving issues of groups. Equally as significant, the system is not adept at co-opting terrorist groups once they appear. The rights of individuals, a major element of democracy, are the same rights that permit terrorism to thrive. Since a solid democratic infrastructure takes generations to develop, nations with a limited democratic history or with a democratic tradition that is interrupted by coups or marked by extreme political fractionalization often have an inadequate infrastructure to respond to terrorism.

Northern Ireland, a situation compounded and driven by religious differences, is at the far end of the democratic scale relative to terrorism. The religious schism has so weakened the infrastructure of that society that the values that militate against terrorism are practically absent. Italy typifies a democratic country with excessive political fractionalization and frequent government changes, a tradition that offers an environment in which violent political dissent is common as is violent crime.

Uruguay is a case study that in many respects is unique to terrorism. The goal of the Castro-type Tupamaros movement was the overthrow of the democratic government of Uruguay. From 1968 through 1972, the Tupamaros escalated their campaign against the government. Major incidents included kidnapping and killing a U.S. Agency for International Development advisor; kidnapping Claude L. Fly, a U.S. agricultural expert; bank robberies; kidnappings and assassinations of government officials; kidnapping of British Ambassador Geoffrey Jackson; and armed attacks against police and military facilities.

Paradoxically, the Tupamaros were the catalyst for a military takeover of the government in 1973. The Tupamaros achieved partial success in that the existing democratic government was overthrown. However, that same success provided the foundation for a repressive military regime that ultimately ensured the demise of the Tupamaros as a viable force. The strong countermeasures initiated by the democratic government in 1972 to combat the intensified Tupamaros violence weakened the political structure and democratic institutions to a point at which the military could intervene. In light of the fact that between 1945 and 1970 Uruguay was rated as the most democratic country in Latin America (along with Costa Rica), the effects of the Tupamaros are insightful and instructive.

The United States and other democratic industrialized nations, such as France, Canada, and Great Britain, have the tradition, values, and societal infrastructures that limit the opportunities for terrorist groups to organize and grow. This limitation is not in terms of repressive laws or restricted civil liberties. It takes the form of an infrastructure that defuses situations and circumstances before the frustration level of participants reaches the point of radicalization. The political system and the economic system (through government programs) is, in its own fashion, responsive to demands of aboveground movements. In essence, the system has an infrastructure that operates to co-opt issues effectively before the decision point for violence.

When terrorist groups have formed in the United States, they have tended to be either single-issue or narrow in focus. While much of the rhetoric of these groups describes revolution, the rationale offered for specific incidents indicates support of issue-oriented ends. For example, the Weather Underground was against U.S. involvement in Vietnam.[3] The Black Liberation Army and Red Guerrilla Family's primary objective in the string of over seventy bombing attacks against Pacific Gas and Electric facilities between 1973 and 1978 was lower power rates for the poor and other concessions to the minority population.

The significance of this limited-objective orientation is that it illustrates that in the U.S. the societal infrastructure and associated values act to constrain terrorism. Another indicator is the discriminate targeting of U.S. terrorist groups.

The vast majority of incidents are bombings against undefended targets, where the danger to human life is minimal. Over 95 percent of U.S. terrorist group bombings between 1969 and 1981 were set in places (outside walls, remote storage areas) and at times (between 1 A.M. and 5 A.M.) when it was highly unlikely civilians would be endangered. In a large number of these bombings, a warning of ten minutes to several hours was provided.

Even the terrorist groups that are not truly U.S. domestic organizations, such as the FALN, the Cuban anti-Castro Omega 7, and U.S.-based Croatian separatists, tend to be discriminate in their targeting. These groups appear to recognize the significance of taking the step to indiscriminate acts in the United States. While indiscriminate violence has not been totally absent (the Wall Street tavern bombing by the FALN that killed three and wounded fifty-six and possibly the LaGuardia terminal bombing that claimed thirteen lives), these incidents have been the marked exception.

On a worldwide basis terrorism is becoming more indiscriminate in its targeting of civilians, with a somewhat declining emphasis on the direct symbolism of targets. An expanding number of right- and left-wing terrorist groups are involving innocent civilians. Previously, innocent civilian involvement was primarily limited to hijackings by most groups. Even the PLO generally avoided indiscriminate acts, except for hijackings. In the past year bombs in Beirut have been repeatedly detonated in areas and at times that guaranteed large numbers of civilian casualties. Similarly, bombs exploded at the Madrid airport and the Milan train station each killed over a dozen civilians.

Indiscriminate terrorism has also extended to random armed attacks on and assassinations of individual civilians. Previously, terrorists avoided this type of targeting, fearing alienation of the general population and support. In recent years the extent of random killing has greatly accelerated. Estimates of terrorism-related deaths in Guatemala in 1980 were approximately 800 civilians, mostly farmers in rural areas. Through November 1981, El Salvador had suffered over 11,000 deaths, according to the Roman Catholic Church in that nation. In the one-year period prior to the military takeover in Turkey, over 1,000 civilian deaths were attributed to terrorism.

Although indiscriminate terrorism is on the rise, many groups are, at the same time, becoming more discriminate in other aspects of their targeting. Specifically, the level of officials targeted has been evaluated. The Red Brigades 1978 kidnapping and subsequent execution of Aldo Moro, a former Italian prime minister, signaled a new plateau for terrorist activity. In 1980 the Archbishop of El Salvador was gunned down. The year 1981 witnessed the attempt on Pope John Paul's life, the assassination of Egyptian President Anwar Sadat, and the alleged terrorist "hit teams" dispatched to kill top U.S. officials, including the president and vice-president.

This discussion of discriminate and indiscriminate terrorism leads back to Figure 2-1, which illustrates that after a terrorist group has formed, its operation tends to follow a pattern of escalation. In the majority of the cases there is a direct correlation between the political, and to a lesser degree, the economic response of the government and the direction of escalation. Initial attacks are usually of low intensity and against undefended, discriminate, and symbolic targets. The frequency of attack is also low, the group waiting and wanting a positive response from the government. For example, the first attack by the Red Brigades was a firebomb placed against the garage door of an Italian industrial executive in September 1970, following a leaflet campaign against that industry. The target was highly discriminate and symbolic, as well as undefended.

At this early stage of the violence, the terrorist group is expressing its "political position." Usually a communique is issued by the group claiming responsibility, articulating its goals and rationale along with revolutionary rhetoric. The statement is often an extension of previous positions of the aboveground movement from which the terrorist group splintered. For example, following the March 1970 accidental destruction of their bomb factory, in which two members were killed, the Weather Underground declared its goals in its May 1970 "Communique No. 1 from the Weather

Underground.'' This communique was in part a restatement of the famous
''You Don't Need A Weatherman to Know Which Way The Wind Blows,''
the Weatherman organization paper that attempted to define an ideology
and goals for the Students for a Democratic Society. SDS was the
aboveground movement from which a Weatherman faction originated later
to become the violent Weather Underground.

A second illustration is the Red Brigades. This group initially attempted
to organize factories in the Milan area into an aboveground movement for
the liberation of the working class from the bourgeois. This legal activity
was aimed at creating strikes and at disrupting industry. When this failed,
the actual Red Brigades terrorist group of less than a dozen was formed.
After the September 1970 firebombing and two similar incidents in
November/December 1970, the Red Brigades disseminated a leaflet accepting responsibility for the attacks and stating their reasons.

Although most groups hope for and want a reconciliating action from the
government, a positive response is not usually possible or in the best interest
of the society. Without addressing the issue of whether terrorism should be
viewed and treated separately from criminal activity within the judicial
system, terrorist violence is, in fact, perceived and responded to as criminal
acts. Thus authorities cannot give credence to this type crime without
undermining the legitimacy of the government and, perhaps, weakening the
infrastructure of society.

Lack of a positive response to terrorist acts generally causes an increase in
both the frequency and intensity of attacks. Incidents still tend to be
discriminate and symbolic against undefended targets. Not a ''wave'' of terrorism at this point, the group still recognizes the need to gain publicity for
its agenda through attacks on targets that will secure this attention with
media coverage.

Two separate but related phenomena seem to take place at this time.
Easiest to explain and understand are the political forces in the system. The
low level and intensity of violence usually results in a governmental reaction
that treats the terrorists as criminals. While not an inappropriate reaction,
the terrorists often see this as an indication that they are not taken seriously
or that all their goals are totally unacceptable. As a result the political forces
impact directly on the terrorist group.

The second phenomenon is associated with the impact mentioned above
and is directly related to the group. Any violent organization is under extreme pressure in terms of members willingness to escalate violence and the
decisions on the direction of escalation. On one hand, certain members will
be unwilling, for example, to kill anyone or innocent civilians. On the other
hand, all members weight the relative attractiveness (in terms of the group's
goals) of acts versus the risk (in terms of being captured or killed or not suc-
ceeding). Obviously, the government's response to terrorism greatly influences the group's actions.

An excellent example of the interrelationship between these two phenomena is the Black Panther Party in 1969-1970. Started in 1966 as part of the civil rights movement, the Black Panthers grew into a viable aboveground movement in the late 1960s with chapters in several major U.S. cities. Violent demonstrations led to a splinter group that issued repeated calls for blacks to arm themselves in the struggle for liberation. The focus of the acts committed by this terrorist splinter group centered on symbols of authority, particularly police officers. Policemen were shot in Philadelphia, Chicago, New York, and Oakland by Black Panthers.

In response to these shootings and other violent acts by the Black Panthers, law enforcement authorities at the Federal, state and local levels took decisive action. Several Black Panthers were killed and wounded in shootouts during the winter of 1969-1970. The result was that a significant portion of the Black Panthers in the splinter group no longer found terrorist violence attractive. In this case, the members opted to cease violent activity rather than risk the consequences should they escalate or even continue their activities.

It should be pointed out that the Black Panther aboveground movement continued, with an orientation toward community work and voter registration. In early 1972 the Black Panther terrorist splinter group formally disavowed violence, almost a year after the organization's last act and after alienating a large segment of the U.S. black community. The Black Panthers are significant as an example because the group's history demonstrates the following:

(1) the evolution of an aboveground movement to a violent splinter group;

(2) the effect of political forces on a terrorist group;

(3) the decision of a terrorist group to discontinue in the face of those political forces, including loss of support in its own movement and community;

(4) the ability of the U.S. political system to respond to a perceived threat and, in turn, accept the subsequent transformation of the terrorist group.

The political statements of groups give way to specific demands as the level and intensity of discriminate violence increases. By this time the terrorist group has become a functioning organization. While not without the stresses discussed previously, the group is past that primary hurdle of organizing, determining direction, defining roles, and generally becoming familiar with the life of a terrorist and violence. Failure of the political system to respond in a positive manner to the group's statements forces them to provide specificity of what they view as necessary.

A prima faci example of this occurring is found in the Red Brigades. After escalation of their attacks between 1971 and 1973, including three kidnappings, a killing, and numerous bombings all aimed at industrial executives or police officials working on the Red Brigades case, the group kidnapped the personnel chief of FIAT. In an attempt to influence a labor negotiation between FIAT and the labor union, the terrorists demanded layoffs be stopped. This was repeated in April 1974 when a judge was kidnapped and demands were made for release of eight prisoners associated with other left extremist groups. Neither set of demands were met.

The Red Brigades is an excellent illustration of a group that has moved toward the far end of the spectrum relative to discriminate violence, without making the step to indiscriminate violence. An explanation of this behavior is found in the genesis of the group and its continuing commitment to mobilizing the workers and to overcoming bourgeois national and multinational industry in the struggle for workers rights. Indiscriminate terrorism, by its nature, would likely also affect the common people, the workers.

The decision to refrain from escalation to indiscriminate violence carries with it a concomitant requirement to maintain the group's momentum, both internally and in the public's view, through discriminate violence. Probably more than any other group in the past decade, the Red Brigades has successfully accomplished this. In the early years bombings escalated to kidnappings, knee capping, and murder. As time passed the length of the period of captivity increased as did the level of the official/businessman kidnapped, although all were Italian. This escalation appeared to peak with the March 16, 1978 kidnapping of the Honorable Aldo Moro, leader of the Italian Christian Democratic Party and former prime minister. Held for fifty-five days, during which demands were made to free Red Brigades members on trial and a dozen propaganda communiques were issued, Mr. Moro was executed on May 9. Slain by numerous bullet wounds, his body was abandoned in the trunk of a car.

Since that time the Red Brigades have continued discriminate attacks, but have broadened their targets to include unions and political parties to a much greater extent than previously. However, the Red Brigades' recognition of the need for a new forum for publicity became apparent with the December 17, 1981 kidnapping of U.S. Army Brigadier General Dosier. He was held captive for forty-two days until he was dramatically rescued by special agents of Italy's central operative security nucleus. His release marked the second time one of the Red Brigades' kidnapping victims was rescued by police. Without question, the likelihood of U.S. businessmen in Italy becoming future targets is enhanced with this act.

The other groups, because of their different orientations and goals, merit illustration with respect to discriminate terrorism and political forces. The Basque Nation and Freedom organization (ETA) has been an active terrorist group seeking autonomy from Spain for over fifteen years and is rooted in centuries of conflict between the Basque region and the Spanish government. Over the years the ETA has been an extremely violent group, ambushing and assassinating government officials and police who are either in the Basque region or associated with Spanish rule. There is no marked pattern of escalation, but rather incidents have been cyclic in frequency and intensity, usually highly discriminate.

ETA typifies groups in a political system that respond to terrorist acts and the accompanying demands. Either implicitly or explicity, ETA acts carry the demand for autonomy. Over the years the Spanish government has tried repression, which resulted in increased terrorist activity, including killing the Army Chief of Staff in Madrid. The government has also taken steps to give the Basque region autonomy. This action, while not totally satisfying the ETA demands for complete autonomy, has resulted in the loss of significant support for the ETA among Basques. Many Basques outside ETA feel that violence at this point is needless and should cease. In fact, the ETA terrorist group has been relatively inactive since autonomy was granted and may become a less important force in the region because of other political forces.

A long-standing terrorist group is the Croatian Revolutionary Brotherhood, a group with the goal of establishment of a separate Croatian state within Yugoslavia. Since the end of World War II the Croatians have wanted an independent state. A rugged mountainous area in western Yugoslavia, the Croatia state has a history of combatting the central government. The Croatians have committed assassinations of Yugoslavic officials and bombed facilities of both the Yugoslavic government and organizations that support it. Over the past ten years Croatian terrorists have assassinated Yugoslavic diplomatic personnel (military and civilian) in most major cities of the world, including Brussels, Paris, Bonn, London, New York, Washington, Madrid, and Belgrade.

The Croatians exemplify groups that have not escalated violence in order to achieve a political settlement. While assassinations are not at the lowest end of the spectrum of violence, the highly discriminate targeting and infrequent attacks of the Croatians mark them as a group whose actions are relatively uneffected by political forces. There are no indications that the Yugoslavic government is ever going to grant Croatia independence. At the same time, the Croatian terrorists show no signs of changing their direction. Thus, the Croatians emerge as a group that wants to keep its goals in the public's mind through political statements associated with violent acts, while recognizing the futility of escalating violence accomplishing any significant political ends. Conversely, by doing nothing, the Yugoslavic government has been a political force that affects the terrorists.[4]

The next critical decision point for terrorist groups is that of escalating to indiscriminate violence. This point is crucial because it causes organizational stress and will result in a new set of political forces, which in turn,

will affect the group. Initiation of indiscriminate attacks is the most difficult step for a terrorist group, next to group formation for violent purposes. At this point members must further commit to killing innocent
civilians. Most people in society, even a majority of the terrorists, are unwilling to do this. The Weather Underground in 1975 became fractionalized
and ineffective at that point in its evolution. Similar examples are found in
the Black Liberation Army and the George Jackson Brigade.

Political forces in society also militate against this program. Risk to the
group members increases as the government is placed in a position where
the fabric of society is endangered by the disruption caused by indiscriminate attacks. Thus, the political response will be more direct and
harsh, if it is within the capability of the government. A prime illustration
of this action and reaction is the FLN in 1954-1956. The FLN terrorist wing
of the revolution moved to indiscriminate violence in Algiers in 1955.
Within eighteen months French paratroopers had ruthlessly suppressed the
terrorists. More recently, the Turkish military takeover in 1980 and its
subsequent actions against terrorists had brought law and order with accompanying economic stability to Turkey.

Generally, terrorist organizations will continue discriminate violence,
albeit at a lower intensity and frequency than immediately prior to initiating
indiscriminate attacks. The government is faced with an increased threat
that may affect the entire society. The IRA and the PLO have resorted to indiscriminate terrorism. In both these cases there has not been a satisfactory
response from those affected. The British government has not been able to
curtail civil liberties to the point that the IRA can be effectively combatted.
Here the political forces of British tradition prevent the implementation of
the extreme measures necessary. The result to date has been over a decade
of violence with no apparent solution. Certain signs of British compromise
are beginning to appear, but the IRA shows no evidence of either losing
strength or resolve.

Unfortunately, the PLO is a case in which terrorism at the indiscriminate
level of violence has been effective. Attacks against not only Israel, but
worldwide targets, dramatized the PLO goals and demands from the late
1960s to the mid-1970s. The world abhorred these acts of hijacking, kidnapping, and murder. However, there was no way short of military action to
counter effectively the PLO terrorist arms, such as Black September and the
Popular Front for the Liberation of Palestine (PFLP).

Perhaps the strong aboveground PLO movement makes this case unique.
The aboveground movement worked toward political solutions, while supporting and being supported by the terrorist groups. Nations of the world
could not agree on measures to combat the PLO. In fact, some nations supported the PLO against Israel, if not the terrorist attacks. Time and again,
captured and convicted PLO terrorists were set free by nations in response

to demands made as part of hostage situations, primarily airline hijackings. Today outside of Israel there is not a single PLO terrorist in jail.

Over time, nations began to recognize the legitimacy of the PLO as an organization. Although recognition as a state is still lacking, the right of the PLO to represent the Palestinian people in world forums such as the United Nations is now established. Most Third World and many Western European nations have recognized the PLO. However, the United States still does not.

Two major points emerge from this discussion of indiscriminate terrorism and political forces. First, at the national level the ability of the government to respond appears directly related to the democratic values and the wherewithal of the government itself. In Turkey the democratic government was ineffective because of politics and the constitutional guarantees. When the military assumed command of the government, suspended certain constitutional rights, and brought the resources of the armed forces to bear, the indiscriminate (and for that matter discriminate) terrorism was suppressed. Conversely, without the more than marginal suspension of constitutional rights that has occurred in Northern Ireland, the British have been unable to stop IRA violence. By way of conclusion, it appears that once terrorism reaches the indiscriminate stage of violence, the ability of government to combat it is inversely related to the strength of democratic norms and values.

The second major point is that at the international level terrorism has a high probability of success if the group can sustain itself over a long period of time. There is a general inability of nations to agree on long-term approaches to countering terrorism. To date, any meaningful agreement on antiterrorism protocols among nations has been lacking. Rather, nations view each case of international terrorism in its own context, with the circumstances of each dictating the political and economic response. International terrorism has often been assisted, even if somewhat indirectly, by the lack of nations to bring concerted political forces to bear on the problem.

The final segment of the spectrum of violence deals with indiscriminate terrorism that brings about societal paralysis. Terrorism, in and by itself, has never resulted in societal paralysis. To date terrorism has never been so rampant in a nation as to stop or significantly affect all activity. However, in conjunction with revolutionary movements, terrorism has been a contributing factor as nations reach that point. For example, the current situation in El Salvador is one in which terrorism from both the right and left is a significant factor. In Guatemala the situation is approaching that point. Similarly, life in Beirut has been severely disrupted by terrorism, but it also is in the context of a civil war.

When the societal situation degenerates to the level where terrorism might cause paralysis, the opportunity for a broader deterioration into general conflict overtakes terrorism and subsumes it. Thus, the political forces affecting terrorism are those associated with making the terrorist movement a part of a larger conflict. The goals of terrorists become, in whole or part, the goals of the forces combatting or supporting the government. In these cases the political system and the infrastructure are no longer capable of containing terrorism, but are fighting for system survival.

Throughout this discussion the economic forces affecting terrorism have been secondary. However, despite the prevalence of political forces, economics are important to the terrorists in two principal respects. First, terrorist movements, particularly those that are domestic to a nation, use economics as a basis for goals. For example, the Red Brigades want to improve the life of workers and combat imperialistic capitalism. The Red Brigades have targeted numerous executives of large Italian companies, bombed industrial facilities and banks, and made economic demands for workers. In Latin America many terrorist groups have established economic goals as well as made economic demands. The majority of ransom kidnappings have been in Latin America. Most graphically, during the 1970s the People's Revolutionary Army (ERP) in Argentina conducted a series of kidnappings of multinational corporations' business executives in which almost $100 million in cash, food, and medical supplies were paid. The food and medical supplies went to the poor, while the cash supported ERP activities.

Second, as mentioned with respect to the ERP, terrorist groups require economic assistance to service. In the early 1970s support for groups usually came from ransom (principally Latin America), bank robberies, and individuals within the group. While linkages existed between groups, particularly in Europe and the Middle East, in the early 1970s, most assistance was in terms of logistics and travel. Over the years these linkages have become deeper relationships involving economic support. For example, it is known that the PLO has provided monetary support to several other terrorist groups in recent years. More significantly, a number of nations, including Libya and Saudi Arabia, have provided monetary support directly to terrorist groups or, as in the case of the PLO, to aboveground movements that support terrorist organizations. Although difficult to measure, it is reasonable to conclude that without economic support terrorist groups would be neither as prolific nor as proficient as they now are.

To this point specific political and economic forces affecting terrorism have been described in the context of the spectrum of violence and by way of example for particular groups. The myriad of forces discussed can be reduced into a manageable set through the classification of group types and their respective goals. Figure 2-3 identifies the group types and defines the primary goal of each type. Clearly, the political goals predominate the classification scheme.

Revolutionary, issue-oriented, and reactionary group types all could be affected by economic forces. Reactionary terrorists generally want to maintain a political and economic status quo that has been to their advantage.

FIGURE 2-3.
Terrorist Group Goals

GROUP TYPE	GROUP GOAL
SEPARATIST	Autonomy for region or establishment of a separate state
REVOLUTIONARY	Change of government and, to some extent, the social/economic system.
ISSUE-ORIENTED	Specific changes in policies relative to the political, economic, or social system
REACTIONARY	Maintenance of status quo or revision to more autocratic system
ANARCHIST	Disruption and overthrow of the government without offering alternative
RELIGIOUS	Establishment of predominance of one particular religion in nation or the eradication of a competing religion/sect
FOREIGN SURROGATE	Terrorist for hire either for money or in return for other considerations

Examples of reactionary groups supporting authoritarian governments are found in Guatemala, El Salvador, and Brazil. Reactionary groups in Spain support the return of the monarch, while Italian right-wing groups are neo-Fascists attempting to keep the government from drifting further left.

Issue-oriented groups, primarily found in the United States and, to a lesser degree, in Europe as antinuclear groups, have a mixed bag of goals. Most U.S. left-wing groups have had some sort of economic goal. For example, after kidnapping Patricia Hearst the Symbionese Liberation Army (SLA) asked for $70 million worth of food to be distributed to California poor people. The Black Panthers goals included more opportunities for blacks, while the Red Guerrilla Family asked for cheaper utility rates for the poor. However, in each case, the goals are viewed as being accomplished through changes in the political system.

Revolutionary groups in other countries are usually oriented toward Marxist-Leninist teachings of the working class struggle against the bourgeois. These groups hope to gain working class support and build the small fragile terrorist group into a broad-based workers movement. From the standpoint of economics being a serious force in revolutionary terrorism, that force is limited to the use of economics as a rallying point and a cornerstone for much rhetoric. A significant point is that workers have seldom followed terrorists, particularly in the early stages of their activities. The Red Brigades were unable to win wide support among factory and auto industry workers. After the killing of Aldo Moro, those that might have been sympathetic to the cause changed their minds. In the late 1960s, U.S.

leftists tried to infiltrate the blue collar work force and win advocates, a scheme that was a dismal failure.

The focus of other groups is dominated by political forces. In each case, the goal of the group type can be accomplished through the political system or through changes in it. Separatists can achieve their goal through a war in which independence is won or through a political settlement, such as in the Basque region of Spain and, potentially, Palestine. Present anarchist groups are oriented toward disruption in the political system. Both the Japanese Red Army and the Baader-Meinhof Gang are considered anarchist.

Religious terrorists direct their attention to establishing the predominance of their religious beliefs. The political system is viewed as a way to achieve this, making political terrorism a means to an end. Iranian terrorists today are religious-based groups that are fighting for survival in a religious-controlled government. Prior to the military takeover in Turkey in 1980, two religious terrorist groups waged war on each other, debilitating the country politically and economically.

In summary, the political forces that affect terrorism are the most significant factor in determining the level and intensity of terrorist violence and the ultimate success or failure of the group. Countries with strong political systems, be they totalitarian, authoritarian, or democratic, have the least problems with terrorism. In these well-developed political systems, the infrastructure as well as unique norms and values have established a society which in its own ways resists the growth of terrorism.

Totalitarian states simply do not permit terrorism, reacting against guilty and innocent populations until it is eradicated. Authoritarian governments carefully measure the impact of government reaction to terrorism in terms of societal and outside perceptions. These governments will avoid drastic action in response to dissent as long as the group and its activities do not threaten the infrastructure and the political system it supports. Once a movement reaches that point, the government then is faced with the lesser of two evils and will act firmly. The stronger the authoritarian system, the earlier the government will feel able to act.

Highly resilient democratic nations are almost equally capable at combatting terrorism. The difference between democratic and authoritarian states is the manner in which it is done. The United States, for example, has a capacity for defusing terrorist movements before they become a danger to society. Mechanisms for defusing terrorism vary from case to case, but all are dependent on a flexible political system that inherently protects itself.

In certain instances, terrorists have been left without a cause. Illustratively, the U.S. withdrawal from Vietnam resulted in the Weather Underground disintegration. In other cases, the cause has been co-opted by government action, such as laws in response to much of the civil rights violence. At times a government policy of no action has been successful, as in the case of the response to the Red Guerrilla Family. The bombings of Pacific Gas and Electric were treated as criminal acts. Finally, the government has shown a willingness to respond with force and public support when it appears the violence might truly affect the ability to govern. Attacks on policemen by the Black Panthers brought a quick and definitive response.

Lack of a better explanation leads one to conclude that the most pervasive force in the United States affecting terrorism is the political system itself and an implicit understanding that certain bounds, such as from discriminate or indiscriminate violence, will not be crossed. On one hand, the system seems to recognize major grievances and responds in some manner. On the other hand, terrorist groups have recognized the bounds of what they can hope to attain and also appear to recognize limits that the system can go to resolve problems.

Notes

1. Fortunately, terrorism has been significantly less of a problem in the United States than most industrialized countries. An explanation of this situation is provided during the discussion in this chapter.

2. The vast majority of contemporary writers on terrorism view it as the commission of violent acts for political purposes or ends.

3. The reemergence of the Weather Underground in the fall of 1981 in armed car and bank robbery incidents in Nyack, New York, appears to be more criminal (for profit) in motivation than terroristic. While an argument can be made that the money was to fund future terroristic activities, the involvement of hardened criminals may suggest that those criminals were using "the cause" and the organization as an umbrella for continued criminal activity.

4. Similar groups are the Armenian (Turkey) and Breton (France) separatist groups, with the former being international in scope and the latter national.

3

The Psychology of Terrorism: Contemporary Views

ROBERT A. FRIEDLANDER

What is a terrorist? Why do they terrorize? How does one explain the practice and perpetuation of terror-violence? Is there an identifiable terrorist mind? Or does terrorism merely represent a change in terminology and a deviance in methodology from older forms of violent, criminal behavior? These questions, and others like them, have occupied the thoughts and attracted the energies of scholars, journalists, and law enforcement officials for half a generation with no discernible agreement or emergent consensus among them.[1]

At the very beginning of the Terror Decade of the 1970s, and looking back to the Guerrilla Decade of the 1960s, Professor Ted Robert Gurr published his seminal study entitled *Why Men Rebel*, which sought to provide a social scientific theory for the causes and processes of political violence.[2] Although terrorism is in part political violence, not all political violence is in fact terrorism. No expert during the past dozen years has been able to come forward with a successful explanation of why terrorists terrorize, although there have been several attempts to do so.[3] Typologies and taxonomies abound in profusion,[4] and one prominent sociologist has even developed a terrorist profile in only three printed pages.[5] Even more confusing is the failure of most of these studies to agree on a definition as to what exactly constitutes terrorism.

There is no denying that our technological, scientific twentieth century has also been a time of terror.[6] Social philosopher Eric Hoffer's belief that "[a] triumphant technology ushers in a psychological age, and history is made not by the hidden hand of circumstances but by men,"[7] gives additional meaning to the various claims that the last eighty years have been an age of anxiety, an age of controversy, an era of violence, an age of conflict, a century of total war, or even the asprin age. The reasons for this are deeply embedded in history, ideology, and what José Ortega y Gasset called the revolt of the masses, and their legacies are to be found in the farthest corners of the globe. Many societal observers, such as Hoffer, have decried the growth of "mindless" terrorism as evidence of modern-day anarchy,[8] but the truth of the matter is that terror-violence, brutal and barbaric though it may be, is far from mindless and more than simply anarchic.[9]

For purposes of this chapter, terrorism can be defined as the intentional use of force, or the threat of force, directed against innocent third parties, motivated by political, psychological, or financial considerations. The immediate victim is not the ultimate target (from which terrorism derives its special horror as well as its undeserved reputation for total randomness). To the terrorist, the ends invariably justify the means. A quintessential element in terrorist victimization is innocence, although this has been confused and confounded by lack of an agreed-upon definition. Three international conventions proscribing interference with air transport[10] have had the effect of making aerial hijacking, or violence against airport terminals, per se acts of terrorism.[11] Likewise, by international and regional conventions, as well as domestic statutes, attacks upon heads of state, certain specified government officials, diplomats, and other internationally protected persons are classified as forms of terrorism.[12] The reasons for this derive from history, custom, and tradition, but the end result has been to obscure the real nature of terrorist activity.

Still another complicating factor is the structural duality of terror-violence. In the technological twentieth century, terror from above, frequently called state or governmental terrorism, became far more pervasive and barbaric (numbering its victims in the tens of millions) than terror from below, often referred to as individual or group terrorism. It is a moot point whether Adolf Hitler, Joseph Stalin, or Mao Zedong was the most successful terrorist of modern times, but totalitarian, authoritarian, and dictatorial regimes have continued to practice mass victimology in numbers that almost defy the imagination.

> It is necessary to smother the internal and external enemies of the Republic
> or to perish with it. But, in this situation, the first maxim of our policy
> must be that one guides the people by reason and the enemies of the people
> by terror.[13]

These words, uttered during the French reign of Terror by Jacobin leader Maximilien Robespierre, proved to be a chilling historical legacy for the contemporary world, as evidenced by Idi Amin Dada, Pol Pot, and the nameless, faceless, Latin-American death squads. However, state terror, particularly when unleashed by a maximum leader, is not the prime focus of this book, and though representing outrageous violations of the UN Charter and the international protection of human rights, governmental terrorism is not—at present—a threat to existing minimum global stability. Violence perpetrated by individual or group terrorist actors is quite another story. The remainder of this analysis is concerned with the latter phenomenon.

As political philosopher Michael Walzer has noted, until the middle of this century, terrorist actors were primarily engaged in political assassination.[14] Tyrannicide, or regicide, had its origins in the ancient world. The Greek philosopher Aristole, during the Alexandrian Age, warned of "those from whom attacks on a tyrant's life may be expected," advising that "they are most to be watched and feared who reck nothing of their own life provided they can take his."[15] From that point forward, self-sacrifice was recognized as a key element in the assassin's mentality. Cicero first attempted to justify acts of regicide on the grounds of political necessity (and was later murdered by his political opponents), but the most influential theoretical justification of the tyrannicide doctrine was provided by John of Salisbury in *Policraticus* (1159), which urged the killing of usurpers and unjust rulers on the basis of natural law and equity.[16] This was broadened into a political declaration of faith four centuries later by the *Vindiciae Contra Tyrannos* (1579), wherein an unknown author ("Stephanus Junius Brutus") argued for the necessity of taking up arms against tyrants, insisting that illegitimate rulers were worse than ordinary criminals and thus merited "a far severer punishment."[17] Not only did French King Henry IV fall victim to an assassin's blade within thirty years of this infamous tract, but throughout the seventeenth-century age of absolutism, and again in the late nineteenth imperial century, assassination became a fatal weapon of dissent aimed at kings, queens, tsars, ministers, and presidents.

"Sic semper tyrannis!" With this triumphant cry, John Wilkes Booth pulled the trigger of the most famous murder weapon in American history, and Abraham Lincoln belonged to the ages. Booth's diary, written during the time of his attempted flight, contains passages reminiscent of the next generation of European terrorist assassins. "I can never repent it," Booth wrote shortly after Lincoln's murder, "though we hated to kill. . . . God simply made me the instrument of his punishment."[18] Looking to history's ultimate judgment (his own being foreordained), Booth averred: "I hoped for no gain. I knew no private wrong. I struck for my country and that alone."[19] How similar this is to Albert Camus's antiheroes in the plays *State of Siege* and *The Just Assassins*, the latter based upon a real historical episode, where the protagonists declare:

To do away with murder we must kill, and to prevent injustice we must do violence.[20]

To die for an ideal — that's the only way of proving oneself worthy of it. It's our only justification. . . . I threw the bomb at your tyranny, not at a man.[21]

As Camus later observed in his classic study of the terrorist rebel, he kills "in the fond conviction that this world is dedicated to death."[22] The modern political assassin is not far removed from Camus's frightening vision. One of the two Irgun assassins of Palestine Governor-General Lord Moyne proclaimed at their 1944 trial: "Our deed stemmed from our motives and our motives stemmed from our ideals, and if we prove our ideals are right and just, then our deed was right and just."[23] Above all else, political assassination is — as the nineteenth-century Russian anarchists well realized — the propaganda of the deed.

Contemporary terrorism, however, has become political warfare "against nations, ethnic groups, religions . . . entire peoples."[24] The present-day terrorist wages war upon innocence. This is terrorism's awful message, and it is terrorism's ultimate challenge. Political or ideologically motivated terror-violence constitutes the major terrorist threat today and the greatest danger to liberal, democratic, pluralistic society. It seeks to undermine and to topple existing regimes by fomenting an uncontrolled societal disorder which invites repression from above and eventual counter-revolution from below. For this reason, in most instances, terrorist victims are, in reality, substitute targets. They represent merely the means to a greater end, or as Brian Crozier observed in a classic statement, terrorism is a highly effective technique for demolishing a state."[25]

If the observation of literary critic and social commentator Irving Howe that "[t]error flourishes on the bones of politics"[26] is correct, then it is necessary, and indeed imperative, to determine the nature of the terrorist carnivore. There are basically two kinds of political terrorists. The most prevalent at the moment, and during the recent past, is the so-called terrorist liberationist, or political secessionist, whom the media frequently mislabels "guerrillas" involved in wars of national liberation.[27] This category includes such terrorist organizations as the PLO, ETA, IRA, SWAPO, FALN, and Moro National Liberation Front, to mention but a few drops in the ocean of political dissidence.

The second group is fundamentally nihilistic and anarchistic, intent on destroying an entire state structure, often motivated by a distorted messianic idealism, and believing that a new Zion can only be created out of the fire and flame of the old order. To the political nihilist, revolutionary violence is a necessary means of moral purification.[28] This latter classification includes especially notorious entities like the Japanese Red Army, the Baader-Meinhof Red Army Faction, the Red Brigades, the First of October Anti-Fascist Resistance Group (GRAPO), and the Tupamaros. A subdivision of this second category is the right-wing, fascist-oriented terrorist bands, reappearing in dramatic fashion during the beginning of the 1980s, and seeking to reestablish a new fascistic political order. Of particular noteworthiness are the Italian Third Position and Armed Revolutionary Nuclei, the French European Nationalist Fasces (FNE) and Odessa, and the German Military Sports Group.[29]

Both types of political terrorists view the nature of established government, whether majoritarian or authoritarian, as a form of organized violence. From this ideological perspective, it is not difficult to view virtually all legal systems as oppressive manifestations of the status quo and repressive instruments of social control. In this twisted line of reasoning, the entire notion of the concept of innocence undergoes a radical transformation. Poltical terrorists now "claim a right to kill anyone; they seek to terrorize whole populations."[30] Self-justification is part of the terrorists' creed, and when they are able to cloak their nefarious deeds in the mantle of political protest, they can and do obtain sympathy and support from groups that identify with their motives if not their methods (such as the IRA and the PLO).

Two Israeli authors of one influential study claim that terrorism is a violent *alternative* to legitimate power.[31] This is what many terrorists would like the world to believe, especially if the term *establishment* is to be substituted for the word *legitimate*. Innocence, however, is nondivisible. Terrorism is neither a mode of self-defense nor an alternative evil. "[T]errorism, because it involves taking innocent lives, is *never* morally justifiable whatever the provocation, and . . . there is always some other means of resistance or opposition even in the most oppressive societies. . . ."[32]

Political terrorism is often a manifestation of ideological fanaticism.[33] Terrorists of the left maintain they are fighting an anti-imperialist war,[34] while terrorists of the right consider liberal democracy as being spiritually bankrupt, racially decadent, and economically stagnant, as well as crumbling from powerful corrosive Communist elements.[35] Both terrorist persuasions have the zealot's obsession with purity of motives, and their very fanaticism tends to encourage their passions as a mystic rite of purification. The Italian Fascist dictator, Benito Mussolini (who, though a political gangster, was not a terrorist), put it succinctly when he declared: "Violence is profoundly moral, more moral than compromises and transactions."[36]

With the attraction of revolutionary violence acting as a motivational aphrodisiac, terrorism becomes a symbolic metaphor and a political statement. To destroy is to create. According to the infamous *Revolutionary Catechism* (1869) of Sergei Nechaev, the terror-revolutionist follows a solitary path to political salvation:

> Day and night he must have one single thought, one single purpose: merciless destruction. With this aim in view, tirelessly and in cold blood, he must always be prepared to die and to kill with his own hands anyone who stands in the way of achieving it.[37]

In the words of French existentialist philosopher, Jean-Paul Sartre, terror-violence has a cleansing effect which "can heal the wounds that it has inflicted."[38] Utilizing this type of Orwellian logic, terrorism is but an avenging sword of the disenfranchised and dispossessed, while death takes on the role of ultimate judge.[39]

One cannot overlook the messianic impulse running throughout political terrorism. In his pioneering study, published nearly thirty-five years ago, sociologist Joseph Roucek stressed the messianism of violence and terror, and the emphasis upon supreme self-sacrifice in which destruction becomes a way of life and a way of death.[40] "My life has absolutely no value," claimed Soledad Brother George Jackson. "I'm the man under hatches, the desperate one. We will make the revolution."[41] In this way terrorism is able to liberate and to legitimate violence, and the terrorist actor "is able to rationalize his own deviation."[42] The immolation of society is merely a necessary evil.

It became fashionable in the early part of the Terror Decade to emphasize the alienation of the terrorist from the society that he abjured, and to view terror-violence as a manifestation of protest on behalf of frustrated youth and the displaced intellectual directed against a suffocating societal control.[43] Political theorist Richard Lowenthal has ascribed the decline and disintegration of institutional authority in the 1970s to a "loss of ties," which in turn led to a desperate anxiety that spawned a willingness to look for any "doctrine that expresses a belief in secular salvation." The root causes of upheaval, he maintained, are to be found in growing societal decay, despair, and anomie.[44] This type of thinking carried to illogical extremes leads to such statements as that of Italian journalist Luigi Barzini, that terror-violence is primarily due to young people admitted to the universities without examination and with implicit promises that they would become future "members of the ruling class without studying," along with incompetent teachers and permissive acquiescence in student revolts.[45]

Actually, concern with alienation has been a long-standing Freudian and non-Freudian analytical focus.[46] Alienation undoubtedly contributes to neuroses, but it is not the central causative factor in terrorist behavior. Nor is irrationality. As British author Rebecca West observed many years ago, assassins and killers are not necessarily insane just because they cannot articulate their aspirations or intentions.[47] To the terrorist, actions often speak louder than words and attract far more attention.

Political scientist James Q. Wilson has noted the tendency to confuse ideologically motivated terrorists with legitimate heroes because their statements and motivations attract serious attention, despite the consequences of their violent acts.[48] (The absurd manifestos of the so-called Symbionese Liberation Army are a case in point.) Excepting the anarcho-nihilists, political terrorists often refer to themselves as soldiers engaged in political warfare.[49] The IRA hunger strikers of Maze Prison, during their unsuccessful six-month siege of self-destruction from March to October, 1981, demanded treatment as political prisoners rather than common criminals.[50] The very name of their organization connotes a legitimacy that they do not possess, and numerous other terrorist groups, including apocalyptic ones, have adopted the word "army" in an effort to gain the color of legitimate aspirations.[51] Rightist assassin Michael Vernon Townley, who on September 21, 1976, booby-trapped the automobile of former Chilean Ambassador Orlando Letelier in Washington, D.C., believed himself to be a soldier merely carrying out contractual obligations for his government employers.[52] Terrorist-liberationists frequently describe themselves as guerrilla soldiers engaged in military combat, and, astonishingly, the two Protocols Additional (1977) to the Geneva Conventions of 1949 take the same view.[53]

At times, certain ideological terrorist entities mask themselves in the trappings of political bandits who rob from the state and its dominant socioeconomic class in order to provide for the downtrodden, needy, and homeless. The Sicilian Red Brigades have recently turned their kidnapping of rich landlords and proprietors like Christian Democrat Ciro Cirillo into ransom demands allegedly demanding housing construction for the poor and protection of squatter's rights.[54] The Colombian terrorist M-19 kidnapped business executives with the alleged purpose of making them pay more money to their employees, and the M-19 also on occasion delivered free milk to poor neighborhoods, thereby enlisting support from the impoverished.[55] The PLO provides jobs, medical assistance, and public aid in Lebanon, which has led one American television correspondent to portray that organization as a proto-welfare state in all but name (omitting to mention PLO attacks on Lebanese civilians and its militant occupation of Lebanese territory).[56]

However, neither morally nor legally do alleged purity of motives excuse wanton and willful criminal conduct. "Murder is murder, no matter what the motives or ends," Pope John Paul II resolutely declared on Irish soil at the end of the Terror Decade.[57] British Prime Minister Margaret Thatcher has been bluntly succinct on the same subject: "Crime is crime is crime."[58] Terrorism thrives on concessions. To concede to the terrorist the possibility of a just cause is to invite disaster. The radical French journalist Régis Debray (now a French cabinet advisor, not all that unusual for successful terrorists and their sympathizers) defiantly taunted the prosecution at his Bolivian trial on charges of guerrilla activities against the state: "I regret that I am innocent of all the charges against me," thereby implying that the acts in question were worthy of any individual sacrifice.[59]

The wrath of the righteous is also reflective of a narcissistic anger. Psychologist Erich Fromm in his classic study of human destructiveness writes in an insightful analysis of aggression and narcissism that

[a] person, to the extent to which he is narcissistic, has a double standard of perception. Only he himself and what pertains to him has significance, while the rest of the world is more or less weightless or colorless. . . .[60]

The terrorist seeks instant gratification from his abominable act,[61] and takes pleasure in the attention occasioned by the consequences of violence. According to Fromm, political terrorists are more interested in destruction than they are in creation. Not only do they hate their enemies, but their destructiveness is a protest against life itself.[62] Terrorism is "a festival of death, a celebration that has its own priest and victims and that carries with it the likely risk that the priest himself will become a victim."[63]

Terrorism, in fact and in theory, has become a psychic religion.[64] Those who worship at the altar of force ultimately make force itself the greater truth. The very act of terror has been ritualized, and destruction becomes confused with salvation. French novelist André Malraux, by his remarkable portrayal of the terrorist mind, has acutely discerned the nexus between ritual and violence: "It was necessary that terrorism become a mystic cult. Solitude, first of all: let the terrorist decide alone, execute alone. . . . "[65] To the terrorist, past and present, violence has been an end in itself. The cult of force becomes significant for its own sake.[66] When the terrorist acts as prosecutor, judge, and executioner combined, the result allows every man to be his own state. Terrorism, truly, has developed into a war against all humanity.[67]

It is relevant to note that the level of frenzy necessary to achieve this attitude of mind, or at least required to stoke the intensity of self-sacrifice, is often heightened by the ingestion of drugs.[68] Nonetheless, to some terrorist-assassins, murder itself is the ultimate narcotic. Intoxicating stimulants are neither a root cause nor an adequate explanation, but merely the means by which mental awareness can be heightened and sustained over an abnormal length of time, and through which irresolution can succumb to excited emotion. One distinguished American psychiatrist, in discussing the profile of presidential assassins, concludes that the murderous act is a form of intimacy between victim and victimizer, with the latter subject to both a "lack of self-esteem and irrational ambition. . . . "[69]

Anonymity is not only the protective shield of political terrorists, but it is frequently characteristic of their method of operation. A bomb is anonymous. It is also per se an act of cowardice.[70] In 1979, the last year of the Terror Decade, bombings accounted for nearly 40 percent of all terrorist incidents.[71] In one week from August 29 to September 3, 1981, there were nine bombing attacks made in Europe, the Middle East, and Peru.[72] (During February and March 1979, there were 19 firebomb-arson attempts on banks and government buildings in Vancouver, British Columbia, alone.)[73] Significantly, American citizens and American property constitute approximately one-third of all terrorist events containing an international element. For example, the Peruvian bombings of several U.S. businesses, in addition to the American embassy and the residence of the American ambassador, were believed to be the work of the Lighted Path, a Maoist terror group opposed to U.S. investment in that country.[74] A similar rationale, plus the desire for ransom, has motivated numerous terrorist kidnappings of American business executives throughout Latin America.

An admixture of politics and desire for financial gain can be seen in many hostage events, including hijacking incidents, such as the five Indian Sikh political extremists who commandeered an Indian airliner at the end of September 1981, and forced a landing in Lahore, Pakistan, keeping forty-five hostages on board. Their demands included freedom for imprisoned colleagues and $500,000 ransom.[75] Thus, a fine line, at times, can be drawn between criminal organizations and terrorist groupings. Almost "every state has its own sophisticated independent criminal gangs, which may or may not have regular international contacts."[76] Without an accepted and workable definition, the truth is that terrorism, at this date, is primarily in the eyes of the beholder.

Like their political counterparts, psychologically disturbed terrorist actors are both alienated and fanatic. In fact, all three terrorist categories are bound together by cruelty, wantonness, and reckless indifference to the value of human life. It is not by accident that John W. Hinckley, Jr., a drifter and nonentity who attempted to assassinate President Ronald Reagan, entered a plea of insanity prior to trial, arguing that he was not criminally responsible for his violent acts.[77] Yet, most terrorists are neither mad nor psychologically aberrant, as one scholar mistakenly argues.[78] The terrorist act is strategically calculated, discriminate in its choice of weapons, and in the selection of the actual situs. The harmful consequences, however, of a bomb, hand grenade, machine gun, or molotov cocktail may be indiscriminate when it comes to the identity of the potential victim.

For terrorists of every variety, violence is a powerful stimulant. All seem to be aware of the effects of publicity and the influential role of the media. The theatrical nature of terrorist events is consciously designed for a maximum impact upon a vast audience.[79] Many so-called terrorist-liberationists (such as the Basques and the Armenians) seek to impose the distant past upon an unwilling present and an indifferent future. Their tiny numbers belie their potential destructive capacity, while modern technology gives such a group an importance far beyond its miniscule membership.[80] In the contemporary world of socially fragmented, ethnically divided societies and cultures, political terrorism has become the last refuge of the hopeless cause. Power is now equated with means as well as with ends. The primary purpose of terror is to terrorize, whatever the motive and regardless of the result.

Neither liberal, pluralist democracy nor the world community has yet come to grips with the terrorist threat. The challenge is ongoing, since terrorism can never be eliminated, although it can be controlled. As long as the terrorist actor is able to wreak his harmful vengeance upon an unprotected public, the world itself remains hostage to future incidents and to further degradations. Terrorism may or may not be contagious.[81] To its victims, terrorism is definitely fatal. To know thine enemy without first taking precautions for survival is not only foolish, it is suicidal.

Notes

1. This is readily apparent from the impressive compilation of Edward F. Mickolus, *The Literature of Terrorism: A Selectively Annotated Bibliography* (Westport, Conn.: Greenwood, 1980), and the slimmer, but still significant volume by Augustus R. Norton and Martin H. Greenburg, *International Terrorism: An Annotated Bibliography and Research Guide* (Boulder, Colo.: Westview Press, 1980).

2. Ted Robert Gurr, *Why Men Rebel* (Princeton, N.J.: Princeton University Press, 1971).

3. See, particularly, David C. Rapoport, *Assassinations & Terrorism* (Toronto: CBC Learning Systems, 1971); Gerald McKnight, *The Terrorist Mind* (Indianapolis: Bobbs-Merrill Co., 1974); Frederick J. Hacker, *Crusaders, Criminals, Crazies: Terror and Terrorism in Our Time* (New York: W.W. Norton & Co., 1977), hereinafter cited as *Terror and Terrorism*; Walter Laqueur, *Terrorism* (Boston: Little, Brown and Co., 1977). Many social scientists have been heard to complain that there is yet much to be done on terrorist theory. Augustus R. Norton, "International Terrorism: Review Essay," *Armed Forces and Society* 7, no. 4 (Summer 1981): 623.

4. Some of the more influential constructs are summarized in Robert A. Friedlander, *Terrorism: Documents of International and Local Control*, vol. I (Dobbs Ferry, N.Y.: Oceana Publications, 1979), pp. 49-58, hereinafter cited as *Terrorism* I.

5. Irving Louis Horowitz, "Political Terrorism and State Power," *Journal of Political and Military Sociology* 1 (Spring 1973): 148-150. Because of the broad nature of the analysis, exceptions can be made to all twelve of Horowitz's propositions.

6. The latter phrase has been borrowed from J. Bowyer Bell, *A Time of Terror: How Democratic Societies Respond to Revolutionary Violence* (New York: Basic Books, 1978).

7. Eric Hoffer, "Works and Days," *Harper's*, October 1978, p. 78.

8. Eric Hoffer, "Beware the Intellectual," in Edison Electric Institute, *Symposium: Science, Technology and the Human Prospect* (Washington, D.C.: The Association of Electric Companies, 1979), p. 11.

9. Brian Crozier, *A Theory of Conflict* (New York: Charles Scribner's Sons, 1974), pp. 127-28.

10. Tokyo (1963), The Hague (1970), and Montreal (1971).

11. See Robert A. Friedlander, "Banishing Fear from the Skies: A Statutory Proposal," *Duquesne Law Review* 16, no. 3 (1977-1978): 283-86.

12. Friedlander, *Terrorism* I, pp. 74-75, 88, and 95; Act for the Prevention and Punishment of Internationally Protected Persons, 18 USC §§112, 116 (1976), reprinted in Robert A. Friedlander, *Terrorism: Documents of International and Local Control*, vol. II (Dobbs Ferry, N.Y.: Oceana Publications, 1979), pp. 521-25, hereinafter cited as *Terrorism* II.

13. Quoted by Jules Mazé, *Sous la terreur* (Paris: Librarie Hachette, 1947), p. 81.

14. Michael Walzer, "The New Terrorists: Random Murder," *The New Republic*, August 30, 1975, p. 12.

15. Aristotle, *The Politics*, ed. and trans. T. A. Sinclair (Harmondsworth: Penguin Books, 1976), bk. 5, chap. 11, p. 230.

16. George H. Sabine, *A History of Political Theory*, 3rd ed. (New York: Holt, Rinehart and Winston, 1961), pp. 246-47.

17. Donald Atwell Zoll, *Reason and Rebellion: An Informal History of Political Ideas* (Englewood Cliffs, N.J.: Prentice-Hall, 1963), pp. 135-36.

18. Quoted in Louis J. Weichmann, *A True History of the Assassination of Abraham Lincoln and of the Conspiracy of 1865*, ed. Floyd E. Risvold (New York: Vintage Books, 1977), p. 209.

19. Ibid., p. 210.

20. Albert Camus, *Caligula and Three Other Plays*, trans. Stuart Gilbert (New York: Vintage Books, 1958), p. 221.

21. Ibid., pp. 246 and 282.

22. Albert Camus, *The Rebel: An Essay on Man in Revolt*, rev. and trans. Anthony Bower (New York: Vintage Books, 1956), p. 285.

23. Quoted by Gerold Frank, *The Deed* (New York: Simon and Schuster, 1963), p. 261.

24. Walzer, "The New Terrorists," p. 13. Cf. *Corriere della Sera* (Milan), Jan. 4, 1981, p. 1, col. 4.

25. Crozier, *A Theory of Conflict*, p. 119.

26. Irving Howe, "The Return of Terror," *Dissent* 22, no. 3 (Summer 1975): 37.

27. Cf. Lesley Hazelton, "Respectable Terrorism: When Its Victims Become Violent," *Harper's*, October 1980, pp. 30-31; George Kane, "Traveler's Diarist," *The New Republic*, March 14, 1981, p. 41; Robert A. Friedlander, "Terrorism and National Liberation Movements: Can Rights Derive from Wrongs?," *Case Western Journal of International Law* 13, no. 2 (Spring 1981).

28. This doctrine was given its most systematic exposition in the twentieth century by Georges Sorel, *Reflections on Violence*, trans. T. E. Hulme and J. Roth (New York: Collier Macmillan Publisher, 1961).

29. On the resurgence of rightist terrorism, cf. Paul Wilkinson, "Still Working 'for the Extinction of Mankind': An Assessment of the Significance of the Resurgence of Fascist Terrorism in Europe," *Across the Board* 18, no. 1 (January 1981): 27-30; Thomas Sheehan, "Italy: Terror on the Right," *The New York Review of Books*, January 22, 1981, pp. 23-26, hereinafter cited as "Terror on the Right."

30. Walzer, "The New Terrorists," p. 13.

31. D. V. Segre and J. H. Adler, "The Ecology of Terrorism," *Encounter* 40, no. 2 (February 1973): 20. See also, William F. May, "Terrorism as Strategy and Ecstasy," *Social Research* 41 (Summer 1974): 296 and 297.

32. Paul Wilkinson, "Can State Be 'Terrorist'?," *International Affairs* (Summer 1981): 468, emphasis in the original.

33. Joseph W. Bishop, Jr., "Law in the Control of Terrorism and Insurrection: The British Laboratory Experience," *Law and Contemporary Problems* 42, no. 2 (Spring 1978): 141, writes that "the terrorist is by definition a zealot." Bishop's

assertion that the terrorist "frequently has little concern for his own skin" is challenged by the CIA and some experts, but recent history supports Professor Bishop.

34. See, for example, the statement of the German Red Army Fraction made after its attack upon NATO military headquarters at Ramstein Air Base in the German Federal Republic. *U.S. News & World Report*, September 14, 1981, p. 31.

35. See Sheehan, "Terror on the Right," pp. 23-26.

36. Quoted by Rebecca West, *Black Lamb and Grey Falcon: A Journey through Yugoslavia* (New York: Viking Press, 1943), p. 613.

37. Quoted by Franco Venturi, *Roots of Revolution: A History of the Populist and Socialist Movements in Nineteenth Century Russia*, trans. Francis Haskell (New York: Grosset & Dunlap, 1966), p. 281.

38. Jean Paul Sartre, "Preface," in Frantz Fanon, *The Wretched of the Earth*, trans. Constance Farrington (New York: Grove Press, 1968), p. 30.

39. The counter to that misguided reasoning can be found in journalist Jack Beatty's aphorism: "Death is true, but it is not the Truth." Jack Beatty, "A Death in the Family," *The New Republic*, October 7, 1981, p. 40.

40. Joseph S. Roucek, "Violence and Terror," in Joseph S. Roucek, ed., *Social Control* (New York: D. Van Nostrand Co., 1947), pp. 339-40.

41. George Jackson, "Bringing the Country to Its Knees," in Thomas Ford Hoult, *Social Justice and Its Enemies* (New York: Halstead Press, 1975), p. 538.

42. Stephen Schafer, *The Political Criminal: The Problem of Morality and Crime* (New York: The Free Press, 1974), p. 115. See also, Herbert Marcuse, *Counter-Revolution and Revolt* (Boston: Beacon Press, 1972), p. 52.

43. Rollo May, *Power and Innocence: A Search for the Sources of Violence* (New York: Delta, 1976), p. 221. See also, Rollo May, *Man's Search for Himself* (New York: Delta, 1953), pp. 28-30, 44-45, and 54; Frederick J. Hacker, *Aggression: violence dans le monde moderne*, trans. Rémi Laureillard and Hélène Bellour (Paris: Calmann-Levy, 1972), pp. 233-34; Marcuse, *Counter-Revolution and Revolt*, pp. 129-32; Stanislav Ardreski, *Prospects of a Revolution in the U.S.A.* (New York: Harper Colophon Books, 1974), pp. 10-22; Kerry L. Milte, Allen A. Bartholomew, Dennis J. O'Hearn, and Andrew Campbell, "Terrorism: Political and Psychological Considerations," *ANZ Journal of Criminology* 9 (March 1976): 4-6.

44. Richard Lowenthal, "The West's Intellectual Crisis: Reorienting Thinking toward an Era of Rapid Change," *Atlas World Press Review*, February 1978, p. 15.

45. Luigi Barzini, "Governing Italian Style," *Policy Review* 12 (Spring 1980): 69. See also, Hoffer, "Beware the Intellectual," p. 11.

46. Cf. Sigmund Freud, *Civilization and Its Discontents*, trans. James Strachey (New York: W.W. Norton, 1961); Erich Fromm, *Man for Himself: An Inquiry into the Psychology of Ethics* (Greenwich, Conn.: Fawcett Publications, 1947); Erich Fromm, *The Sane Society* (Greenwich, Conn.: Fawcett Publications, 1955).

47. West, *Black Lamb*, p. 8.

48. James Q. Wilson, "Thinking about Terrorism," *Commentary*, July 1981, p. 38.

49. "Frederick J. Hacker Interview," *Penthouse*, November 1977, p. 138, hereinafter cited as Hacker interview.

50. *The Blade* (Toledo), October 4, 1981, Sec. A, p. 1, col. 2.

51. H. H. Anthony Cooper, "The Terrorist and the Victim," *Victimology: An*

International Journal 1, no. 2 (Summer 1976): 239, maintains that "[t]he terrorist has a great need to rationalize his violence."

52. John Dinges and Saul Landau, *Assassination on Embassy Row* (New York: Pantheon Books, 1980), p. 362.

53. Yoram Dinstein, "The New Geneva Protocols: A Step Forward or Backward?," *The Yearbook of World Affairs* 33 (1979): 265-83.

54. Pier Vittorio Buffa, "Quanto Pesa Cirillo? Centomila Vani," *L'Espresso*, May 17, 1981, pp. 28-31.

55. Cynthia Gorney, "Voices from a Bogota Jail," *The Washington Post*, June 7, 1981, p. D 5, col. 1.

56. *ABC-TV World News Tonight*, Mike Lee reporting, "The PLO," September 9, 1981.

57. *New York Times*, September 30, 1979, sec. 1. p. 28, col. 2.

58. *Time*, May 4, 1981, p. 34.

59. Régis Debray, *Strategy for Revolution*, ed. Robin Blackburn (New York: Monthly Review Press, 1970), p. 227.

60. Erich Fromm, *The Anatomy of Destructiveness* (New York: Holt, Rinehart and Winston, 1973), p. 201.

61. Tom Morgan, Book review, *Psychology Today*, August 1977, pp. 88-89. See also, Fromm, *Anatomy of Destructiveness*, pp. 201-5.

62. Fromm, *Anatomy of Destructiveness*, p. 269.

63. May, "Terrorism," p. 297.

64. Albert Parry, *Terrorism: From Robespierre to Arafat* (New York: Vanguard Press, 1976), p. 535. See also, André Malraux, *Man's Fate*, trans. Haakon M. Chevalier (New York: The Modern Library, 1934), p. 196.

65. Ibid., p. 246.

66. West, *Black Lamb*, p. 1104.

67. Bernard-Henri Levy, "The War Against All: Every Man His Own State," *The New Republic*, February 11, 1978, p. 14. See also, David B. Tinnin, "Terror, Inc.," *Playboy*, May 1977, p. 166.

68. Cf. Hacker interview, p. 140; Bommi Baumann, *Terror or Love? The Personal Account of a West German Guerrilla*, trans. Gilbert Shelton (London: John Calder, 1979), pp. 49-56; Parry, *Terrorism*, p. 29; and the generalized observations of Fromm, *Anatomy of Destructiveness*, pp. 275-76.

69. Interview with Dr. Lawrence Z. Freedman, "In His Own Work," *People Weekly*, June 5, 1978, p. 40.

70. President Ronald Reagan was not far off the mark when he declared, in a fit of exasperation, that "the civilized world has got to find a method to protect ourselves from terrorists, who I think are the most cowardly of the human species." *CBS-TV Evening News*, The White House, March 12, 1981.

71. National Foreign Assessment Center, *International Terrorism in 1979* (Washington, D.C.: Central Intelligence Agency, 1980), p. 6, reprinted in Robert A. Friedlander, *Terrorism: Documents of International and Local Control—From the Terror Decade of the 1970's to the Dangerous Decade of the 1980's*, vol. III (Dobbs Ferry, N.Y.: Oceana Publications, 1981), p. 63.

72. *Time*, September 14, 1981, p. 48; *U.S. News & World Report*, September 14, 1981, p. 31.

73. *New York Times*, March 6, 1979, p. A 8, col. 4.

74. *U.S. News & World Report*, September 14, 1981, p. 31.

75. *The Miami Herald*, September 30, 1981, p. 12 A, col. 1.

76. Richard Clutterbuck, *Kidnap and Ransom: The Response* (Boston: Faber and Faber, 1978), p. 28.

77. *Washington Post*, September 29, 1981, p. A 1, col. 5.

78. Parry, *Terrorism*, p. 35.

79. For a detailed discussion of this issue, see Robert A. Friedlander, *Terrorism and the Media: A Contemporary Assessment* (Gaithersburg, Md.: International Association of Chiefs of Police, 1981).

80. The Basque terrorist ETA, for example, reportedly does not exceed 200 members. GRAPO is supposed to have only 50 activists. Vittorfranco S. Pisano, "Spain Faces the Extremists: Cannons to the Left and Cannons to the Right," *Terrorism, Violence, Insurgency Journal* 2, no. 6 (July 1981): 10 and 13.

81. See Manus I. Midlarsky, Martha Crenshaw, and Fumihiko Yoshida, "Why Violence Spreads: The Contagion of International Terrorism," *International Studies Quarterly* 24, no. 2 (June 1980): 262-98. A *contra* position is taken by Edward Heyman and Edward Mickolus, "Observations on 'Why Violence Spreads,'" ibid., pp. 299-305.

4

Businesses Becoming Increasing Targets

CHARLES A. RUSSELL

Terrorist attacks against business facilities and personnel have increased steadily since the mid-1970s. As a result, business today is the single largest category of activity targeted by terrorist groups worldwide. Of all major actions recorded in 1980 and the first six months of 1981, 29.4 percent of the 3,982 terrorist operations involved business facilities and personnel. By comparison, terrorist actions directed against other high-risk target categories during the same time span were significantly less. Police and military installations/personnel were involved in only 22 percent of all incidents, governmental personnel and facilities 18.1 percent, and diplomatic establishments or individual diplomats 3.8 percent.[1]

An Evolution in Terrorist Targeting

As radical political groups in Europe, Asia, the Middle East, and Latin America turned increasingly toward terrorism as a revolutionary tactic during the early 1970s, the initial targets attacked by these groups were those directly linked to governments they opposed. Policemen, military personnel, high-ranking public officials, police posts and government offices all were high on terrorist "hit lists" throughout the 1970-1973 time span. By mid-1973, however, this strategy of direct confrontation was an obvious failure. In contrast to the pronouncements of terrorist theoreticians, governments did not collapse or bow to revolutionary demands and police were quick to shoot back when assaulted. Accordingly, by early 1974 most terrorist targeting had shifted rather definitively to attacks against diplomatic establishments and the abduction of foreign diplomats. Again, the terrorist belief was that governments would accede to their demands as a result of the leverage gained through such operations. Additionally, actions of this type had the obvious advantage of almost certain large-scale media coverage. Such coverage gave small terrorist organizations a means of publicizing their objectives and goals to both national and international audiences.[2]

Despite acute embarrassment in many cases, governments did not give in to the terrorists. Instead, they often increased security measures and began active counter-terrorist programs. Further, terrorist groups soon learned that diplomatic establishments also could be "hardened" against attack. By 1975, most diplomatic facilities in high-risk areas had implemented effective security systems, while individual diplomats were assigned ever larger protective security details by the host nation as well as by their own. In brief, within the short span of two years (1974-1975), diplomatic targets had become almost as difficult and costly to attack as police, military, and governmental facilities/personnel were during the early 1970s.

Faced with these developments, most terrorist groups active since 1975 have directed a significant percentage of their operations against business installations or personnel—targets that by their very nature cannot "harden up" or restrict public access to their installations and representatives. In contrast to police, military, governmental, and diplomatic offices, all of which can and have implemented rather rigid security procedures in high-risk areas, businesses were and are unable to follow suit. For them, and almost all commercial ventures, unrestricted public access is vital. Any real restraint upon this traffic flow is tantamount to going out of business. Similarly, corporate executives or managerial personnel surrounded by heavily armed security details are virtually useless in dealing with potential customers or even colleagues.

Recognizing these vulnerabilities and the necessarily open nature of commercial and business operations, terrorist groups worldwide have focused one-third or more of their efforts since 1975 on business targets. During the years 1976-1978, 41 percent of all recorded terrorist actions involved business facilities or personnel. In 1979 the comparable figure was 33 percent, with 30 percent reported for 1980 and the initial six months of 1981. Viewed in terms of total incidents, 3,449 of the 10,054 recorded terrorist operations reported between January 1, 1976 and June 30, 1981 targeted business (34.3 percent for this five and one-half year period). Thus, business facilities and personnel remain the largest single category of activity attacked by terrorist groups worldwide.[3]

While the inherent vulnerability of business operations was an important factor in moving most terrorist groups to attack these targets, a less quantifiable strategic consideration also seems to have been significant. This was particularly true in the case of terrorist organizations espousing a radical Marxist political philosophy. (Eighty-one percent of all terrorist groups active since 1975 have been radical Marxist in political orientation.) For these groups, the concepts of revolutionary theorists such as Abraham Guillen and Carlos Marighella had a special appeal. Particularly attractive were those aspects of their writings calling for an attack on the economic foundations of a government rather than overt elements of the regime itself (police, military, governmental targets). These new ideas were perhaps best articulated by the Italian Red Brigades in their February 1978 strategic resolution entitled *Brigate Rosse: Rizoluzione della Direzione Strategica.* In this and other similar writings, capitalism, led by the United States, is seen as the economic foundation of virtually all "repressive" states. As noted at the outset of the Red Brigades document, "Multinational imperialism (directed by the United States) thus emerges as a system of global domination in which various national capitalisms are merely its organic fingers and toes."[4] Accordingly, to strike at the very heart of such a state, eliminate the government, and lay the basis for a future Marxist society, this "capitalist network" must be destroyed. To accomplish this, terrorist assaults on domestic, foreign, and U.S. business firms—as integral parts of the capitalist system—are indeed attacks upon the very foundations of the state itself. They injure, at one and the same time, capitalism and the state. Thus, for terrorists of a radical Marxist persuasion, operations against business targets remain high on their priority list.[5]

Terrorist Tactics: Operations Against Business

Since the early 1970s, business personnel and installations worldwide have been attacked by revolutionary groups using a wide variety of tactics. Three of these, however, have been particularly in evidence since 1975 and currently (1981) account for almost 90 percent of all terrorist actions directed against business. The three are bombing, kidnapping, and attacks against facilities. All take maximum advantage of the necessarily open nature of commercial activity and the inability of business to implement severe security restrictions that would reduce public access to its facilities or personnel.

The extensive use of bombing, kidnapping, and facility attacks as tactics for operations against business targets is quite clear from Table 4-1.

BOMBING

As Table 4-1 indicates, 42.2 percent (451 incidents) of the 1,069 significant bombing actions reported worldwide in 1979 involved business. In 1980, 48.7 percent (490 acts) of the 1,006 bombings that year also targeted business, as did 46.4 percent (188 incidents) of the 405 bombings recorded in the first six months of 1981. Total known losses in terrorist bombing actions over this two and one-half-year period were $165,013,800. Of this figure, more than 60 percent involved business targets with U.S. business losses reaching $45,518,500.

In operations against business and other targets during the 1980-1981 time span, explosives rather than incendiary devices were used in 83 percent of all operations. The explosive favored by most terrorist groups is plastique. Ideally suited for clandestine use, plastique is very stable and easily adaptable for a wide variety of operations. It also possesses extremely high

TABLE 4-1.
International Terrorist Activity, 1979-June 1981, by Category
  of Attack and with Business Target

Total Terrorist Incidents			*Initial Six*
Worldwide	*1979*	*1980*	*Months 1981*
Incidents Broken Out			
by Tactic			
Bombing	1,069	1,006	405
Kidnapping	132	124	50
Facility Attack	790	768	447
Assassination	546	843	295
Maiming	37	18	7
Hijacking	11	14	5
Percent of Above Targeting Business			
Bombing	42.2	48.7	46.4
Kidnapping	52.7	46.0	42.0
Facility Attack	32.6	22.9	14.8
Assassination	11.7	13.8	9.2
Maiming	45.9	33.3	28.6

destructive power and is readily available, through theft, from most military facilities.

Unusually stable in transit, plastique has been taken almost everywhere. It has been smuggled into various European nations placed behind the lining of suitcases checked aboard aircraft as well as packed around the chassis of cars and trucks. Jolts, bumps, and even burning will not cause detonation. Resembling coarse putty in consistency and appearance, plastique can be molded into any form. As a result, it is easily placed around structure-bearing supports, making it an ideal tool for bombing high-tension towers and electrical power plants—priority targets for many terrorist groups today.

Exploding at 26,500 feet per second, plastique is extremely destructive with a very high brisant (shattering) effect. Four ounces, for example, will demolish a large American-made sedan. As a result, a relatively small quantity of this explosive is necessary in most terrorist bombings. Finally, as mentioned earlier, plastique is stored in most major military installations worldwide. Terrorist thefts from such facilities have been frequent since the early 1970s. Within the first five years of that decade, for example, terrorists in the Federal Republic of Germany took significant quantities of the explosive from U.S. military storage areas in that country. More recently, in July 1980, a unit of ETA, Spain's most active terrorist organization, carried out the largest theft of plastique in history—17,600 pounds taken from a military warehouse near Santander.[6]

Examining terrorist bombing operations directed against business on a country-by-country basis, twelve nations have accounted for 81 percent of these actions over the past two and one-half years. Within Europe, business bombings have been focused in Spain, France, Italy, and Northern Ireland, while critical countries in Latin America are now and have been El Salvador, Chile, Colombia, Guatemala, and Peru. Within the Middle East, most business bombings have occurred in Iran, Israel, and Lebanon, while in Asia significant actions have been reported only in the Philippines. During the same time span, U.S.-based corporations were bombed most frequently within the continental United States, as well as Puerto Rico, El Salvador, and Spain.

KIDNAPPING

While terrorist bombings account for the largest number of actions affecting the business community as a whole, perhaps even more disrupting to any corporate structure is the abduction for ransom of key executive and management personnel. During the past eleven years, operations of this type have accounted for slightly more than 47 percent of all terrorist abductions and over the last two and one-half years, the comparable percentage was 45.1 percent (138 of 306 total kidnappings, January 1, 1979 through June 30, 1981). By way of contrast, the other three categories of high-risk terrorist targets (police/military, governmental, and diplomatic officials) taken together accounted for only 21 percent of all abductions worldwide in the same 1979-1981 time frame.

Currently, Risks International of Alexandria, Virginia, has data a\ ailable on ransoms demanded and paid in 32 percent of the 710 total terrorist kidnappings between January 1, 1970 and June 30, 1981. This information reflects ransom demands in these cases of $405,256,000 and known payments totalling $156,666,400. (It is emphasized these figures pertain to only 32 percent of all recorded abductions. Accordingly, actual ransom payments obviously were much higher.)

As is evident from the above data, paid kidnap randoms are a primary source of revenue for many terrorist groups worldwide. Within Latin America, and to a lesser extent Europe, the abduction of businessmen for ransom is particularly widespread. During 1980 and the initial six months of 1981, for example, 77 (48.7 percent) of 158 total abductions in the two regions involved business personnel.

Illustrative of the important role played by funds generated via business abductions are the cases of El Salavdor, Italy, and Spain. In El Salvador, a substantial portion of the financing required to support present-day guerrilla/terrorist groups operating against the national government was derived from a series of four business abductions carried out between August 14 and December 14, 1978. On August 14, 1978, Kjell Bjork, technical director of the Swedish firm Telefonico L. M. Ericson, was kidnapped by the Armed Forces of National Resistance (FARN) and later ransomed for a reported $1 million. Slightly over three months later, Fritz Schuitema, manager of operations in El Salvador for the Dutch-based Phillips Corporation, also was kidnapped by the FARN and later released after payment of some $4 million. Six days after the Schuitema affair, Ian Massie and Michael Chatterton, manager and assistant manager of the British-owned Bank of London and South America, were taken by the FARN on November 30. After being held prisoner for several months, the two bankers were freed following payment of a reported $8 million ransom. The final victim of FARN abductions was Takakuzu Suzuki, manager of the joint Japanese-Salvadoran textile firm Insinca. Kidnapped on December 8, 1978, Suzuki was released after payment of a reported $5 million ransom. (With the release of Suzuki, following the earlier kidnap-execution of his predecessor Fujio Matsumoto, all Japanese personnel were withdrawn from El Salvador and Insinca ceased operations.) Thus, in the short space of four and one-half months, Salvadoran terrorists abducted and later ransomed five foreign businessmen for reported paid ransoms of at least $18 million—more than sufficient funds to lay the financial basis for the current revolutionary effort in that country.[7]

In Italy and Spain, similar developments took place during 1979 and 1980-1981. Italian terrorists abducted twenty-two businessmen in 1979—75.9 percent of all kidnappings reported in Italy that year. Known paid ransoms in these cases exceeded $4 million—again more than enough to replenish depleted terrorist coffers.

Within Spain, four businessmen were abducted for lucrative ransoms during 1980, and in 1981 a single kidnapping provided the ETA with between $4.5 and $5.6 million in ransom payments according to reports of the Spanish Ministry of the Interior. This operation took place on January 13 and involved the abduction of corporate chief and multimillionaire Luis Sunyer Sanchis from his company (Avidesa) offices in Alcira (Valencia province). Taken by a five-member ETA kidnap team (four males and one female) armed with submachine guns, Sunyer Sanchis was held for ninety-three days until ransom demands were met. Faced with declining contributions from revolutionary elements in the Basque provinces of Spain, ETA appears to have conducted this action for the sole purpose of replenishing its depleted treasury.[8]

While the abduction of business personnel is almost always carried out to obtain operational funds, terrorist groups also have conducted such actions to force the release of imprisoned associates or to obtain other political goals. Although these cases are relatively rare, two such actions stand out in recent years. The first involves the kidnap-murder of Dr. Hans-Martin Schleyer, chairman of the board of Daimler-Benz. Abducting Schleyer in Cologne, Federal Republic of Germany, on September 5, 1977, his kidnappers demanded the release of several key terrorist prisoners. When these demands were not met, the automobile executive was killed and his body left in Mulhouse, France, on October 19, 1977. More recently, José Maria Ryan, an engineer for the Iberduero Corporation in Spain, was abducted from his office at the Lemoniz nuclear reactor site near Bilbao. Iberduero is Spain's largest electrical contracting firm and is responsible for reactor construction. Following the kidnapping by an ETA team late in January 1981, the terrorists demanded an end to site construction as well as demolition of all work completed. When these demands were refused by the Spanish government, Ryan was murdered on February 6, 1981 and his body left in a field near Bilbao.[9]

Although the abduction of businessmen for purely political purposes is rare, it is interesting to note such individuals almost invariably share the same fate as governmental, police, or military personnel taken for similar reasons. In almost 90 percent of these cases, the victims are killed when terrorist demands cannot be met. By way of contrast, businessmen abducted for ransom almost always are freed in reasonably good health once the ransom is paid.[10]

As indicated earlier, most business abductions since 1978 have occurred in Latin America and Europe. Latin America, however, is by far the real focal point for such operations. During 1979, 52.7 percent of all kidnappings within that region involved businessmen. (Of the fifty-five total actions of this type in Latin America, twenty-nine concerned business personnel. These took place in El Salvador, Nicaragua, Colombia, and Guatemala.) This same trend continued in 1980 with 50 percent of all abductions in the region involving businessmen. Deleting Nicaragua, again Colombia, Guatemala, and El Salvador remained the most active states that year. The initial six months of 1981 also continued the pattern with 57 percent of all abductions in Latin America targeting business (sixteen of twenty-eight operations). As in the past, Colombia, Guatemala, and El Salvador led all other nations of the area.

As a concluding note in regard to terrorist kidnappings, there has been remarkably little change in the pattern followed for such operations over the 1970-1981 time span. The "normal" kidnap team consists of three persons (usually including a female), the single victim is the rule rather than the exception, and the action most often involves taking the target from a chauffeur-driven vehicle while he or she is en route to or from work.[11]

FACILITY ATTACKS

A final tactic of interest to the business community is the facility attack. Defined as an assault, by a terrorist commando unit, upon a physical installation such as an office, police post, political party headquarters, etc., the facility attack differs from a bombing operation in that it is an open attack as opposed to the clandestine placement of an explosive device. Frequently involving a team of six or more persons armed with submachine guns and explosives, this type of action is essentially paramilitary in nature. While over 50 percent of such actions during the 1970-1981 time period targeted police, military, or governmental installations, 31.8 percent involved business. Within recent years, however, although the total number of facility attacks per year has increased substantially when compared to the 1970-1978 time period (790 in 1979 and 768 in 1980 versus 952 for the entire nine years, 1970-1978), the percentage of these actions affecting business has declined steadily (Table 4-2).

TABLE 4-2.
Percentage of International Terrorist Facility Attacks Directed
   Against Business, 1970-June 1981

Time Period	Total Facility Attacks	Percent Directed against Business
1970-1978	952	46.1
1979	790	32.6
1980	768	22.9
1981 (6 mos.)	447	14.8

The substantial percentage decrease in facility attacks involving business targets during 1979-1981 reflects a change in terrorist targeting for this type of operation from business to police, military, and governmental facilities. This change was most pronounced in Latin America, the region in which most facility attacks take place. Of the 1,215 such operations recorded between January 1, 1980 and June 30, 1981, a total of 71.9 percent occurred in Latin America. Almost 70 percent of these targeted police, military or governmental installations rather than business.

In evaluating the above-described change, a January 1981 analysis of facility attack operations prepared by Risks International states,

> When facility attacks are at a relatively low level, terrorist groups are usually limited in capability and focus most of their operations against business targets. However, as the number of facility attacks increase in relation to total incident count—particularly attacks against police and military objectives—this shift in tactics and targeting usually indicates improved group capabilities. At the same time, it normally results in a drop in business targeting as the terrorists place greater emphasis on attacking police and military elements of an incumbent government. It is thus interesting to note the greatest threat to business does not occur during an all-out terrorist/guerrilla offensive but rather in the period in which revolutionary groups are building their forces.''[12]

While the number of facility attacks affecting business has declined in recent years as a percentage of total operations, these actions remain an important source of operational funds for many terrorist groups. Although detailed data is available concerning funds stolen in only 10 percent of the 2,510 facility attacks carried out between January 1970 and the close of 1980, thefts in this small percentage of all cases still amount to $44,788,642. ($18,323,062 taken 1970-1978; $17,846,300 in 1979; and $8,619,280 for 1980.) Robberies from U.S. corporations during the same time span (again based on only 10 percent of all such cases) reached $3,793,698. Quite clearly, total thefts exceeding $44,000,000 over an eleven-year period were of substantial benefit in providing operational funding for the groups involved.

Although facility attacks affecting business have been less frequent in the past two years, the bulk of these actions continue to occur in the same countries. During 1980-1981 business firms were hit most often in El Salvador, Turkey, Spain, Colombia, Chile, Guatemala, Italy, and France. U.S. corporations were attacked in El Salvador, France, Guatemala, and Puerto Rico.

As a closing note on facility attack operations, these are among the most lethal and costly (in terms of losses) of all terrorist actions. Again, based upon data in 10 percent of the 2,510 facility attacks reported 1970 through 1980, total dollar losses (from damages and funds stolen) were $224,333,502 ($20,887,238 for U.S. corporations). Total fatalities in all 2,510 actions were 4,944 killed and an additional 2,911 persons injured.

Targeting by World Region

Since February 1980, Latin America has led all other world regions in the total number of recorded terrorist actions, including those directed against business. In that month, for.the first time since January 1970 (the initial year reported in the Risks International data base), Latin America recorded more incidents than Europe. By the end of 1980, looking at the year as a whole, 56.5 percent of the 2,773 reported terrorist operations worldwide occurred in Latin America versus 21.5 percent in Europe, 15.4 percent for the Middle East-North Africa, and much lesser percentages for Asia, Sub-Saharan Africa, and North America. This same trend continued throughout the first six months of 1981 with 63.2 percent of all 1,209 reported terrorist actions worldwide taking place in Latin America, followed by Europe with 20.8 percent, the Middle East-North Africa at 6.5 percent, and the other world regions with significantly lower figures.

Although the steadily expanding scope of terrorist/guerrilla activity in El Salvador accounted for a very substantial portion of the rising incident count for Latin America in 1980 and the first half of 1981 (50.4 percent of all 2,331 operations in the region for this period), growing revolutionary activity in Guatemala, Colombia, Peru, and Chile also provided significant additions to the regional total. In fact, for most of 1980 and the initial six months of 1981, Guatemala was the second most active nation worldwide, led only by El Salvador. During this eighteen-month period, five hundred significant terrorist operations were reported in Guatemala. For the same time span, Colombia also ranked high among the more active states, varying from third to sixth on a monthly basis for total reported terrorist actions.

Paralleling this overall rise in the Latin American regional incident count was an expansion in the number of operations targeting business. During 1980, a total of 47.6 percent of all such actions worldwide took place in Latin America as did 54.2 percent in the first six months of 1981. Thus, more than half of all terrorist actions targeting business today are occurring in a single region.

Within Latin America, as might be anticipated from the concentration of regional terrorist activity in El Salvador and Guatemala, these nations also led in actions targeting business. During 1980 and the first six months of 1981, there were 317 antibusiness incidents reported in El Salvador, 112 for Guatemala, and 43 in Colombia. Other states with a significant number of actions directed against business targets were Chile (43) and Peru (38). In all, 615 antibusiness operations were recorded in Latin America during the eighteen-month period extending from January 1, 1980 through June 30, 1981. Overall, of these 615 operations, 553 took place in the five countries mentioned above.

Looking at the five most active Latin American nations from the standpoint of those tactics used in attacks against business over the 1980-1981 time span, bombing was preferred by terrorist groups in El Salvador (195 incidents, the largest number directed against business in any single nation worldwide). Also favoring bombing were revolutionary groups in Peru (34 incidents) and Chile (27). In the assassination of business personnel, Guatemala was the regional and world leader with 46 such actions. El Salvador was second worldwide with 28 incidents of this type. As in assassinations, Guatemala was the most active state worldwide for business kidnappings, reporting 28. Colombia was second in the region with 16 followed by El Salvador (9). Finally, in facility attacks targeting business, El Salvador again ranked first worldwide, reporting 74 such actions. Second in the region and world was Guatemala (27). Chile held third place in Latin America with 16.

As pointed out earlier, a significantly smaller percentage of total terrorist actions as well as those affecting business have taken place in Europe. Of the 3,982 terrorist operations worldwide between January 1, 1980 and June 30, 1981, only 831 occurred in Europe. Of these, 316 (38 percent) involved business targets. Spain, France, and Italy accounted for 71.5 percent of the 316 antibusiness incidents.

While reporting a regional high of 109 operations against business for the January 1980-June 1981 time frame, Spain also led all other European nations in terrorist assassinations involving businessmen as well as in business kidnappings, facility attacks targeting commercial organizations, and bombings directed against business installations. In connection with the assassination of businessmen, twenty-four such operations occurred in Spain, compared to eleven in Italy and two for France. For business abductions, seven were recorded in Spain versus two in Italy. As for facility attacks, Spain reported fourteen contrasted to twelve in Italy and nine for France. Finally, Spain also led in bombings, targeting business with sixty-four actions of this type, compared to fifty-three in France and twenty-eight for Italy.

Within the Middle East-North African region, terrorist actions targeting business in 1980 and the initial six months of 1981 totalled 137 incidents. Of these, 120 (87.6 percent) occurred in Turkey, Lebanon, Israel, and Iran. Turkey alone reported 39 antibusiness actions and 38 took place in Iran.

The number of terrorist operations involving business targets was substantially lower in Asia, Sub-Saharan Africa, and North America. In Asia, forty-nine such actions occurred during the eighteen months between January 1, 1980 and June 30, 1981. Thirty-six of these took place in the Philippines and Thailand. For Sub-Saharan Africa, during the same time span, thirty-one antibusiness operations were reported. Twenty-seven of these took place in four nations: South Africa, Zimbabwe, Uganda, and Namibia. Finally, within North America, twenty-two terrorist acts involving business occurred in the above-mentioned eighteen-month period. All took place within the continental United States (Puerto Rico is excluded from this total).

Targeting by Corporate Nationality

An examination of the 1,170 terrorist incidents targeting business between January 1, 1980 and June 30, 1981 disclosed 89.2 percent (1,044 actions) affected companies owned by nationals of the country in which the action took place (domestic corporations). Firms controlled by foreign nationals (excluding U.S. citizens or companies) were involved in 83 terrorist attacks (7.1 percent of the 1,170 incidents) and U.S.-owned corporations were targeted in 3.7 percent (43 actions) of the 1,170 operations.

In the case of domestic corporations, thirteen countries accounted for 77.5 percent of the 1,044 actions involving such firms. The most dangerous nation for domestic business was El Salvador (305 actions) followed by Guatemala (99 incidents), Spain (92), France (50), Chile (38), Peru (36), Turkey (34), and Italy (34). Other states with more than 20 attacks on domestic business firms over the eighteen-month period included Colombia, Iran, Israel, Northern Ireland, and the Philippines.

For foreign-owned corporations, five nations accounted for 45.8 percent of the eighty-three attacks on these firms. Leading all other states was France, followed by Italy, Lebanon, Spain, and Guatemala. Additional nations reporting three or more operations against foreign firms were Greece, Turkey, and Switzerland.

In regard to U.S. corporations, thirty-three of the forty-three terrorist actions directed against these companies over the January 1980 through June 1981 time span occurred in El Salvador (12), Guatemala (11), the continental United States (6) and Spain (4). Other nations or areas recording at least two operations against U.S. firms were France, the Philippines, Honduras, Colombia, and Puerto Rico.

As for tactics used against domestic, foreign, and U.S.-owned corporations, bombing was preferred in all three cases. It was the most popular in operations against foreign corporations accounting for over 60 percent of all such actions during the January 1980-June 1981 time period. For incidents involving domestic firms, bombs were used in 55 percent of these cases and in 51 percent of those affecting U.S. corporations.

Facility attacks were second in line of tactical preference for terrorists operating against domestic and foreign firms. Over 24 percent of all actions against domestic businesses involved facility attacks with 15 percent the figure for foreign corporations. In the case of U.S. firms, executive kidnapping replaced facility attacks as the second most popular tactic. Corporate managerial and staff personnel were abducted in over 18 percent of all terrorist incidents involving U.S. firms, compared to 8 percent for foreign corporations and 5 percent for domestic businesses.

The final tactic of interest in connection with terrorist actions against domestic, foreign, and U.S. firms is assassination. The percentage figure for this type operation was highest for foreign corporations. Slightly over 14 percent of all actions affecting these firms involved the murder of corporate personnel, compared to 12 percent for domestic businesses and 11 percent in the case of U.S. companies.

Outlook: Terrorist Targeting in the 1980s

Trends in terrorist targeting over the last six years suggest that business firms will remain high on the priority lists of most revolutionary groups. Overall, it is anticipated business will be the target hit most frequently by terrorist organizations worldwide, accounting for at least one-third of all actions by such groups. As in the past, most of these operations will involve domestic firms with significantly smaller numbers affecting foreign and U.S. corporations. Barring substantial and unanticipated governmental successes in coping with terrorist/guerrilla groups, Latin America should remain the focal point for most attacks on business with Spain, France, and Italy continuing as key countries in Europe.

In looking at possible business targets during the next year or two, it now appears some of the most likely might be (a) electrical power plants (conventional, nuclear, and hydroelectric); (b) electrical transmission systems, including substations and power lines; (c) telephone and microwave communication systems; (d) water purification facilities; and (e) petroleum pipelines, and pumping and storage stations.[13]

Targeting trends during the last six months of 1980 and the first half of 1981 show a steady rise in operations directed against these targets, particularly in nations with active terrorist movements. In Spain, for example, Iberduero Corporation, that country's largest electrical supplier, has been a continuing terrorist target. During the last month of 1980 and the first in 1981, Iberduero losses directly attributable to terrorist actions exceeded $7 million. More than sixty high-tension towers were destroyed as well as power stations in Oyarzun, Ibaeta, Urrechu, San Sebastian, and Zumarranga, all cities in the northern Basque provinces. Power outages forced the suspension or curtailment of operations at the Altos Hornos de Vizcaya steel fabrication plant, the Somorrostro refinery, and at plants of the Campesa and Petronor corporations. Also affected was the electrified Ortuella-Abanato rail line. To maintain minimum public services, power had to be rerouted into the area from central Spain.[14]

Additional actions against Iberduero included the May 1981 kidnapmurder of the company's chief engineer at the Lemoniz nuclear reactor site. This installation was designed to provide much of the electrical power for northern Spain. In recent years, damages to the Lemoniz facility, being built by Iberduero, have exceeded $6 million.

Within other active terrorist areas, including El Salvador, Colombia, Guatemala, Chile, and Peru, electrical generating and transmission facilities as well as petroleum pipelines and pumping stations have been popular targets. In El Salvador, damage to electrical generating plants, substations, and high-tension line towers has been high. During January 1981, seventy-five high-tension line towers were destroyed at a loss of over $3 million. In February five substations were demolished and by May losses to power facilites alone exceeded $12 million. As a result, San Salvador often was without power or on a reduced usage schedule. During mid-August, one outage blacked out that city as well as ten others for over three days. Business losses during this period exceeded $150 million.[15]

Within Guatemala and Colombia, petroleum pipelines have been preferred targets. The critical 160-kilometer line from the new Guatemalan oil fields along the Mexican border to the port of Matias de Galvez was bombed three times during a fifteen-day period in late April and early May 1981. In Colombia, pipelines were attacked early in 1981, cutting the oil flow to Bucaramanga and Barrancabermeja. This action resulted in reduced oil flow to four departments, Cesar, Bolivar, Norte de Santander, and Santander.[16]

During late 1980 and the first six months of 1981, attacks on electrical power lines in Peru and Chile blacked out temporarily a number of municipalities including the Chilean cities of Santiago, Valparaiso, and

Viña del Mar as well as Ayacucho, Chiclayo, Cajamarca, and Huancavelica in Peru. The Peruvian government estimate of losses during late 1980 and early 1981 for destroyed or damaged microwave relay equipment and high-tension towers was $12 million.[17]

Current terrorist interest in utility targets appears predicated upon their vulnerability as well as the substantial public impact resulting from damage to or the destruction of such installations. High-tension line towers or microwave relay facilities scattered across a nation's isolated rural areas as well as metropolitan centers are almost impossible to protect. They can be toppled with only a few pounds of plastique explosive, blacking out cities or essential communications and creating economic havoc.

Equally attractive as terrorist targets are petroleum pipelines stretching across jungle or barren areas and subject to rupture by only six to ten ounces of plastique explosive, again creating serious problems for a nation's commercial sectors and manufacturing facilities. Other targets such as electrical power stations, microwave relay installations, and electrical generating plants are equally vulnerable to attack by groups using weapons such as the Soviet-designed RPG-7 grenade launcher (effective range, 800 meters), a device now available in the arsenals of most terrorist organizations worldwide.

In addition to the clear vulnerability of utility targets, the trend toward expanded operations against these facilities is fostered by a growing belief on the part of many terrorist groups that a government often can be attacked more effectively in an indirect rather than a direct manner. Continued assassination or other actions targeting police, military, and governmental personnel—particularly in a democratic state—frequently alienate a populace from terrorist objectives. (In Spain, for example, the bloody twenty-year Basque terrorist campaign, which relied primarily on the public assassination of government personnel, failed totally in gaining even Basque backing for terrorist goals. Instead, it strengthened popular support throughout Spain for the democratic regime in that country.)

As a result of the Spanish experience and similar developments in several other world areas, some terrorist organizations have questioned the validity of this direct approach, or at least relying upon it exclusively. As noted earlier in the 1978 strategic resolution of the Italian Red Brigades, the best indirect method of bringing down a national government involves attacking its economic foundations. Since these foundations are the "economic heart" of a nation, they can be destroyed most effectively by severing the fragile and almost totally unprotected telecommunications, electrical, and petroleum networks that tie them together. Once these links are interrupted or rendered inoperative, the economic foundations of a state will collapse and with them the national government they support.

In short, a growing number of terrorist groups today see cutting those highly vulnerable power and communication systems that link together a nation's major cities and economic centers as the most effective means of bringing any country to its knees. When these systems are interrupted even temporarily by natural causes, a development that has taken place in New York, Mobile, Miami, Los Angeles, and many non-U.S. locations, the result is usually confusion, a loss of governmental authority and control, and in some cases, political/economic chaos. Should such outages be of substantial duration and the result of terrorist action, the impact would be significantly greater and public pressure demanding a capitulation to terrorist demands might be overwhelming. It is upon this theoretical and practical basis that many terrorist organizations today are looking at electrical generating and distribution systems, communication linkages, and petroleum storage, processing, and pipeline installations as among the most rewarding targets to strike in the near future.

Notes

1. All statistics, percentages, and other numerical materials used in this chapter were obtained from the computer data base of 12,096 terrorist incidents (as of June 30, 1981) maintained by Risks International, Alexandria, Virginia. Materials contained in the data base relate only to significant actions carried out by terrorist groups operating in the United States and abroad. Actions by purely criminal elements are not recorded.

Incidents included in the data base are categorized by type of activity. Categories used are (1) kidnapping, (2) hijacking, (3) assassination, (4) maiming, (5) attacks against facilities and (6) bombing. Only selected bombings are reported: those where the damage/casualities are significant, the device unique, or the method of emplacement unusual.

Each individual incident in the data base is recorded by date and time of occurence, country and city where the action took place, target, nationality of target (if an individual, the corporation or organization represented and his or her position therein), name of the group carrying out the action, number of persons in the attack team, type of weapons or explosives/incendiaries used, ransoms demanded or paid, hostages taken, disposition of hostages, and demands made.

Information in the data base is derived from foreign and U.S. government publications, police reports, and the foreign/English language press. News service reporting by Reuters, *EFE* (Spanish), and Agency France Press also is used. Data relating to damages, persons killed and injured, and hostages taken are dependent upon the accuracy of such reporting. In many nations, government policies preclude the publication of such data. Accordingly, the figures cited for these categories can only give a relative approximation of human and material losses.

2. The importance of publicity to terrorist groups has been evaluated by a number of authors. For a useful summary on this subject see Yonah Alexander, "Terrorism and the Media: Some Considerations" in Yonah Alexander, David Carlton, and Paul Wilkerson, eds., *Terrorism: Theory and Practice* (Boulder, Colo.: Westview Press, 1979).

3. The evolutionary process in terrorist targeting during the years 1970-1976 is reviewed in more detail in "Terrorism: An Overview 1970-1978," *Executive Risk Assessment* 1, no. 2 (December 1978)

4. *Brigate Rosse: Rizoluzione della Direzione Strategica*, 1978, p. 2.

5. Additional detail is found in "Business Targeting: The Ideological Basis" in *Regional Risk Assessment: Europe* (Alexandria, Va.: Risks International, 1979).

6. See *EFE* (Spanish news agency) report datelined Santander, July 26, 1980, entitled "Roban en Santander 8 Mil Kilos del Explosivo Goma 2." Additional information on this incident can be found in a July 28, 1980 *EFE* wire service report from Bilbao captioned "Ofrecen Recompensa a Quien Aporte Datos sobre el Robo de Explosivos en Santander." Also see *EFE* report dated July 31, 1980 from Bilbao entitled "Se Responsabiliza ETA con el Robo de los Explosivos."

7. The four abductions are examined in detail in *Regional Risk Assessment: Latin America* (Alexandria, Va.: Risks International, 1979), pp. 60-61.

8. The Sunyer Sanchis incident is reported in the following *EFE* wire service reports: "Se Encuentra Secuestrado el Ciudadano que Declaró más Ingresos a la Hacienda Española," Valencia, January 15, 1981; "Pide ETA $2 Millones y Medio para Librar al Millonario Industrial Luis Sunyer Sanchis," Alicante, January 17, 1981.

9. The Ryan kidnap/murder is discussed in the following *EFE* wire service reports: "Provoca Unánime Repulsa el Secuestro de Ingeniero de la Central Nuclear de Lemoniz," Bilbao, January 31, 1981; "Condenan Partidos Políticos el Asesinato de un Ingeniero," Madrid, February 7, 1981.

10. It might be added that when ransom is not paid, or when police attack a safehouse in which a kidnap victim is held, the result *usually* is death for the detainee, no matter what his or her position or occupation. The August 13, 1981 murder of U.S. executive Clifford Bevens is a case in point. Manager of the Goodyear affiliate in Guatemala (Compañia Centroamericana de Neumáticos), Bevens was abducted by terrorists from his home in Guatemala City on December 7, 1980. When police assaulted the safehouse in Santo Domingo Xenacoj (a small town 65 kilometers west of Guatemala City) where he was held, his abductors killed their captive.

11. Data regarding team size, the number of victims taken per incident, and the location of most kidnappings were obtained through a July 1981 computer run by Risks International of the 710 kidnapping incidents recorded in their data base for the period January 1, 1970 through June 30, 1981.

12. "Terrorist Operational Patterns," *Executive Risk Assessment* 3, no. 1 (January 1981)

13. The vulnerability of utility and energy targets has been analyzed by several authors. See Maynard M. Stephens, "The Oil and Natural Gas Industries: A Potential Target of Terrorists," in Robert Kupperman and Darrel Trent, *Terrorism: Threat, Reality, Response* (Stanford, Calif.: Hoover Institution Press, 1979). A good brief summary regarding the vulnerability of all types of utility and energy targets is contained in Chapter Two of the above-mentioned text. The author, in association with Bowman H. Miller, also examined this problem in "Terrorism and the Corporate Target" in Yonah Alexander and Robert H. Kilmarx, *Political Terrorism and Business: The Threat and Response* (New York: Praeger, 1979).

14. Data on losses sustained and targets hit are based upon *EFE* and Agency

France Press wire service reporting, June 1, 1980 through June 30, 1981. A summary of some 1981 losses is contained in a May 1, 1981 *EFE* report from Bilbao captioned "Vuelan Planta Eléctrica de Iberduero cerca de Bilbao."

15. Damage and loss figures are based upon Reuters, UPI, Agency France Press, and *EFE* reporting, January 1 through August 20, 1981. Clipping files maintained by Risks International were used.

16. For Guatemala see "Vuela la Guerrilla por Segunda Vez un Importante Oleoducto," *Diario las Américas* (Miami), May 2, 1981, p. 7 and "Atentado en Guatemala contra un Oleoducto," *Diario las Américas* (Miami), May 10, 1981, p. 7. Reporting on Colombia can be found in "Destruyen Oleoducto en Atentado Terrorista," *Diario las Américas* (Miami), June 29, 1981, p. 2.

17. Damage estimates for Peru, as stated in an interview with Senator and Second Vice-President Javier Alva Orlandini, are reported in "Aumenta el Terrorismo en Lima," *Diario las Américas* (Miami), May 14, 1981, p. 2. For other recent information on microwave relay and communication system damage in Peru see "Azota a Lima una Ola de Atentados," *Diario las Américas* (Miami), May 7, 1981, p. 3 and "Un Millón sin Electricidad por Obra de Terroristas," *Diario las Américas* (Miami), May 6, 1981, p. 10. For Chile see "Culpan a Comandos Terroristas por los Atentados Dinamiteros," *Diario las Américas* (Miami), November 15, 1980, p. 2, and "Cazan a los Terroristas que Desataron una Ola de Atentados en Chile Anoche," *Diario las Américas* (Miami), November 14, 1980, p. 2.

5

Preparing and Protecting Personnel and Property Prior to a Terrorist Attack

JOSEPH A. MALLEY

This chapter describes a program for preparing and protecting personnel and property prior to a terrorist attack. It consists of four sections which address planning, management, personnel security, and property protection. The main objective of this personnel security and property protection (p^2) program are to: prevent or deter acts of aggression; reduce personnel losses and/or minimize property damage when an incident occurs; and expedite return to normalcy or recovery following a terrorist attack.

As the probability of terrorist attack(s) increases, management's attention to the security force readiness should increase proportionately. Accordingly, greater importance should be placed on background investigations and screening, training should be increased, post orders should be reviewed, supervision should be improved, weapons firing exercises should occur, and additional inspections, drills, and tests should be conducted.

Security programs have several components such as manpower, construction materials, electronic systems, alarms, other equipment, plans, and operating procedures. The degree to which each component is developed will depend upon a number of factors, the most important of which are the risk assessment and the costs. Obviously, if the level of threat is low and the operation is not critical, then the security program will have few components and may not cost much. However, if the level of threat is high and the operation is critical, then the security program should have many well-developed components and will be costly. Therefore, the decision as to the extent of the security program is a fundamental resource allocation type decision and should be made by the top management in each country after completion of an extensive risk assessment.

The p^2 program consists of a variety of security measures designed to counter a wide spectrum of potential threats including terrorism, kidnapping, hostage situations, extortion, arson, bombings, civil unrest, and disorder. A description of this program follows.

Planning

Planning for the security of personnel and protection of assets prior to a terrorist attack is both a corporate and a country management responsibility. At the corporate level, resources, in terms of the time and expenses of qualified staff, must be committed to prepare the series of plans required for an effective security program. This process includes preparing the risk assessment, developing the physical security program, preparing contingency plans, providing personnel indoctrination and training, and conducting tests and audits. Further, periodic inspections are required to ensure that plans and programs are being maintained properly. At the country management level, this obligation involves establishing and maintaining relationships with appropriate U.S. and host government authorities; allocating the necessary resources to fund the preparation and maintenance of adequate security programs; establishing and maintaining an intelligence gathering and risk-assessment capability; keeping these plans in a current status; orienting, training, and rehearsing employees and those included within the protective program; and maintaining a posture of readiness to execute the applicable plans when required.

The architectural addage that form follows function applies in preparation of security plans. Accordingly, each plan should be based upon the requirements of a particular country and a specific location.

PREPARING THE RISK ASSESSMENT

To have a cost-effective security program usually requires use of a risk-management approach by completion of the following work program. First, the personnel and property to be protected should be inventoried. The number of personnel, their location, the work environment, travel patterns, and the living, shopping, and entertainment accommodations should be identified, and the plant, office, and home reviewed. The current book and replacement value of each asset should be determined. In essence, that which is to be protected and its value should be clearly understood.

The external environment should be reviewed. In doing so, the following factors should be considered: terrain and weather; crime rate and history; population characteristic/attitudes; socioeconomic factors; customs of country; local laws and regulations; transportation network—air and land; communications system; availability of mutual aid from other companies; response and cooperation of local authorities, police, and military; proximity, sympathy, and capability of nearest U.S. or friendly nation response force facility and safehaven; guidelines, plans, or procedures recommended by the U.S. State Department and/or host nation and/or local police.

Third, it is necessary to evaluate the threats. Security programs are designed to counter general and specific threats. Based on historical perspectives and future probabilities, the nature and extent of these threats should be examined. Each facility is exposed to threats in varying degrees.

The threats including those due to terrorists, common criminals, vandals, and dishonest employees should be identified and defined. A probability of occurrence should be assigned for each threat identified.

Next, vulnerabilities should be determined. Vulnerability assessment involves an evaluation of the various threats as well as the security systems' weaknesses identified during the inventory of personnel and property to be protected. Specific security surveys should be conducted at each facility concentrating on requirements for and provision of security management, guard force operations, physical security improvements, electronic security systems, and contingency plans, where applicable. Based on these surveys, vulnerabilities should be identified and the requirements for the physical security program and contingency plans defined.

Finally, the annual loss expectancy should be developed. Potential losses should be estimated. The critical aspects of the operation should be identified and a dollar value placed on the potential losses. Losses should be grouped into categories such as for damage to facilities; destruction/damage to vehicles; injury to personnel; loss of production/disappearance of product; and loss of tools, supplies, and parts. The loss potential should be estimated based on the cost to replace the damaged facility, vehicle, product, or tool.

A matrix of potential losses and threats should be prepared. Potential losses should be considered for each threat. The annual loss expectancy is calculated by multiplying the loss estimate by the probability of occurrence for each threat. This provides the cost base against which the benefits of the physical security measures can be evaluated. Since this is not an exact process, results should be reviewed from a relative importance and common sense point of view and adjustments made to estimates and probabilities where appropriate.

DEVELOPING THE PHYSICAL SECURITY PROGRAM

Based on the risk assessment including the requirements specified in the vulnerability analysis, the physical security program should be prepared. The components for a typical physical security program to protect the company's personnel, plant, equipment, and information resources are security management, guard force operations, physical security improvements, electronic security systems, and contingency plans. Where applicable, alternative approaches should be developed and the relative advantages and disadvantages of each considered.

At this stage, the cost-benefit analysis can be prepared. Estimates of the installation costs, annual operating costs, and life-cycle costs should be prepared for each protective measure. Based on these estimates, the annual costs of the physical security measures can be calculated. By combining the annual loss expectancy with the costs of the physical security measures, the cost-benefit analysis can be prepared. Alternative protective measures can be considered against loss expectancy data. When an alternative measure is evaluated, the amount of the reduction in loss expectancy will be estimated. The amount of that reduction is the benefit. Following this procedure, alternatives can be evaluated and cost-effective options selected, where applicable. Based on a comparison of the cost and benefits, the physical security program can be formulated.

PREPARING CONTINGENCY PLANS

As part of the planning process, contingency plans should be prepared as appendices to the physical security plan, including plans for executive protection, bomb threat, fire, disaster/emergency preparedness, and evacuation. Each appendix satisfies a specific requirement and provides part of the overall program to counter terrorist and related threats.

The development of these plans includes site surveys, interdepartmental cooperation, draft plan preparation, internal management review, external organizational approval, and liaison with official representatives of the U.S. State Department.

An executive protection plan is designed to afford life-safety and property protection for selected executives and their families. The main objective of the program is to prevent any act of aggression against executives and their families. The secondary objective is, in the event of a hostile act taking place, to set into motion prescribed actions already established to meet such an eventuality. The scope of the program includes protection at work, at home, and while travelling.

A bomb threat plan is intended to provide guidance and direction for officials and employees before, during, and after bomb threat conditions. The plan provides for preparation and actions during a crisis situation, and has objectives to prevent or reduce injury or harm to personnel, damage or destruction to equipment and facilities, and loss of plant operations.

A fire plan should establish guidelines for a fire protection program. This plan should detail:
• responsibilites of management
• organization including floor wardens and fire brigades
• coordination with other departments
• liaison with local fire department
• insurance program
• evacuation procedures
• instructions to guards and watchmen
• maintenance and inspection programs
• location of potential hazards
• special requirements for flammable and toxic materials
• location of emergency exits, with automatic sprinklers, hydrants, extinguishers, hoses, standpipes, alarm bells, smoke detectors and manual alarms
• emergency situation communication procedures

- adequacy of water supply, reserve storage, etc.
- training, testing, aand drills
- control room/command center
- diagrams/instructions for building occupants
- emergency power and lighting.

The purpose of an emergency preparedness plan is to provide for an orderly transition from normal to emergency operations, to delegate authorities and assign responsibilities, to assure continuity of operations, and to expedite recovery. This plan should specify:

- chain of command
- command and control center
- mutual aid
- liaison with local authorities including police, fire emergency, medical, civil defense, power company, public works, national guard, and Red Cross
- personnel contact and notification procedures
- emergency provisions, including rations, water, blankets, tools and lights
- standby power source
- transportation means
- evacuation routes
- provision for security during emergency
- shutdown responsibilites and procedures
- fire protection system
- vital records protection
- emergency finances-payroll
- insurance provisions
- communications
- damage assessment and control
- training and testing
- emergency medical services
- messing and billeting plans
- all clear and start-up procedures.

An evacuation plan represents a modification of an emergency preparedness plan and could be annexed to an executive protection plan. This contingency plan should provide for: liaison with a U.S. State Department representative; registration with the local U.S. consulate; security of property while vacant; designation of "safehaven" assembly area; transportation means; authority to order; authentication of order to evacuate; company and personal property to be evacuated; emergency finances; evacuation routes; designation of those eligible for evacuation; emergency communications systems; and shutdown and close-up procedures.

PROVIDING PERSONNEL INDOCTRINATION AND TRAINING

Orientation and training are essential elements of this protective program. Even though drills and rehearsals occur during implementation, indoctrination and training should be provided for as part of planning. Accordingly, as soon as plans are approved, training programs and materials should be developed for general orientation to security and contingency plans for all employees; security force basic training program; weapons training and familiarization for security force; security force supervisor training program; general orientation to security and contingency plans for dependents; special training for fire wardens and brigade; and rehearsals and drills for bomb threats, fire, emergency preparedness, and evacuation plans. Course outlines, lesson plans, demonstrations, tests, and course notebooks should be prepared for each orientation and training program.

CONDUCTING TESTS AND AUDITS

Inspections also are an essential element of this protective program. These too occur during implementation and operations and should be provided as part of the overall planning process.

Management

This section describes three management activities considered essential for the personal security and property protection program including special functions, security program management, and security force administration.

SPECIAL FUNCTIONS

Certain countermeasures are required to reduce the impact of terrorist activities. Special efforts should be made to collect information and monitor terrorist activities in those countries included within the protective program. Sources of data should include: subscribing to a local newspaper; obtaining periodic reports from the country or area desk of the U.S. State Department, and subscribing to publications of firms specializing in reporting on terrorist activities. Files should be maintained. Reports should be interpreted and the results disseminated at the corporate and country levels. In summary, someone should follow and analyze the events in each country to anticipate turmoil.

A corporate crisis management team should be established to deal with hostile acts against personnel and property. This team should consist of the chief executive officer, legal executive, financial executive, administrative executive, and the international executive. The chief executive officer should be designated as the team leader and, in turn, should designate an alternate, most probably the international executive. The team leader should be responsible for notifying the team of any threats or other hostile acts received to evaluate the information received. If the threat evaluation is positive, the team will institute preplanned courses of action. The legal executive should determine the limits to be set on the team's action and be in a position to indicate to the board of directors that the proposed responses are in conformance with legal requirements of the various countries involved and the corporate charter and by-laws. The legal executive should review insurance coverage and confer with the directors, for example, as to the amount of corporate assets that can be committed under a kidnap situation. He or she should arrange for the crisis management team to be empowered to authorize special action in the event of a kidnapping or similar event and should assure that the board has made a formal resolution which is covered in the official corporate minutes. The financial executive should provide availability of funds, access to cash, and have the appropriate authorization from the corporation to negotiate with the financial institutions that could be involved. The legal and financial executives should be responsible for all financial and insurance matters. The administrative officer should be responsible for direction of the corporate security program and the command post. The international executive should be responsible for administration of the intelligence program.

Furthermore, the corporate legal executive should maintain confidential personal files about all executives and their families. These personal files should contain data relative to physical characteristics, activities, habits, and life-style. This information should include: full name; physical description (height, weight, color hair, color eyes); birth date; scars/marks; address of family residences; telephone number; physician's name and address; and clubs and hobbies. Similar information should be maintained for wives and children. Data should be kept on personal vehicles such as make, year, model, color, license, and serial number. Moreover, other information should be maintained including: individual photographs, fingerprints, voiceprint, sample of handwriting, special medical requirements, and a copy of an individual's driver's license. Importantly, these records should be kept current, treated strictly confidentially, and stored in locked files in secure offices.

Because terrorists strike at leaders, the existence of a board-approved management succession plan is essential.

In planning and preparing for terrorist attacks, liaison should be established with local municipal officials, host country officials, local police and fire officials, other U.S. corporate executives, U.S. embassy or consulate, and nearest U.S. military base, where applicable. While all these sources can be helpful in gathering intelligence, details of evacuation plans should only be discussed with an official representative of the U.S. State Department.

SECURITY PROGRAM MANAGEMENT

A member of management should be designated as responsible for security. This individual should function in a staff capacity reporting directly to the country or plant manager. Depending on the size of the operation, the requirements of the position, amount of attention, and the qualifications of this person may vary. However, in a large operation, prior experience in security management, municipal police, or military service should be a prerequisite for the position. In the absence of this background, then the assistance of the corporate security director or a qualified security consultant should be obtained. Typically, the functions of this security manager should include:

- structuring and staffing the security organization
- administering the security force
- preparing contingency plans
- conducting special investigations
- maintaining liaison with law enforcement agencies
- reviewing and approving electronic security systems
- maintaining an incident reporting system
- designing security programs for new facilities
- serving as a corporate staff officer
- preparing policies and procedures for the security program
- conducting security surveys and quality control audits
- conducting background investigations for new employees
- developing and conducting security orientation and awareness training program for new employees
- administering the lock and key control program
- administering the employee identification badge system
- providing protection for top executives
- providing guidelines and advising line managers on security and loss prevention matters
- administering the fire protection plan and program.

SECURITY FORCE ADMINISTRATION

Certain aspects of security force administration should be emphasized in providing security and property protection prior to a terrorist attack.

Security officers should be selected from applicants as a result of interviews and background checks. Preference should be given to applicants with previous experience in either the military or police work. The specifications for security officers should include: no criminal record; in general good health; acceptable vision and hearing; capable of performing normal physical duties; and be physically fit. Some sort of preemployment investigation should be made for all security officers.

Officers should be provided a basic training program including classroom and on-the-job portions so they will have the knowledge and ability to perform the duties assigned. This training should include the organization and functions of the security force, legal authority and responsibility, procedures for search and seizure, first aid, procedure for handling incidents, safety requirements, bomb threat procedures, fire procedures, lock and key system, and logs and reports.

Another element of security force administration is post orders, written instruments that outline the general instructions and specific duties for each post. General orders define functions such as protecting life and property; being alert for fires, accidents, or sabotage; patrolling designated areas; checking unoccupied offices and buildings; and reporting unusual or emergency situations. The specific duties will usually include boundaries of the post, emergency procedures and contact list, patrol rounds, work schedules, administrative controls, locking procedures, fire protection procedures, and telephone procedures.

Job supervision is another important element in the security force operation. The supervisor should be selected for his or her ability to oversee the security force properly on a day-to-day basis. This individual should be responsible for proper scheduling of personnel, maintaining time reporting systems, and ensuring approved patrol procedures have been followed. This supervisor should conduct frequent inspections of the security force during day and night shifts to check for appearance, alertness, and the knowledge of general orders and specific instructions.

The security force should be furnished with uniforms of a certain color and style to project the appearance of a well-organized, equipped, and disciplined organization. Care should be taken to assure materials are of sufficient quality to maintain durability and appearance and that uniforms fit properly. A sufficient number should be issued to each security officer to allow proper rotation and cleaning.

Weapons should be issued to the security force with caution. No member of the security force should be issued any firearms until the security officer has a valid license and has been qualified on an approved range. Specific training and procedures should be provided concerning carrying the weapon, ammunition, and conditions when it may be used. For example: at no time should weapons be used, carried, or fired except in the line of authorized duty. Extreme care should be taken when handling weapons.

Additional equipment such as vehicles, radios, watch clocks, batons, and mace should be issued as required. Other equipment should not be issued until the security officers have been trained and are fully qualified to use it.

A log book should be maintained by each security officer at each post to record violations of security, fire, safety, and incidents.

Generally, the use of sentry dogs increases security and provides an additional psychological deterrent to attackers. Certain precautions should be taken when using sentry dogs. Only trained and qualified handlers should work with a sentry dog. A training program should be conducted for handling the dogs. The dogs should have a physical conditioning program. Importantly, the corporation should have adequate liability insurance coverage.

Finally, inspections should be conducted routinely by the supervisor to monitor individual and unit training and operations; maintain standards of performance and appearance; check on uniform and weapon conditions; and ensure compliance with security directives. Periodically, simulated contingency drills should be held to check on security force readiness. Similarly, communications and electronic security systems (alarms) should be tested monthly to ensure operability. Written reports and records should be maintained for these inspections, drills, and tests. Copies should be distributed to the plant and country manager.

Personnel Security

Personnel security includes protective measures at work, while travelling, and at home. It concentrates on security for executives and plant managers, as they have been most affected by terrorists attacks.

SECURITY AT WORK

The executive and/or administrative offices should be surveyed and security improvements installed. Typically, security can be improved considerably for moderate costs. Doors and partitions should be constructed to control traffic and access into the executive and/or administration areas. Receptionist desks should be positioned to observe those approaching the area. Impact-resistant security glazing/safety glass should be used on basement and first floor windows in high-security areas.

Those officials and employees working in the executive/administration areas should use a card access system with card readers and appropriate cards. Card readers should be positioned at key access locations to control traffic effectively. Since many card access systems have zoning (or area) capability, one system should be able to service a whole plant with one zone and limited access in the executive/administration area.

Silent duress alarms should be installed at the desks of selected secretaries and executives, at the reception desk, and in meeting rooms. These duress alarms should be monitored in the command and communications center. In addition, all executive and administrative offices, meeting rooms, and the reception area should be provided with approved smoke and/or heat detectors. Fire-resistant safes and vaults should be provided for storage of company confidential or sensitive materials.

In addition, a number of general operational procedures can be carried out, some at little or no additional cost. For example, background investigations should be conducted on all support staff working in the executive and administrative areas. All visitors to the executive offices should be registered and under escort at all times, and special telephone screening procedures should be established. Switchboard operators, receptionists, and secretaries should be given training in handling bomb threat and extortion telephone calls. Packages and large envelopes should not be opened in executive offices unless the sender or source is positively known. Janitorial closets, service openings, and telephone and all electrical rooms should be kept locked at all times, as should rest rooms in executive areas. Special procedures for control or observation of cleaning personnel should be initiated, and trash receptacles should be emptied daily and the contents shredded or burned. Work papers should not be left on desks, especially overnight, but locked in file cabinets. Finally, all name signs outside executive offices and specific room identification in lobby directories should be removed.

SECURITY DURING TRAVEL

A high percentage of kidnappings have occurred during travel. Accordingly, effective countermeasures are important. The choice of which to use depends on the level of threat.

All executives are vulnerable while travelling in cars and when out of contact with their home or office. Therefore, all cars should be provided with a two-way radio which is monitored on a twenty-four hour basis. These two-way radios should be linked to a company-operated central post. The range of the two-way radio voice communication system should approximate fifteen miles in favorable terrain. Prearranged codes should alert the monitoring group that an emergency exists.

Vehicle drivers should be carefully selected and trained in defensive and antiterrorist driving techniques at a reputable school. Loyalty and ability are the two chief prerequisites for this individual.

Although reinforcing a vehicle is an expensive proposition, the cost will be economical if it prevents one kidnapping/ransom situation. Vehicle armor includes reinforcing the front bumper, protecting the radiator and battery, installing bullet-resistant glass, adding a roll bar, armoring the door panels, and using heavy-duty tires with some sealing capability. The engineering aspects of vehicle armor are critical. Additional weight must be balanced. The basic vehicle needs several heavy-duty options such as radiator-cooling system and battery. Importantly, the vehicle must have sufficient horsepower to accelerate out of potentially dangerous situations and be sufficiently balanced for high-speed maneuverability. These vehicles must receive proper preventive maintenance.

These vehicles should be equipped with special features such as inside hood latch, locked gas caps, inner escape latch on trunk, heavy-duty disc brakes, heavy-duty air conditioning, and standard commercial tamper indicating alarms with locally audible sounds of attempts at breaking and entering. Moreover, the vehicles should carry safety equipment including fire extinguisher, first aid kit, flashlight, and spare tire.

Additionally, the driver and chief occupants should wear body armor similar to that used by U.S. municipal police. Vehicles should be equipped with a pistol and/or shotgun, provided the driver and chief occupant are properly trained and qualified in their use.

Travel times and routes should be varied in an attempt to deny would-be attackers surprise or ambush opportunity. In addition, reserved parking places should not be used. Executives should vary their parking spots, and numbered spots should be assigned on a random basis. Spaces showing executives names at plants and offices should be removed. All cars should be locked and kept in a locked garage when not in use. Cars should not be left unattended.

Executives should use pseudonyms when making air, train, hotel, and car rental reservations.

Boats and aircraft should be equipped with security devices including two-way radios, vehicle tampering protection, body armor, and weapons.

Finally, depending on the threat assessment, executives should consider the use of bodyguards or escorts. Loyalty, age, training, and physical condition are the key prerequisites for bodyguards. Situations when weapons should be used must be clearly understood.

SECURITY AT HOME

Residences of key personnel, including weekend retreats and vacation homes, should be surveyed and security improved. Generally, security in most homes can be increased considerably for relatively moderate costs. Several factors should be considered. The external grounds should be enclosed with a fence of sufficient height and gauge to serve as a deterrent and have gates that can be locked. The grounds should be cleared of high bushes to permit observation and have protective lighting and listening devices, so outside activities can be observed and monitored.

Doors should be constructed of materials adequate to prevent immediate entry by an intruder. Hinges should be on the inside rather than the outside of the exterior doors. Windows should be constructed of safety or bullet-resistant (not proof) glass. Deadbolt locks should be used on all exterior doors. Gates and protective screening should be used on basement doors and windows.

Homes should be equipped with duress, fire, and intrusion detection alarms which should be connected to and monitored by local police and the command and communications center at the plant. An intrusion detection system with a control unit should be installed with magnetic contacts on doors and windows. Where appropriate, motion detection units should also be installed. These alarms should be turned on nights and weekends and when the home is not in use. Smoke and/or heat detection units and silent duress alarms should be installed at several locations throughout the house. Fire extinguishers should be positioned in several locations throughout the house.

Two-way radios should be maintained for communication with the communications center at the corporate plant. Certain supplies and equipment should be stored in a protected area within the home. These should include water, gasoline/diesel fuel, first aid kit, flashlights, blankets, change of clothing, extra fire extinguishers, canned food, money, weapons, radios, flares, and maps.

Other elements of domestic security include background investigations on all domestic help to ensure loyalty, the use of trained watchdogs around the home, and the cooperative neighborhood watch program, one of the oldest and best ways to protect any home and family.

Property Protection

This section presents the basics of an industrial plant protection program. The extent to which each component of the property protection program is used depends on a number of factors, such as geographic location, local terrain features, size and criticality of the operation, industry, value of product, etc. Plant managers should have a physical security survey conducted by qualified personnel to identify vulnerabilities and recommend specific protective measures.

SECURITY ZONES

In developing a protection program, the property (land, roads, waterways, and buildings) should be divided into security zones based on the relative importance/criticality of the building or equipment to the overall operation. Typically, a large multiple building site should have three security zones with increased levels of access control. The three-zone system improves security and provides defense in depth. Instead of having "tight" control over the whole facility, the zone system is economical, in that it allows levels of protective measures within a site increasing from low to moderate to high depending on, but not interfering with, operational requirements. Delineation of these zone areas by protective barriers and control of access into each area are further prerequisites of the zone security system.

PERIMETER SECURITY

Perimeter barriers define the boundaries of, or an area within, the facility and restrict access to the facility. These protective measures deter unauthorized entry, delay intruders, and direct the flow of traffic. Importantly, these safeguards reduce the requirements for manned guard posts. Barriers may be natural or man-made products such as fences, walls, floors, roofs, gates, and screens. To be effective, these barriers must be used with other elements of the perimeter security program including lighting, alarms, surveillance cameras, and patrols.

Fencing provides a psychological deterrent, channels the flow of personnel and vehicles, and impedes unauthorized access. To be effective, chain link fence should be of certain wire gauge, height and mesh, such as 0.11 gauge, seven-foot height and 2-inch mesh. It should be topped with a

45-degree outward and upward extending arm bearing three strands of barbed wire stretched taut or double razor ribbon wire spaced to increase the vertical height one foot. Fence post should be embedded in concrete. Fence bottom should meet solid ground or touch a concrete strip.

Adequate lighting is an essential element of a perimeter security program and serves as a deterrent to intruders. The specific position of each light pole as well as the height and type of lamp should be engineered. Lights should provide 0.5, 1.0, or 2.0 foot-candles of illumination at ground level at the perimeter fence and vehicular and pedestrian entrances, respectively. Lighting systems should be inspected routinely and properly maintained. Wiring systems should be located underground and sufficiently inside the perimeter to prevent tampering. An auxiliary source of power should be available in the event of an emergency. If closed-circuit television (CCTV) is to be used as part of perimeter security, detailed light meter readings should be made to ensure that the correct type of cameras will be installed and that light will be adequate for CCTV cameras to function properly. Moreover, the specific positions of the lights must be provided in relation to the specific positions and span of the CCTVs.

Perimeter barriers (fence) should be observed. Depending on the degree of security required, observations can be periodic or continuous. Periodic observations should be provided by patrols. Continuous monitoring can be provided by guards in watch towers or by use of closed circuit television (CCTVs). Properly positioned with correct mounting equipment and cabling, low-light level outdoor cameras with weather-proof housing, pan-tilt capability zoom lens control, and adequate lighting, such as with high pressure sodium lights, can be effective tools for day or night observation. The number and location of each camera, whether outdoors or indoors, should be carefully engineered to achieve anticipated results. Cameras are an expensive component of a security system and should be used judiciously.

Perimeter fences should also be equipped with alarms. Depending on the situation, particularly the terrain and weather, perimeter alarms can be selected from among the following: capacitance fences, photo electric beam barriers, infrared beam barriers, E-field fence motion detection, coaxial cable devices, magnetic detector, differential pressure sensors, seismic barriers, microwave devices, acoustic detectors, laser systems, and E-flex cable.

In high-security areas, redundant or dual detection systems are used to ensure reliability of alarms. This system might include a free-standing five wire E-field combined with coaxial cable mounted on the chain link fence. The two intrusion detection systems (E-field and coaxial cable) can be integrated into one alarm output which can be monitored at the security central command post.

Generally, a large perimeter fence is segmented into zones of 100 to 150 meters to facilitate identification of areas. These lengths coincide with equipment capability and assist in detecting intruders and directing the response force.

SECURITY FORCE

The security force consists of fixed posts, foot and/or vehicular patrols, and response elements. Fixed posts might be at the main gate or entrance to the plant. Foot patrols might occur inside buildings, while vehicle patrols may occur at the perimeter and throughout the property. The number of posts, patrol routes, hours of operation, shifts, and size of the response force will vary depending on the size of the facility, criticality of operation, and extent of threat. Having a response capability available at all times is an essential element in any property protection program. In some locations, that response may come from the local police. However, in other areas, each plant may have to provide for its own contingent force, even if it comes from a "standby" watch of off-duty production workers. Regardless of the source, someone must provide backup to the guards at the gate and/or the patrols.

Importantly, each guard should have a continuous communications means with a central command and control station.

ACCESS CONTROL

Access control is an essential component of a security program and includes employee identification and visitor and traffic control. All employees should have background investigations completed as part of employment screening. Typically, a background investigation will include a criminal or police records check, an educational check, a prior employment check, and a residential or character check. Once employment screening is completed and the employee is determined to be trustworthy, then a photo-identification badge should be issued. These badges should be worn in visible locations for gate guards to inspect on entering or leaving the plant. Gate guards should be instructed to admit only employees with valid photo-identification badges.

Visitors should be directed to a visitor control point, usually a receptionist, who can determine the validity of their visit by contacting the individual to be visited. Visitor logs should be maintained and visitor passes used. Visitors may be escorted or unescorted, based on the level of security required.

In addition, employees and visitors may be further screened through the use of metal detectors, x-ray machines, and brief case and/or body searches depending on the level of security needed. Gates should be staffed at time of shift change to perform these procedures and still allow a reasonable flow of employees into and out of the plant.

Similarly, vehicles need to be controlled. Employee parking should be outside the plant, usually in a lot across the street. This area should be secured with adequate fence, lights, and gates. Many firms have roving patrols on duty in employee parking areas. Visitors vehicles should be routed to the visitors parking area by signs and gate guard. Delivery trucks should be directed to receiving areas after paperwork has been checked and the trip authenticated by the guard at the gate. Depending on the security requirements, the cab and trailer may need to be inspected prior to entering the plant.

MATERIAL, PACKAGE, AND PROPERTY CONTROLS

Procedures should be established for control of materials, packages, and property entering and leaving the plant. A property pass system should be used to control materials leaving the plant. Guards at the exit gates should have lists and signatures of the department managers authorized to approve removal of materials and/or property from the plant. Anyone seeking to take something from the plant must be required to obtain an authorized property pass. Certain gates should be designated for entrance and exit of materials and packages.

LOCKS AND KEYS

Locks are one of the basic security measures. Buildings, rooms, cabinets, vaults, and safes with critical operations or sensitive materials should have locking devices and be kept locked when not in use. Several types of locking systems are available such as key locks, combination locks, and cipher locks. Control of locks and keys is important. Someone should be designated as responsible for key control. Records should be maintained for each lock and key. Inventories of key systems should be conducted annually. Reserve locks and keys and duplicate keys should be stored in a locked cabinet. Use of master keys should be limited. Locks and combinations should be changed periodically, when employees using them terminate, or when keys or combinations are lost or compromised.

BASIC CONSTRUCTION MATERIALS

The basic materials (concrete, steel, and brick) of a facility can provide a degree of protection. In developing a security program for a plant, the basic construction materials should be reviewed. Particular attention should be paid to gates, doors, and windows in vital areas, and the floors, ceiling, and walls of the command and communications center and any safehavens. Where needed, the doors, floors, ceilings, and walls should be reinforced with steel or concrete. Similarly, selected windows can be reinforced with bullet-resistant glass, where required.

Since reinforcing the basic construction material could be an expensive process, the benefit and costs of these site "hardening" techniques should be evaluated carefully prior to undertaking any renovations.

FIRE PROTECTION

Because terrorists frequently use fire bombs as a means to initiate a disturbance, plants should be equipped with adequate fire detection and protection systems. Buildings and vital areas should have smoke and/or fire detection monitoring devices wired to the central command center. Buildings and vital areas should have approved automatic sprinkler systems, hydrants, fire hoses, manual alarm systems, and extinguishers. Special precautions should be taken relative to chemicals and toxic materials.

Each plant should have a fire plan, fire force, and conduct rehearsals and drills. Large plants may have their own fire trucks and fire department. Liaison with the local fire department is an important action in preparation of a fire protection plan. Compliance with local building and fire codes is also an important step in any fire protection program.

COMMAND AND COMMUNICATIONS CENTER

Each plant should have a security command and communications center (SCCC). Many plants have some location where the operation is monitored on a twenty-four-hour-a-day basis. Oftentimes, the functions at these SCCCs can be expanded to include security requirements during the second and third shifts. If not, a separate center should be established.

The SCCC should have radio communications with the security guards and perimeter patrols, as well as with outside agencies such as the local police. Additionally, the center should have the capability to monitor electronically the plant protective systems including (where applicable) controls for CCTV equipment, video switching systems, alarm requesting/annunciating, perimeter fence protective system, video tape recording, fire alarm, and intercom master station, and monitors for video surveillance, video sequencing, access control system, utility control system, fire alarms, and toxic gas detection system.

It should be constructed of "hard" materials and access to it carefully controlled. The SCCC should be staffed with highly qualified personnel following approved procedures. All alarms should be monitored and authenticated by the SCCC.

EMERGENCY POWER AND WATER

Since terrorists are apt to damage or destroy the municipal power generation and/or portions of the distribution system, industrial plants should have an emergency power generator to provide backup capability and assistance during crises situations. As the probability of terrorist attack increases, it would be wise to collect water in storage containers.

Summary

This chapter outlines a comprehensive approach for preparing and protecting personnel and property prior to a terrorist attack. Subsections deal with planning, management, personnel, security, and property protection. As described in each subsection, security programs have many components. The extent to which each component is developed will depend upon several factors, of which the risk assessment and costs are the most important. In terms of capital and operating investment, security programs can cost a few thousand dollars for an individual home, a few hundred thousand dollars for a moderate sized office building, and a few million dollars for a large plant. In comparison to the potential loss of life and the value of the property, these types of capital and operating expenditures for protective programs represent prudent investments. However, the extent to which the security program should be developed in each country is a fundamental resource allocation-type decision which should be made by top management based upon a thorough risk evaluation. Importantly, it is assumed in this analysis that each company has an intelligence-gathering capability and the ability to perform a comprehensive risk assessment.

6

Terrorism and the Media: Observations from the American and British Experiences

ABRAHAM H. MILLER

The purpose of this chapter is to explore the relations between law enforcement and the media as they deal with terrorist actions. Among the byproducts of contemporary terrorism has been conflict between law enforcement and the media. This is especially true of situations in which law enforcement and the media are brought together during in-progress terrorist operations. For their part, the media have been concerned about getting firsthand, on-the-spot coverage of news as it is being made. That kind of coverage calls for relatively free access to the scene where news occurs. In contrast, ongoing terrorist scenes usually elicit a police response of control and containment. The different mandates of law enforcement and the media are bound to result in some type of conflict, as each sees the other as interfering with its functions and social responsibilities.

At times, in their attempts to obtain news, the media have interfered with police operations. Similarly, in their attempts to bring a threatening situation to speedy conclusion, the police have ignored the needs and the potential contributions to be obtained from having an active media disseminating information and squelching rumors.

The author wishes to gratefully acknowledge the assistance of the following people who in various ways contributed to this research: The members of the Charles Phelps Taft Memorial Committee who made it possible for me to travel to England to conduct interviews; Robert Friedlander, Ohio Northern University, who has been an endless source of wisdom and intellectual stimulation throughout this and other projects; Walter Jaehnig, University of Wyoming, whose work on terrorism and the media in Great Britain was a source of departure and inspiration for this research; Peter Neivens, Scotland Yard, for his insights, reflections, and kindness; Richard L. Clutterbuck, University of Exeter, for his theoretical and empirical observations and his hospitality; and the Rt. Hon. Lord Shackleton for his reflections on the prevention of terrorism acts (1974 and 1976).

The most common and often the most intense conflict between the media and law enforcement has come about during ongoing terrorist operations involving hostage and barricade situations. However, by no means is this the only arena of conflict. The media and law enforcement have at times found themselves at odds over the manner in which the media have portrayed terrorists or their operations. Law enforcement has seen some of this portrayal as providing terrorists with legitimacy for their activities and a forum for their propaganda.

In this chapter, we will examine the points of view of both protagonists, how they have defined the issues, how they have attempted to resolve those issues, and what the United States might learn from the British whose experience with this conflict has been longer, if not greater, than that of America and whose discussion of the issues has been every bit as intense as the commitment to finding solutions.

Although many readers will be accustomed to definitions of terrorism that restrict such activity to political violence, it is generally recognized in both law enforcement and media circles that the motivations behind an act are less important than the nature of the act itself. Thus, the present discussion will be based on a view of terrorism that is more appropriate to both law enforcement and media circles than it is to the scholarly community, namely, violence, assassination, bomb throwing, or similar acts which are designed to intimidate a population or government into granting demands. The motivations may stem from political or nonpolitical concerns. The motivation is far and away less important than the general perception by the media, law enforcement, and the public that the act itself is generally what they would consider to be an act of terrorism.

Two Perspectives

The heated and at times fruitful dialogue that has come out of this controversy usually results in the aftermath of situations where the media in their attempts to gather news have interfered with police operations during an ongoing siege. In such situations the problem is unavoidable. What the police see as intrusion the media see as the performance of their traditional role to gather information and disseminate it. What the police see as important tactical procedures—control and containment—the media see as unnecessary restrictions which violate the media's constitutionally guaranteed right to publish. For the media have generally been quick to argue that without the right to gather information freely the right to publish is meaningless. The first amendment, the media assert, not only guarantees the right to publish; in so doing it guarantees the right to gather news and to be at the spot where news is being made.

From this position the police dissent. The police argue that the right to life and limb precedes the public's right to know, especially when it is not the information itself that is being interfered with, but the speed at which it is being transmitted. Invariably and inevitably, so the police argue, the public will know, but in the meantime the rights of the victims of the terrorists constitute law enforcement's more immediate concern.

Newspaper publisher James Hoge, one of the most eloquent spokesmen for the media's point of view, argues that the police have overreacted to those episodes in which the media have intruded on police operations. The police, Hoge contends, have tended to perceive the nature of the media's performance in their coverage of ongoing terrorist situations from the perspective of the media's intrusion. Hoge argues that much of the reaction seen in police circles tends to be a generalization from police experience with the behavioral excesses of the few which has overshadowed the responsible behavior of most reporters.[1] In continuing to see the media from this perspective, the police, Hoge and Police Foundation President Patrick V. Murphy argue, have failed to properly appreciate and utilize the beneficial aspects that flow from media's coverage.[2] Hoge further argues that the media's coverage of terrorism can be beneficial and that the proper response of government should be to encourage more rather than less coverage.[3]

Patrick V. Murphy is not the only member of the law enforcement community to agree with Hoge's point of view. H.H.A. (Tony) Cooper, staff director of the National Advisory Committee Task Force on Disorders and Terrorism, has addressed what he perceives as the greater mischief of partial revelations, half-truths, and frightening speculation that occur when there is not comprehensive media coverage of an extraordinary, media-attracting event such as a terrorist siege.[4] Similarly, Richard Clutterbuck, an astute student of media coverage of terrorism in the United Kingdom, has argued, "The overwhelming majority of the public detest political violence and terrorism and wish to help the police to defeat them. So, given the chance, the media will reflect that feeling."[5] Clutterbuck maintains this view despite being one of the strongest critics of the media's role in terrorism in the United Kingdom.

Experienced police officials like Patrick Murphy and former Washington, D.C. police chief Jerry Wilson have generally come to the conclusion that civil authorities have everything to gain by cooperating and working with the media rather than interfering with the transmission of information by the media to the public.[6] As the British have learned through their long and painful experience in Northern Ireland, the policy of prohibiting the ordinary soldier from talking to the media was a mistake. Once the policy was changed, the British public found that their enlisted soldiers in Northern Ireland were not insensitive, violent "fascist pigs," as they had been portrayed.[7]

There is, however, strong evidence that the perspective of the National Advisory Committee Task Force on Disorders and Terrorism, generally recognized as a law enforcement perspective, is not the dominant one among police chiefs in the largest cities of the United States. A survey undertaken by Michael and Heidi Sommer, which assessed the opinions of police chiefs in the thirty largest American cities, told quite a different story. The chiefs believed that television coverage of terrorist events has been insensitive and has served to encourage further acts of terrorism. When the data on police chiefs was compared with similar data obtained from members of the media, the differences were profound. One of the sharpest differences concerned the extent to which live television coverage of terrorist acts constituted a threat to hostage safety. As one might guess, the police saw live television coverage of a hostage episode as constituting a substantial threat, while the journalists saw such coverage as constituting only a minimal threat to the safety of the terrorists' victims.[8]

Many police do not share the view that the press has played a functional role in its coverage of terrorist episodes. That the press has dispelled rumors, replaced half-truths with accurate information, and kept hundreds from descending on the scene of a terrorist incident through accurate on-the-spot reporting is an assertion that is objected to in many police circles, especially by individuals with hands-on experience in hostage negotiations. One such outspoken critic of the media is former deputy-chief Robert L. Rabe of the Washington, D.C. police. During his tenure as the force's chief hostage negotiator, Rabe was considered one of the best and most successful hostage negotiators in the country. If at times his criticism appears strong, one should remember that it is based on actual experience—experience encountered while life hung in the balance.

One of Rabe's major complaints is that reporters have too often intruded on the police in their attempts to bring a terrorist operation to a swift and safe conclusion and, in so doing, the media have not been mere observers and reporters of events, but they have become part of the news themselves. To Rabe this means not only that reporters are prone to lose their valued objectivity but that their involvement may bring about a change in the course and direction of events themselves, usually for the worse.[9]

Rabe's criticism of the media is not restricted merely to the media's intrusion into ongoing events but is also strongly directed at the media's portrayal of terrorists. Rabe, like others, is concerned that the media have often portrayed terrorists on their own terms, making them appear to be heroes, daredevils, and idealists waging battles against oppression. Such portrayals not only demoralize the police who are called upon to risk their lives to combat terrorists, but they create a climate where others may emulate the terrorists or be inclined to support them.

The points Rabe makes about intrusion are widely shared by police both in the United States and abroad. Ironically, Rabe's concerns about how the media have at times portrayed terrorists are most widely shared among the fraternity of journalists themselves.

Access and Portrayal: Two Issues

In a broad sense the issues of access and portrayal are what divide the media and the police when it comes to the questions of how the media should deal with terrorism. Although we generally view these issues as ones that separate the police and the media (and that observation is usually accurate), when we move to more specific aspects of the issue, we see that neither the police nor the media have uniform positions on these issues. As we have already noted, Police Foundation President Patrick V. Murphy has called upon his fellow police officers to be more flexible and creative in their response toward the press and to learn how to utilize the press to dispel rumors, provide accurate information, and give the public a close enough view of the scene to keep them glued to their television sets and out of harm's way. As Murphy has challenged his fellow officers to be more creative in their response to the press, some of the strongest criticisms of the media come not from the police but from the media themselves, challenging co-workers to have value commitments that extend beyond getting a story or keeping a friendly source happy by permitting portrayals that serve the interests of the source more than the objective interests of reporting.

Within these variations in opinion, one can find the framework for the continuation of the ongoing dialogue between the police and the media. To sustain such a dialogue it is important to have some idea of the specifics involved. Let us begin by looking in detail at some of the problems related to the issue of access.

In 1974, a group of convicted felons attempted to escape from the District of Columbia courthouse by seizing hostages in the cellblock located in the courthouse basement. Unbeknownst to the hostage takers the police were able to observe through a two-way mirror what was happening in the cellblock. Moreover, the police were able to direct sniper fire right through the mirror if the hostages' lives were at any time jeopardized. Discovering the logistics of the situation, local media made that information public and the hostages were rapidly dispatched to tape over the mirror.

In the course of this same situation, a young, aggressive reporter conducted lengthy telephone interviews with the hostage takers and tried to get himself admitted by them into the cellblock. When I asked him if he had ever, through the course of those telephone conversations, thought of accidentally setting off the terrorists, he openly said that it was the furthest thing from his mind. He was concerned solely with getting a scoop, something worthy of the front page.

In the October 1977 hijacking of a Lufthansa airplane which ended in the daring raid by West German police at Mogadishu, Somalia, the plane's captain was summarily executed by the terrorists and his body dumped ignominiously from the plane. According to Thomas M. Ashwood, chairman of flight security for the International Pilots Association, the media were responsible for the pilot's death.[10] Apparently, the pilot had cleverly and skillfully passed information to authorities through the normal radio transmissions overheard by the terrorists. The media aired the story of the captain's bravery and cost him his life. A similar episode took place in November 1974, when a British Airways plane flying to Dubai from Libya was hijacked for an exchange involving thirteen terrorists incarcerated in Egypt. An aircraft arrived in Cairo supposedly carrying the freed terrorists. As the exchange was about to take place, a reporter broadcast that the operation was a trap and that there were no freed terrorists aboard the Egyptian aircraft. The terrorists selected a West German banker from among the hostages and in retaliation executed him.

In the course of the delicate negotiations between Deputy-Chief Rabe and Chief Maurice Cullinane with the Hanafi Muslims who seized hostages at three separate locations in Washington, D.C. in March 1977, arrangements were made for food to be brought to the hostages being held in the B'nai B'rith building. As a truck pulled up and police began to carry out the large boxes of food, a reporter broadcast that the boxes contained weapons for the special weapons team which was preparing an imminent assault on the building. The aired misinformation was received by the Hanafis, and it took some convincing before the Hanafis were prepared to believe that their trust in the police negotiators was not misplaced and that the radio report was false.

Almost every major police department can recall its own series of experiences when police operations have been intruded upon and for the sake of a story the media have been willing to put the lives of hostages at risk. These are the events that come to mind when the police talk about the need to restrict the access of the media to in-progress terrorist operations.

For their part the media have not been entirely unresponsive to these issues. A number of the more responsible segments of the media have worked long and hard on creating a climate of professionalism which would bring such abuses by the media to an end. In the aftermath of the 1977 Hanafi Muslim episode, then-U.N. Ambassador Andrew Young publicly criticized the media for glorifying terrorism. President Jimmy Carter was called upon by the media to comment on Young's criticisms. In response, Press Secretary Jody Powell issued a statement which challenged the media to respond to the problem as "a powerful and responsible institution in our society."[11] In the context of these events, the National News Council issued a statement to the media calling for a reexamination of live coverage of terrorist events, for a reconsideration of the practice of obtaining interviews with terrorists during an ongoing situation, and for the continual development of guidelines to ensure ethical and responsible conduct by the media during their coverage of terrorist events.[12]

News agencies individually evidenced their concern by promulgating internal guidelines and by sponsoring conferences to bring together journalists and law enforcement personnel to discuss the issues that divide them. There are some who argue that for all the evidenced concern about solving these problems that the news media have demonstrated, their prime concern is still for getting a story. How one gets a story is a consideration that is secondary to getting it. Legal scholar Robert Friedlander concluded from an intensive analysis of the media's coverage of the Iranian hostage crisis that ". . . throughout the Iranian captivity these guidelines were ignored to a far greater extent than they were observed. All three television networks, taking advantage of the Iranian drama, developed a blind eye to professional, ethical considerations in a fervent competitive quest for audiences."[13] Professor of journalism Walter Jaehnig has pointed out that most of the guidelines for the coverage of terrorism are nothing more than a restatement of the common basics of good journalism taught in virtually every journalism curriculum. Why are they ignored when they are most needed?, Jaehnig asks of his fellow journalists.

Most of the emphasis of the guidelines is directed at the coverage of ongoing terrorist events and at keeping the media from either intruding on the police operation or overly sensationalizing the event itself. The guidelines, to a significantly lesser degree, address the issue of how journalists might portray terrorists. To understand both the significance and complexity of this issue, it is necessary to look at and understand some of the fundamental difficulties reporters continually face in trying to get a story and then trying to assess its accuracy. Commenting on this difficulty, Edward Jay Epstein, a longtime observer of the media, has noted, "The problem of journalism in America proceeds from a simple but inescapable bind: journalists are rarely, if ever, in a position to establish the truth about an issue for themselves, and they are therefore entirely dependent on self-interested 'sources' for the version of reality they report."[14] To underscore his point Epstein alludes to the widely circulated story in 1969 alleging that local police and the Federal Bureau of Investigation were jointly involved in a systematic campaign of genocide against the Black Panthers. The story emanated from sources in the Black Panther hierarchy. The allegations even claimed that twenty-eight Panthers had already been killed in this campaign. One news source after another picked up the story without commentary, without even attribution, exactly as the Panthers had told it. It soon became part of the public perception of the "truth." On the basis of that story, civil rights leader Ralph Abernathy accused the nation of waging genocide. In truth, after close examination of the numerous violent shootouts between the Panthers and the police, only two remotely showed that they might have been executions under the cover of law. This number was far less than the ten policemen known to have been killed by the Panthers. The discrepancies were known to some of the reporters who had been working on stories about the Panthers and had obtained access to them. Not one of those reporters came forward to dispute the Panthers claims. To do so would have jeopardized their special access to Panther information and future stories.

This reluctance to jeopardize privileged access might just explain correspondent Louis Rukeyser's observations about American news coverage of Arab terrorists: "American news coverage of the Arab guerrillas in recent years has resembled nothing so much as American news coverage of the Black Panthers—and in neither case has my profession covered itself with journalistic glory. With both groups there is a fascination with the reality and threat of violence. With both there was a tendency to overrate their influence and to take with grave seriousness the most nonsensical extremes of rhetoric."[15]

In all fairness, it is necessary to point out that source dependency does not just occur on one side of the street. A different kind of dependency occurs because of the willingness of some members of the press to become a mechanism for the uncritical dissemination of government versions of the "truth." In the post-Watergate and post-Vietnam eras, it is common to have an image of the media as critic of information that originates with government sources. However, this image too easily overlooks the often symbiotic relationships that typically develop between journalists in search of a story and government officials looking for outlets for self-serving news. An example of this dependence can be seen in Simon Hoggart's observations about British press accounts of the situation in Northern Ireland. As Hoggart notes: "When the British press prints an account of an incident as if it were an established fact and it is clear that the reporter himself was not on the spot, it is a 99 percent certainty that it is the army's version which is given."[16]

The media's dependency on sources and access has been incorporated in the British government's very adroit response to the media in Northern Ireland. Journalists are treated as important guests by a large network of both army and government press corps. Those who adhere to the official line and seek news from official sources are rewarded with continued access and even an occasional scoop. Those inclined to strike out on their own are cut off from official sources and may find themselves harassed out of Ulster.

Biases do occur from both directions. Perhaps, to some degree biases are almost unavoidable. The extreme forms of bias are readily discernible. There are, however, those less well defined areas that are not clearly seen as biases, but are nonetheless. Consider, for example, that calling a person a "terrorist" instead of a "guerrilla," "freedom fighter," or "commando" already establishes a point of view. Similarly, when the media says that a police officer is "executed," or that he has simply "perished" at the hands of terrorism, a connotation is created that something other than murder has occurred.

Consequently, how the media depict terrorists and their actions will always possess some bias or other. Some are subtle and, given the nature of journalism, almost unavoidable. As Walter Lippmann reflected in an assessment of the biases of his own profession, "The final page is of a definite size and must be ready by a precise moment.''[17] Such biases as the limitations of time, space, and human energy are understood and easily discounted. What cannot be so readliy discounted are those situations in which the media have become devices for the uncritical dissemination of terrorist propaganda and where the media have been all too willing to portray terrorists in a fashion that gains for them sympathy and legitimacy, if not outright emulation.

We will look more specifically at this issue, as well as the issue of access, in terms of the British experience with terrorism in Northern Ireland and its spillover throughout the United Kingdom. The British have had a long and tragic experience with the issues of concern in this chapter. They have made themselves felt in poignant and dramatic circumstances which have caused societal reaction and debate far beyond media and law enforcement organizations. It is to these examples that we will now turn.

Law Enforcement and the Media in the United Kingdom

Terrorism crossed the Irish Sea in 1972 and arrived on the shores of England with the deafening roar of an explosion which ripped through the British Army officer's mess at Aldershot and killed seven people. Aldershot was an ominous beginning portending greater violence to come. It did in November of 1974 when bombs ripped through two crowded pubs in Birmingham, killing twenty-one people. The British public, accustomed to the violence in Northern Ireland as something one casually digested with other news, now found that terrorism had taken root on home soil. The Birmingham bombings brought cries of public outrage and demands on government for protection. Parliament responded to the public's will with the 1974 Prevention of Terrorism Act, a measure described by the British Home Secretary as "draconian" and "unprecedented in peace time."[18]

The act was directed at the Irish Republican Army, but a number of its provisions had profound implications for journalists working on stories involving the IRA. Section I of the act prohibited anyone from soliciting or providing financial or other support for the IRA. This not only prohibited "checkbook journalism," but it raised serious concerns about news stories that might appear to invite IRA support. Section II made it a crime for a person not to come forward when he or she knowingly had information that would prevent an act of terrorism or lead to the arrest of a terrorist. This wiped out any claims a journalist might make for a privileged relationship between a reporter and a confidential source. This same issue was dealt with by the American Supreme Court in Zurcher v. Stanford Daily, and the court concluded that the Constitution of the United States did not confer upon the press a special immunity from testimony. The Stanford Daily decision followed from precedent established in an earlier case, Branzburg v. Hayes et al. in which the court ruled that a reporter could not claim special privilege to protect a confidential source from a grand jury proceeding. The 1974 act of Parliament embodied the same philosophy toward the idea of reporter's privilege.

Other provisions of the act appeared to prevent newsmen from attending a press conference or briefing held by the IRA or for camera crews to request IRA supporters to wave placards before the television lights. The language of the act, however, was not directed at the news media; nonetheless, the plausible interpretation was ever present that the act had implications for the manner in which the news media conducted itself when reporting stories about the IRA.

The chilling implications of the act for civil liberties were acknowledged by Lord Shackleton in his 1978 review of the operation of the act. However, Lord Shackleton refrained from addressing the implications of the act for the civil liberties of the media. The British National Civil Liberties Council, citing a long series of abuses of fundamental civil liberties by the act, came out strongly against it. Arguing in a vein common to many who have anguished over the effects of strong antiterrorist measures on the democratic foundations of the society, the NCCL noted, "We oppose emergency legislation because it diminishes the rights of all citizens by providing Government, the police, and the army with powers unchallengable in the courts, and by corrupting the standards which are central to the administration of justice."[19]

In 1981 the NCCL came out for the repeal of the prevention of terrorism act. Citing in detail abuses of almost all of the act's provisions, the NCCL, which had montitored the act since its inception, hoped to alert Parliament to the desire if not the necessity for repeal. Despite its detailed list of abuses, the NCCL said little if anything about the implications of the act for the press.[20] Even Lord Shackleton's earlier review of the operations of the act, which he wrote in 1978, said nothing about the press.[21] In large measure, this was not a result of the act having no consequences for the conduct of the press, but rather it was due to the press not being specifically mentioned in the act. That was more of a curse than a blessing, for those who would use the act against the media could easily do so, while those who sought to assess the implementation of the act tended to ignore the implications for the media because they were not mentioned specifically.

The media were in a rather vulnerable position. The act by implication could be used to prohibit a number of the media's traditional mechanisms used in obtaining a story. The Metropolitan Police, however, demonstrated a profound and uncanny understanding of the situation. Contrary to expectations, they did not seek to regulate the media through the act. Instead, recognizing that the impression most British subjects have of both terrorists and the police is filtered through the media, Sir Robert Mark and his successor, Sir David McNee, Commissioner of Scotland Yard, followed a policy of cooperating with the media. Both commissioners sought to increase the dissemination of information to the media and to make access to the police by the media more readily available. In a fashion strikingly similar to that of Patrick Murphy and James Hoge, Mark, and later Mc-Nee, advocated a functional role for the media to be brought about through a policy that emphasized cooperation between the police and the media.

Mark and later McNee also had the political acumen to negotiate, with the news industry, "gentlemen's agreements" which now govern the media's reporting of terrorism. Walter Jaehnig, who has studied the application of these agreements in some depth, reports that both the police and the media have found that the voluntary agreements not only clarify matters that have generally put the two institutions at odds with each other, but because the agreements were voluntary, the media retained ultimate discretionary authority over what they published and the agreements were infinitely preferable to relationships that might have been based on the act.

Thus, possessing legal power that would have been the envy of many an American police commissioner, Robert Mark and David McNee sought to follow a course that opened up police operations to the press far beyond what was required of the police.

The agreement, however, was not one-sided. For its part, the Yard sought and got cooperation from the media it might not otherwise have received. In a democratic society such as Britain, even under the constant threat of the terrorist's bomb, even with the legal support of such legislation as the 1974 Prevention of Terrorism Act, the tradition of civil liberties is not readily or easily pushed aside. The image of the police in conflict with the press gains little for the police. Even in instances in which the press had clearly violated the act, the Yard has been reluctant to request prosecution, and in other instances when the request has been made, the attorney general respectfully declined prosecution. Thus, in 1980 the government invoked section II of the act and requested prosecution of BBC (British Broadcasting Company) for airing news from a Provisional IRA roadblock at Carrickpergus. Mindful of the societal and political repercussions of such a prosecution, Sir Michael Havers, the attorney general, refused to carry forward the prosecution.

Despite both the gentlemen's agreements and the general sense of civility that governs police and media relations in Great Britian, as the police and the media pursue their respective goals conflicts still occur. Some of these are every bit as involved, complicated, and impassioned as what have been experienced in the United States. We present one of the more noteworthy and more controversial of these conflicts below.[22]

Six Days at the Iranian Embassy (London)

At 11:32 A.M. on April 30, 1980, seven men calling themselves "The Group of the Martyr" burst into the Iranian Embassy across from

London's tranquil Hyde Park. Trevor Lock, the constable on duty, saw glass from a bullet-sprayed outer door shatter around him. Glass splintered into his face as three men rushed and grabbed him, but not before the valiant constable got out a distress signal. A warning light flashed in Scotland Yard's monitoring room and the sergeant at the console instantly ordered members of the diplomatic protection group to the scene. Three minutes later they were outside the embassy. As they took up positions, the air was punctuated with sounds of police sirens.

At 11:45 Deputy Assistant Commissioner Peter Neivens, the Yard's chief press officer, was attending a conference at Church House, Westminster. Ironically, the topic of the conference was "Terrorism and the Media." Neivens was called out of the conference at about the same time that Deputy Assistant Commissioner John Dellow, the officer in charge of day-to-day operations, was en route to the Iranian Embassy. For the next six days, Dellow would direct the tactical procedures employed against the terrorists.

American police, had they witnessed the scene, would have quickly noted striking similarities between their tactics and those implemented by the British. Procedures of "containment and control," so frequently associated with the tactics of American special weapons teams, were being put into place. Streets were being cordoned off, buildings were being evacuated, and the Blue Berets, the Yard's crack marksmen, had taken up their positions. A "sterile area" was being created.

At 5:30 P.M. the gunmen used two of the captives, both journalists, to transmit the terrorists demands to the BBC by telephone. Earlier the *Guardian* had come on the embassy's telex line, but after the *Guardian's* questions moved into areas that the terrorists did not wish to discuss, they pulled the plug on the machine.

The police negotiating team consisted of four men, later augmented to six because the pressure became too severe. Only one of the terrorists negotiated with the police and he maintained a remarkable presence of self right up to the end.

On the second day of the siege, the lead terrorist, a man known as Oan, asked Mustapha Karkouti, a Syrian journalist who was taken hostage, to telephone the BBC World News to repeat the gunmen's demands and to repeat to the British public that nothing was going to happen to the non-Iranian hostages. Colin Thatcher, a BBC editor, seized the opportunity for an interview. Some excerpts follow below:

BBC: There has been a phone call [a reference to the phone call from the Iranian Foreign Minister Quotbzadeh received the night before]. What was the message? Oan: The message—I think he says: we will not yield to the demands of the group. BBC: What is your reaction to the message? Oan: Just a minute. (Pause) I think he will regret for this statement. BBC: Can you go into details? What do you mean 'he will regret it'? Oan: I mean, after the deadline, we will kill everybody here. All the hostages. BBC: And the deadline is twelve today? Oan: Twelve noon today. This is what Quotbzadeh wants, because they are nothing to him. He doesn't care for the Iranian hostages.[23]

Colin Thatcher was behaving as a journalist in search of a story. The opportunity had been dumped in his lap. Who could blame him for wanting an interview with Oan? What journalist would have passed up the opportunity? Yet, those familiar with the process of negotiation will recognize some of the dangers involved in this exchange. Asking for details about the telephone call from Iran and more important the gunmen's response to it, placed a gunman in a position of having to talk tough. The gunman now had to have a response. Initially, Oan had Syrian correspondent Karkouti place the call to reassure the public that the non-Iranian hostages would not be harmed. What started out as a benign act on the part of the terrorist escalated when the BBC's Thatcher pursued the opening for an interview that began with Karkouti and ended up with Oan taking over the phone and threatening the lives of all the hostages, something which up until that point he had conspicuously avoided. No doubt, the fate of the hostages was all the worse for Thatcher's intrusion.

Thatcher's intrusion, however, would not be the worst aspect of the conduct of the press throughout this siege. Coming on the heels of the ill-fated American attempt to free its nationals from the American Embassy in Tehran, the seizure of the Iranian Embassy in London, by Arab nationalists seeking self-determination for the Iranian province of Khuzistan, was a media event. The world's media descended on Kensington like a spring flood.

Deputy Assistant Commissioner Peter Neivens sought to follow policies that would secure the media's assistance and squelch rumors surrounding the situation. Neivens also sought to utilize the press to communicate to the terrorists that the British were neutral in the situation and were deeply and optimistically committed to a nonviolent solution. Neivens expected that there would probably be some difficulties with the foreign press. What Neivens could not anticipate was that the police operation would be jeopardized by the local media.

As the spokeman for Scotland Yard, Neivens had a great deal of experience with the media. Witnessing the deluge of reporters, especially foreign reporters, on the scene, Neivens' concerns were directed toward the foreign press. After all the local journalists were party to a gentlemen's agreement between the Yard and the media. Whether the foreign reporters, many of them unfamiliar with Britain and the history of relations between the media and police, would stay out of trouble was entirely another matter.

Yet, Neivens' concerns were misplaced. It was not the foreign press but British Independent Television that almost ruined the police assault against the terrorists. On the afternoon of the first day of the embassy's siege, a special antiterrorist unit from the legendary Special Air Services had been called to the scene. This group had distinguished itself from the battlefields of North Africa to the IRA-infested counties of Northern Ireland. Its training grueling, its demands relentless, its men rare; there was no question that once called into action, the SAS were not going to be called to negotiate.

As the SAS waited in ready, it appeared that they would not be called. After all, the negotiations had appeared to go very well; several hostages had even been released. Besides, no one really believed that the terrorists themselves wanted anything more than publicity. They certainly could not have thought that the Ayatollah Khomeini was going to give them autonomy because they had seized an embassy. Then, the inexplicable happened: On Monday, May 5, the sixth day of the siege, the terrorists shot one of the Iranian hostages.

On the morning of May 5, Professor John Gunn, who had been advising the police negotiators, began to worry about their morale as the crisis continued. Gunn anticipated that the siege would last only another few days before the terrorists capitulated. He had already rearranged appointments for Tuesday and Wednesday. However, at about 1:30 in the afternoon, shots rang out. The terrorists alleged to have shot one of the hostages, and at that point the SAS knew that an assault on the embassy was inevitable. There would be no negotiations with killing—not in Britain.

Attempts at bringing the situation to a negotiated conclusion continued through the afternoon, but at 6:50 P.M. more shots rang out, and the dead hostage who had been shot earlier was thrown out the door.

At 7:23 P.M. the sound of explosives shook the building. The embassy filled with the stench of smoke, accompanied by a chorus of shattering glass. The SAS attacked. They came down ropes from above, from the house next door, where, several days earlier, the bricks separating the common wall had been cautiously removed one at a time; and they came from the front where they had planted charges to crash in the windows. It was the frontal assault that was transmitted live to every television set in Britain tuned to ITV.

For earlier, ITV in its quest for a dramatic story had infiltrated the sterile area with a camera crew. The SAS assault which was so heavily dependent on the element of surprise was going off live. Had the captors in the embassy turned on their television set, they could have watched the assault. The media could have been the eyes and ears of the terrorists and the lives of the hostages and the brave men who had come to their rescue might have been lost.

The Yard was infuriated! ITV claimed that there had been a two-to-three-minute delay in the transmission. The Yard claimed that not only did that cut it close but that it only occurred because a decision had to be made whether to interrupt an ongoing program. Moreover, the decision to transmit was made by whomever happened to be at the station at the time. It was a major decision which involved absolutely none of the station's highest-ranking decision makers.

The SAS assault was a dramatic success. During the assault, five gunmen were killed, two hostages wounded, one hostage killed, and the remaining hostages released unharmed. Three members of the SAS sustained minor injuries. The elation that Britain and the rest of the free world felt was only marred by the intrusion of ITV which nearly jeopardized the assault. As usual some of ITV's strongest criticism came from the press itself. Clive James, the *Observer's* television critic, called for a ban on the reporting of sieges where the lives of hostages were at risk. Members of the print media looked upon ITV's behavior as the kind of excess typical of the electronic media in search of an instant story. In the final analysis, the siege pointed up once again the dramatic differences in goals that separate the police and the media in the handling of terrorist episodes.

Some Observations

The six days at the Iranian embassy demonstrate the complexity of relations between the police and the press during an ongoing violent incident. In the annals and discussions of police/press relations, the siege will be remembered primarily in terms of ITV's intrusion into the sterile area and their placing of the rescue operation at risk. Law enforcement will probably say that image is as it should be. The press would argue that once again the excesses of one team of journalists have subsumed the highly professional behavior of all other members of the press, both foreign and domestic, who followed the procedures established by the police. In fact, the behavior of one journalist, Tony Crabb of the BBC News, was nothing short of exemplary. Crabb had put a camp bed in his office on Thursday night. It was decided that someone with authority would be on call at all times at the BBC should the need arise for a high-level decision. The need came the next morning when the police received a call from Sim Harris, a BBC newsman held hostage at the embassy. Harris had asked to speak to John Exelby, the home news editor, and the police wanted him down at the embassy immediately. Exelby was unavailable and Crabb went in his place.

Crabb arrived at the embassy about 9:30 A.M. Friday and went with Superintendant Ray Tucker, one of the police negotiators, to a ground floor window where Crabb spoke with fellow journalist Harris. The discussions resulted in Crabb becoming immediately aware that some of the captors' demands had not been transmitted to the media. After the discussion with Harris, Crabb was asked by the police to keep his silence about this information and he did. What Crabb learned was that the captors demanded the presence of Arab ambassadors as mediators between them and the police. For a variety of complex reasons, the police, with the approval of Prime

Minister Margaret Thatcher, were not disposed to comply with that demand. Crabb had a real scoop, but publishing the story would have thrown the negotiations into chaos. Crabb decided not to risk the lives of the hostages for a story.

If we are to remember the siege at the Iranian Embassy because of the intrusion of ITV, we should also keep in mind the behavior of Tony Crabb. It is vital and necessary to create mechanisms that will prevent another ITV type of intrusion, but we must learn to balance those mechanisms against the utility of maintaining harmonious relations between law enforcement and the media. Those kinds of relations make it possible for law enforcement to be able to have the assistance and trust of someone like Tony Crabb.

We might also keep in mind that the 1974 Prevention of Terrorism Act gave Scotland Yard a great deal of control over the media, had the Yard sought to use it. While some American police officers might look upon the Prevention of Terrorism Act with envy, we are reminded that the Yard opted for gentlemen's agreements between themselves and the press rather than for the enforcement of the act. Despite media excess, both parties are pleased with the informal agreements and the continuing interaction, both formal and informal, that permits the press and the police to air and attempt to resolve their differences.

In a democratic society even when the police are given, under emergency conditions, the power to behave undemocratically and to implement procedures that have authoritarian overtones, there are institutional, political, and even moral constraints on their ability to use those powers. If we in the United States are going to find a mechanism that will lessen the probability of press intrusion into ongoing police operations and make the press more aware of the consequences of some of their romantic portrayals of terrorists, it is going to have to come about through more dialogue and interaction between the parties involved and by basically convincing the press to live up to the professional ethics they have so frequently espoused. The greatest ally law enforcement might have in this pursuit is those people in the media who have shown by their own positions and conduct to stand for a strong commitment to implementing the ethics of good journalism. Differences between law enforcement and the media are bound to continue to exist, but those differences should not obscure their mutual interests in the preservation of a free and orderly society.

Notes

1. James W. Hoge, "The Media and Terrorism," in Abraham H. Miller, ed., *Terrorism, the Media, and the Law* (Dobbs Ferry, N.Y.: Transnational Publishers, 1982), pp. 90–91.

2. Patrick V. Murphy, "The Police Perspective," in *The Media and Terrorism:*

A Seminar Sponsored by the Chicago Sun-Times and Chicago Daily News (Chicago: Field Enterprises, 1977), p. 11.

3. Hoge, "The Media and Terrorism," p. 94.

4. National Advisory Committee on Criminal Justice Standards and Goals, *Disorders and Terrorism: Report of the Task Force on Disorders and Terrorism* (Washington, D.C.: LEAA, 1976), pp. 236-39.

5. Richard Lewis Clutterbuck, *Guerrillas and Terrorists* (London: Faber and Faber, 1977), p. II.

6. Cited in Hoge, "The Media and Terrorism," p. 97.

7. From a personal conversation with Richard Lewis Clutterbuck, August 3, 1980 at Thorverton, England.

8. Michael Sommer and Heidi Sommer, "The Project on Media Coverage of Terrorism: A Summary of National Surveys and other Investigations, 1977-1979," in Miller, ed., *Terrorism*, pp. 166 and 179.

9. Robert L. Rabe, "The Journalist and the Hostage: How Their Rights Can Be Balanced," in Miller, ed., *Terrorism*, p. 70.

10. From a personal conversation with Thomas M. Ashwood, November 17, 1977 at the City University of New York.

11. Cited in John Herbers, "Carter Says Coverage of Siege Is Problem for the News," *New York Times*, March 15, 1977.

12. The National News Council, "Paper on Terrorism," in Miller, ed., *Terrorism*, pp. 133-147.

13. Robert A. Friedlander, "Iran: The Hostage Seizure, the Media and International Law," in Miller, ed., *Terrorism*, p. 59.

14. Abraham H. Miller, "Terrorism, the Media and the Law: A Discussion of the Issues," in Miller, ed., *Terrorism*, pp. 13-50.

15. Louis Rukeyser, American Information Radio Network, March 4, 1977.

16. Cited in Philip Elliot, "Reporting Northern Ireland: A Study of News in Britain, Ulster and the Irish Republic," in *Ethnicity and the Media* (Paris: Unesco, 1976), pp. v-5.

17. Walter Lippmann quoted in Edward Jay Epstein, *Between Fact and Fiction: The Problem of Journalism* (New York: Vintage Press, 1975), p. 5.

18. Cited in Walter B. Jaehnig, "Terrorism in Britain: The Limits of Free Expression," in Miller, ed., *Terrorism*, p. 109.

19. Catherine Scorer and Patricia Hewitt, *The Prevention of Terrorism Act: The Case for Repeal* (London: National Council for Civil Liberties, 1981), p. 5.

20. Ibid.

21. Rt. Hon. Lord Shackleton, *Review of the Operation of the Prevention of Terrorism (Temporary Provisions) Acts 1974 and 1976* (London: Her Majesty's Stationery Office, 1978).

22. For this section, I have relied on George Brock et al., *Siege: Six Days at the Iranian Embassy* (London: *The Observer*, 1980) and from interviews with Deputy Assistant Commissioner Peter Neivens of Scotland Yard.

23. Brock et al., *Siege*, p. 46.

7

Negotiating with Terrorists

GEORGE S. ROUKIS

Terrorism will not diminish during the 1980s but will increase in intensity as international and regional instability continue and pose problems for governments and business organizations. While small groups of terrorists could cause incalculable damage to economic facilities such as offshore platforms, central oil and gas pipelines, and refineries if they carefully concentrate their efforts on economic disruption, the kidnapping of corporate executives will still continue to be a profitable activity.[1] It provides the financial means to support the terrorist organization and is relatively risk free. It exposes the terrorists to only a limited time of danger and if successful, the executive can be held safely in the underground quarters. If the demands have not been met, the terrorists could kill or release their hostage.[2]

In 1979, 35.1 percent of all international terrorist attacks on U.S. citizens or interests were directed against American executives and corporate property, and the average for the years 1968-1979 was 36.2 percent.[3] The odds show that there is almost an 80 percent chance that the members of a kidnapping team will escape capture and close to an even chance that all or part of the demands will be conceded. For a political group contemplating this form of terrorist activity, it could conclude that it had an 86 percent chance of actually seizing hostages; an 86 percent chance of success when safe passage of themselves or others was the sole demand; and a 100 percent probability of gaining extensive media exposure. It is a thoughtful activity and the ransom process is manageable.[4]

Terrorists believe that firms can pay ransom with minimal inconvenience and justify their demands on ideological grounds. If, in addition to acquiring a large sum of money from the target corporation, they can force the same company to distribute food, clothing, and medicines to the local population, an ancillary revolutionary objective has been achieved, which expiates the criminal nature of the kidnap act. Such beneficence rationalizes the terrorist attack.[5] In the early 1970s Argentinian terrorist groups amassed over $150 million in ransom and correlative extortion payments, and thus demonstrated that kidnapping is lucrative.[6] For example, the Ejercito Revolucionario del Pueblo (ERP), an Argentinian terrorist group, received $14 million for the release of an oil executive in 1974 and $60 million for the release of two Bonge and Born heirs in 1975. The latter amount was the most lucrative ransom ever paid in one country. In addition to the aforementioned sum, which was estimated to be the equivalent of one-third of the military budget of Argentina, the company was also required to distribute more than $1 million of food and clothing to the workers and place in all the Bonge and Born factories the busts of General and Eva Peron.[7]

There are limits to capitulation. In democratic societies, where negotiating flexibility exists, it would be imprudent to succumb always to terrorist demands or compromise on vital positions that are inherently antithetical to the government. It would create a dangerous precedent and would encourage more terrorist activities. Yet, we should not rule out negotiation, if the release of the hostage-victim or the political demands posed does not handicap the government involved or expose it to further terrorist demands. For corporate executives exposed to this danger, it becomes important for them to understand the dynamics of the kidnapping process and above all to learn how to negotiate their survival in captivity. If the government or local law enforcement authorities are unsuccessful in securing the release of hostages, they must depend upon their own resources for survival. It might well be politically necessary for the government, which officially observes a tough nonconcession policy, to express concern for the hostage's life, but the executive, of necessity, must save his or her own life. Executives are perceived as a means of financing the terrorists' cause and a vehicle for broadcasting their political demands. Hostages cannot presuppose a rational bargaining relationship with their captors since these victims are expendable in the conflict process. A precipitate police rescue attempt could mean sudden death if the terrorists turn on the hostage, or if he or she is accidently killed during the assault. However, the chances of survival are high, if executives understand what is involved and prepare themselves for this ordeal.

Initially, when the kidnapping attack takes place, the executive is disconcerted and in a state of shock, which admittedly precludes the deliberateness characteristic of planned negotiations; but he or she should remain calm, cooperative, and avoid a competitive relationship. If the hostage attempts to escape or disputes the ideological merits of the kidnap attack, his or her own life will be endangered. This is especially true in a barricade-siege-type crisis. Survival depends primarily upon a willingness to follow orders and the avoidance of aggressive, uncooperative behavior.[8]

Local police forces, who are usually the first to arrive on the scene, have developed fairly sophisticated crisis-management techniques to deal with a barricade-hostage situation. Quality, of course, differs among jurisdictions depending upon experience and public funding. In the United States, where hostage negotiation training is more pronounced, a higher degree of preparedness exists, but other countries have improved their capabilities as well. The police are concerned with containing the terrorist attack, gathering intelligence about the terrorist group, negotiating the release of the hostages, and terminating the barricade crisis by persuasion or force, if necessary, depending upon the circumstances. They play a pivotal role in the barricade negotiating process since they control the sealed off area and communications with the outside world, and their initial response to the crisis determines the course of the negotiations. The terrorists' motivation will, at first, determine the parameters of the agenda, but time and skillful police negotiating tactics will change the situation.

If an impasse develops that the terrorists perceive as foreclosing the success of their mission, negotiations might appear to be the only reasonable alternative to securing at least secondary or symbolic goals. The police are in a position to structure a negotiating climate that is closer to the collective bargaining model, in which the mixed tactics of coercion and cooperation are successful and the trade-offs do not compromise the host government's deterrence policy, while the kidnapped executive can attempt to develop a cooperative relationship with the captors.

The terrorists' dependence upon the police for basic necessities such as food and water becomes stronger as fatigue and uncertainty disorient their perceptions and they become more receptive to bargaining. However, the unpredictability of the situation and the lack of rationality, which is the essence of labor-management negotiations, is not present to ensure that commitments are observed. There are no institutional processes to enforce these conditional promises like the National Labor Relations Board, but the exchange of necessities for the release of hostages is a reasonable bargain and police negotiators should be trained to recognize the practicality of these environmental variables.[9] Making minimal concessions and extending negotiations provides the needed maneuverability that is essential for reaching agreement.

On the other hand, the kidnapped executive should not try to confuse or excite the terrorists or direct their attention away from the police. Until the status quo sets in, the executive should remain calm and cooperative and slowly attempt to change the terrorists' mind set. Such attitudinal change developments cannot be accomplished at the inception of the barricade siege, but over time, the subtle, measured cooperative responses could begin to modify the terrorists' perceptions. The executive should try to know the captors, but not at the price of inciting a competitive relationship. In New York City, the police hostage negotiating team under the leadership of Captain Frank Bolz has deservedly earned a worldwide reputation as an effective hostage negotiating model. The team's style and methods have been adopted by other law enforcement agencies, and Captain Bolz's success in terminating hostage crises has become legion.[10]

In barricade situations, executives should not get into philosophical discussions with the terrorists since hostages are the most disadvantaged party, but they should be as helpful as possible to get the terrorists to like them. In captivity, the most important goal for the executive is to neutralize the politicized antipathy of the terrorist and win him or her over. This does not, however, require that the executive grovel before the captors, but he or she should not be careless.[11] The terrorists will invariably set time limits when they are surrounded by the police to create pressures favoring their positions, but experience shows that they are willing to modify these time limits if negotiations do not appear threatening. The police are in a stronger position to shape the negotiating process and, if they are able to defuse the hostile response of the terrorists and create a negotiable climate, which permits the cooperative interests of the parties to dominate, then the executive has the time to act simultaneously on the terrorists' attitudes and affectations. The police and the terrorists have competitive interests regarding the nature of a settlement agreement and cooperative interests regarding the fate of the hostages and the publication of the terrorists' demands. Emphasizing the competitive aspects of the negotiating process or viewing the barricade crisis in either/or terms will escalate the conflict, since cooperation will be ruled out. The mixed-motive bargaining approach, with emphasis on the cooperative aspects, is more appropriate. If a cooperative relationship can be established that permits the terrorists to reformulate their position, then an outcome favorable to all the parties might result.[12]

In the United States, where experience with political hostage taking is somewhat limited, the Hanafi seizure of hostages at the national headquarters of B'nai B'rith, the District of Columbia's City Council offices, and the Islamic Center on March 10, 1972, is a classic example of traditional mixed-motive bargaining. Moreover, it shows that a flexible response to a barricade siege can produce satisfactory face-saving results.

Two of the three demands initially proposed by Hanass Abdul Khaalis, leader of the Hanafi Muslim sect, were amenable to a negotiated settlement, while the third demand was patently nonnegotiable. The Hanafis wanted the government to release to their custody the five Black Muslims convicted of the brutal 1972 Hanafi murders for purposes of vengeance, but this demand was not pressed. The movie *Muhammad: Messenger of God*, which was offensive to the sect, was not publicly exhibited in the theaters, and the $750 fine Khaalis paid, when he was disruptive in Judge Leonard Brahman's court during the Black Muslim murder trial, was returned to him. In addition, a federal judge agreed to release Khaalis on his own recognizance, pending trial for his terrorist offenses.[13]

District of Columbia Police Chief Maurice J. Cullinane, who ably directed the containment and hostage negotiation, involved the Islamic ambassadors of Egypt, Iran, and Pakistan in the talks when requested by the Hanafi, and their active assistance facilitated the trust-building process needed to terminate the crisis. The siege lasted thirty-eight hours and the hostages were released, though not without distressing consequences. A newspaper reporter was killed, a security guard was wounded, and a city councilman was shot in the chest, along with others who were needlessly assaulted.[14] But apart from these tragedies, the negotiation in toto demonstrated clearly that resiliency, timing, and symbolic trade-offs enhanced the bargaining process. The terrorists had an opportunity to assess their predicament, modify their position, and accept a face-saving agreement that was also acceptable to the police. A behavioral norm was established that governed the content and direction of the bargaining agenda and was supported by the parties changed attitudes. To be sure, there were significant differences between them, but they were not exaggerated or exploited. The police managed to avoid an aggressive-defensive reaction that would have been harmful to the hostages and transformed a threatening crisis into a positive outcome. In effect, the parties organized their perception of the ambiguous environment by the negotiation categories they imposed upon that environment and a convergence of interest developed. This prevented further violence and demonstrated the efficacy of negotiations in barricade-siege crises.

Time, which is the most important variable in barricade situations, permits both the police and terrorists to negotiate a cooperative understanding while minimizing the competitive elements of their relationships. If the terrorists believe that their political message has been widely publicized and this was really their key bargaining objective, then there is a better chance of ending the siege.

If the terrorists' demands also include the freeing of political prisoners, ransom payments, and safe passage to a third country, the competitive aspects of bargaining predominate, thus forcing the national government into the bargaining process and the dangers to the hostages increase. The local law enforcement agencies at the scene cannot negotiate political concessions and the media, which sees the incident as a major news event, compounds the problem, if the police try to minimize its significance. It is at this point that the hostages' efforts to structure a transference effect are put to the test. If they are successful, the hostages will have saved their lives. They have no other options, other than to modify the terrorists' perception of them. Above all, hostages must not create conditions that preclude their survival.

On August 23, 1973, an escaped Swedish convict named Jan Erik Olson held up the Sveriges Kreditbank, one of Stockholm's largest banks, and took hostages, including two women. During the six days of captivity, the prisoners developed an affection for the kidnapper and a suspiciousness toward the authorities, which became known as the Stockholm Syndrome or Transference Effect. Psychologically, it represents a return to the state of infancy, when children found themselves dependent upon their mothers for sustenence and protection and in the case of hostages, their recognition that they are totally dependent upon the captors.[15] The terrorist is not viewed as evil or criminalistic, but instead perceived as needing understanding and empathy. Women sometimes develop a romantic attachment toward their captors, while older victims are more statesman-like in their behavior. Age and sex are critical variables and the duration of captivity, quality of interaction, and the captive's predisposition to relate to the terrorist affect the development of the transference effect. Transference, however, will generally not take place if strong racial and ethnic hostilities exist.[16]

Interestingly, as more is known about terrorism and hostage survival tactics, the terrorists themselves will be studiously avoiding a transference effect relationship. This eventuality, however, should not deter the kidnapped executive from structuring a cooperative relationship with the captors. Time is an important concomitant of the attitudinal restructuring process and should be used diligently to encourage a cooperative atmosphere. The terrorists' demands will be stridently articulated to ensure that a worldwide audience is aware of their attack and they will be clearly predisposed to violence. If a barricade siege leads to a stalemate, which permits negotiations to take place, the hostage should begin to change the relationship in the direction of more cooperation. In the life-threatening situation that victim and terrorist face, their recognition of their common fate might lead to an acceptable accommodation. Sharing the same physical space and experiencing the stress of a barricade siege helps build the emotional closeness that acts as a deterrent against violence. Executives should be aware of the transference effect and if unfortunately kidnapped, they should carefully strive to develop a cooperative bond. It is possible that the terrorists will not reciprocate these cooperative overtures, but this should not prevent hostages from trying. They have no other alternative in this environment.

In a nonbarricade situation, when the kidnapping attack has been successful, captured executives, who are usually senior corporate officers, are faced with different survival options. They are now in total captivity, although free from the dangers of the barricade siege, but held by persons who are indifferent to their concerns. The hostages are simply chips to be traded for ransom money, similar to King Richard I Coeur de Lion, when he was captured by the Duke of Leopold on his journey home from the Crusades in 1192.[17] For executives who have known status and financial independence, captivity is a dehumanizing ordeal. They will experience claustrophobia, time disorientation, sleeplessness, and gastronomical disturbances. The captors will humiliate them and justify the captivity on ideological grounds. However, chances of survival are good.[18] Of a reported 567 persons kidnapped during the 1970-1978 period, 35 were killed and one-fourth of these deaths were attributable to resistance. The average period of captivity is thirty-three days, but some executives were held longer than six months. An Owen-Illinois executive, for example, was held for three and one-half years.[19] This is, however, a notable exception.

Since executives are not political officials, it is easier to negotiate their release. The kidnappers are seeking funds, not major political concessions, and the victim's company is usually willing to pay the ransom. It is the political demands that elicit firm no-concession policies. At times, however, the host government's policy prohibits the payment of ransom which affects the negotiating process. If the business firm pays the ransom, it could contravene the laws of the host government and invite litigation, but this is still an unanswered question. While ransom insurance is a growing business and a presumption arises that terrorists seize insured corporate executives, there is no evidence that this occurs. Insurance carriers have established strict policies regarding insurance disclosure and policies will be cancelled if it is known that ransom insurance exists.[20]

In captivity, executives have no power to enforce their views or to create a bilateral bargaining relationship since the terrorists are in full control of the stressful drama, but these hostages are not confronted with the dangers that exist in a barricade siege. They have time to adjust to their captivity and to build cooperative relationships with the captors. Discerning temperature changes, environmental noises, and the spacing of meal breaks will help captives get a handle on time and permit them to make needed situational inferences, when secrecy surrounds the terrorist operation.[21] Meditative exercises will induce relaxation and heighten mental clarity and they are easy to learn. Once hostages become familiar with their surroundings, however, and develop a more focused time orientation, they should begin to act on their captors' perceptions. Captives should move the kidnapped relationship in the direction of cooperation and trust, but they should not adopt the terrorists' belief system in the interest of securing their release or receiving better treatment. They are still instruments of a planned mission, not colleagues, and are held solely for ransom. Their captors will usually provide them with radical reading materials, which should enable the hostages to understand the captors' position and motives, an insight that is valuable for politically unsophisticated executives. If captured executives can demonstrate that they also share the terrorist belief that poverty should be abolished, an attitudinal modification has occurred. This does not mean that the hostages have changed their political philosophy, but merely shows that they are concerned with social problems. They might recognize that unemployment is high in the host country and agree with the terrorists that economic growth is essential. A common background, such as being of the same faith or national ancestry or a pronounced fondness for a particular genre of literature or music, or even fishing, can be helpful and should be constructively exploited to build a trustful relationship. This produces a de-escalatory spiral which incrementally reduces the level of hostility and minimizes the uncertainties that flow from the asymmetrical power relationship. It stresses the value of congeniality by understating the parties' differences.[22] Captured executives, however, must never become competitive or try to impose their views on their captors. Power resides only in the terrorist.

To secure personal safety, hostages must subtly orchestrate the attitudinal change process and threats and sanctions have no place in this milieu. Occasionally, the captors will provide a minor comfort, which should not go unnoticed. Extending a compliment or expressing appreciation for these courtesies will strengthen the cooperative bond. It is instrumental goal-focused behavior, which may be the only way to affect the attitude change process. If a captive's company pays the ransom, which is usual in these situations, he or she will be released unharmed. In essence, captives must provide cues that encourage the formation of a shared cooperative orientation since this would increase the probability of a trustful relationship. They should not manifest behavior that is viewed as an opposition of interest, since this would surely anger the captors. Hostages have no power to influence the terrorists' orientation and hence, must unilaterally identify the situational characteristics that facilitate trust development. It is a form of tacit bargaining that produces an awareness of a common bond and it must be skillfully exploited. If the host government's security forces or national government complicate the process, the efforts spent in nurturing a cooperative relationship could save the captive's life. He or she is viewed as a human being.

The kidnapping of Sir Geoffrey Jackson by the Uruguayan Tupamaros in 1971 illustrates this point. As the British ambassador to a country that was experiencing widespread political kidnappings, Sir Geoffry Jackson believed that he would eventually become a victim. When his prediction became reality on January 8, 1971 and he remained in captivity for 244 days, his adjustment behavior was remarkable and a persuasive indication that a person could prepare oneself for captivity. During his long stay with the Tupamaros, he developed a repertoire of adjustment activities that preserved his integrity and permitted him to interact with his captors without being abjectly submissive. He exercised, read books, sketched caricatures of the terrorists, learned as much as he could about them, and showed consideration when it was appropriate. This conferred status, which was not an endorsement of their conduct, but it produced a mutually respectful relationship. His adaptive responses have been carefully assessed by students of political kidnapping and demonstrate that a cooperative, life-saving relationship can be developed in captivity. For corporate executives assigned to countries with high incidences of kidnapping, his personal account of his experiences should be required reading.[23]

In collective bargaining, in which the process is legitimized and regulated by law, the parties stand on an equal footing in negotiating an agreement.

Tactics of persuasion, coercion, bluff, and threats are thoughtfully used to consummate an acceptable labor contract, and disinterested third-party mediation is available to help the parties reach agreement when an impasse is declared. This is not the case in hostage situations. There are no written procedures for resolving terrorist-hostage conflict or internationally acceptable mediators, who have the confidence of the terrorists, hostages, and governments involved. When American corporate executives are kidnapped for ransom in a foreign country or for that matter in the United States, and the assault results in a barricade siege, they have no power to negotiate their release. They must depend upon the skills of the local police and the terrorists' perception of their predicament for survival. If tactical mistakes are made, the captives may well pay with their lives. They should not, however, gratuitously waive it. Experience shows that if captives do not resist their captors at the point of the assault or in the barricade area or attempt to distract the captors from the police, the victims will preserve their lives. If the barricade siege lasts a few days and the police negotiators are trained to understand the changes that occur in behavior when the terrorists are deprived of sleep, food, and water, then negotiating a positive sum-type agreement might be possible. If the terrorist group has a strong penchant for media exposure, then releasing their manifesto and program might be equally as acceptable under the circumstances. This, however, requires that the police and security forces have an accurate profile of the terrorist group's philosophy and motives and an understanding of the hostage-negotiating process. Artfully weaving into the negotiating process the political beliefs of the terrorists, to reduce the competitive aspects of the barricade negotiations and to use the leverage acquired to build a more cooperative relationship, is the sine qua non of successful bargaining. If the terrorists believe that the police negotiators are credible, the captors will consider the feasibility of settlement options. This will most likely occur when the terrorists perceive their condition as untenable and find that symbolic trade-offs are more valuable than no solution at all or extinction.

Trust is the prime ingredient of the negotiating process and it should be thoughtfully cultivated by both the police and the hostage. Trust facilitates open communication and predictability and provides the flexibility needed to devise acceptable options. A win-win outcome, even in appearances, is more preferable than a win-lose outcome, since the latter will lead to violence. Police negotiators should avoid engaging in short-term win-lose behavior, which to authoritarian officials appears more realistic than unhurried and cooperative overtures, since it would provoke antagonistic responses. Rather, the police should try to manage the crisis by controlling the process and substance of the negotiating agenda. Asking questions to determine the needs and conditions of the terrorists permits the police to control the flow of negotiations and to formulate and introduce settlement proposals when appropriate. In the meantime, the kidnapped executive has the time to create a transference effect, which if successful, saves his or her life and aids the police in their negotiating efforts. Unless the hostages' lives are plainly endangered and a police assault is required to end the crisis, time should be used to build the trust that encourages productive negotiations.

Terrorist groups have improved their organizational and tactical effectiveness, and nuclear and biological threats are no longer unthinkable. The fragmented nature of world politics will increase the level of political violence and corporate executives must learn how to cope with these dangers. Kidnapping is a profitable terrorist venture, but with adequate preparation and an understanding of the kidnapping-negotiating process, business officials can survive.

Corporations should provide training for their executives, which simulate the disquieting conditions of a barricade-siege or long-term captivity to acquaint them with the stresses and dynamics of a kidnapping situation. There are indications that terrorist groups are beginning to behave like criminal organizations as evidenced by the marked similarity between the Mafia kidnappings of executives in Italy and the politically motivated kidnappings of foreign corporate executives in Latin America.[24] Commenting on this parallel development, terrorist experts Robert Kupperman and Darrell Trent stated in their seminal book, *Terrorism: Threats, Reality, Response* that:

> The latter have proved so profitable an industry that they could easily continue without the indictment of "crimes against the people" made by various revolutionary tribunals, or they could simply maintain their revolutionary trappings as a mask for activities of an essentially criminal nature. This suggests the emergence of a "quasi-political crime syndicate engaged in criminal activities" such as kidnapping, protection rackets, and other forms of extortion, while maintaining a political profile to exploit mass resentments or revolutionary sympathies within the populace. This potential development represents one of the ways in which a terrorist subculture could become a permanent fixture in our world.[25]

If this assessment is a reasonable accurate portent of the future, it is imperative for corporate executives to learn how to survive this severe experience. The dangers will multiply as more executives are assigned to manage overseas subsidiaries and corporate managements should prepare for these likely contingencies. Additionally, corporations should organize a special crisis management team to deal with the media and law enforcement agencies. This is an important function which complements and supports the organization's negotiating efforts. To be effective, the team should be limited in size to ensure that decisions are promptly made independently of the corporate hierarchy and provided unrestricted access to the organization's resources. Procedures should be developed to guide the corporation's media and law enforcement relationships and an articulate team member should be chosen media spokesperson. Credibility is important, since inaccurate information or glossed-over public relations releases could endanger the negotiating process and rescue operations. A well-trained corporate crisis mangagement team could avoid disastrous mishaps.[26]

Notes

1. Maynard M. Stephens, "The Oil and Natural Gas Industries: A Potential Target of Terrorists," in Robert Kupperman and Darrell Trent, eds., *Terrorism: Threat, Reality and Response* (Stanford, Calif.: Hoover Institution Press, 1979), p. 222. Stephens notes that while these facilities are vulnerable to sabotage, federal and state authorities have not adequately addressed these possible contingencies.

2. Brian Jenkins, Janera Johnson, and David Ronfeldt, "Numbered Lives: Some Statistical Observations from 77 International Hostage Episodes," *Conflict: An International Journal for Conflict and Policy Studies* 1, nos. 1 & 2 (1978): 80.

3. John E. Karkashian, "Terrorism and the Overseas Executive," *New York Times*, Sunday, May 18, 1980, p. 16 F.

4. Jenkins et al., "Some Statistical Observations," pp. 71-72. These figures are derived from an examination of ninety international hostage incidents from August 1968 to December 1975. While they represent the kidnapping of foreign government officials or demands made on governments, they indicate persuasively that kidnapping is a successful terrorist activity.

5. U.S. Congress, House, Committee on Internal Security, Terrorism Hearings, Part 3, 93rd Congress, Second Session, 1975, pp. 4025-28. Summary report, provided by Robert A. Crandall, Counsel to Majority Staff, entitled, "Summary of Information Derived from Officials of U.S. Industries with Large Foreign Operations." These findings were based upon the information provided by corporate executives whose companies experienced political terrorism, extortion, and kidnapping. These officials did not testify at the hearings because they believed that any public identification would invite terrorist attacks.

6. Karkashian, "Terrorism and the Overseas Executive," p. 16 F.

7. Caroline Moorehead, *Hostage to Fortune: A Study of Kidnapping in the World Today* (New York: Atheneum: 1980), pp. 151-53.

8. Brooks McClure, "Hostage Survival," *Conflict: An International Journal for Conflict and Policy Studies* 1, nos. 1 & 2 (1978): 25-27. This is an excellent article which corporate executives should read. It is pragmatic, realistic, and provides survival rules for hostages.

9. Stephen Sloan, *Simulating Terrorism* (Norman, Ok.: University of Oklahoma Press, 1981), pp. 101-2.

10. For a detailed lively account of how Captain Bolz's team successfully resolved several well-known hostage incidents see Captain Frank Bolz and Edward Hershey, *Hostage Cop: The Story of the New York City Police Hostage Negotiating Team and the Man Who Leads It* (New York: Rawson Wade Publishers, Inc., 1979). Thoughtful suggestions for surviving a barricade siege are provided in the appendix, entitled "What to Do If You Are Taken Hostage," pp. 313-16.

11. McClure, "Hostage Survival," pp. 28-29.

12. Morton Deutsch, *The Resolution of Conflict: Constructive and Destructive Processes* (New Haven: Yale University Press, 1973). For an informative theoretical treatment of mixed motive bargaining, see Chapter 8, "The Effects of Threat and Communication upon Interpersonal Bargaining: Initial Studies," pp. 215-48.

13. Abraham H. Miller, "Negotiations For Hostages: Implications from the Police Experience," *Terrorism: An International Journal* 1, no. 2 (1978): 125-45. This is the best account written of the Hanafi incident, particularly as it addresses the negotiating process. As Miller states, "It is the perception of the hostage scenario as a ritual with subsidiary benefits to the hostage takers resulting without complete capitulation by authorities that the strategy of negotiations begins to take on meaning and is comprehensive. To see hostage taking as a plus-zero game where only the authorities or the hostage takers can win, is to reduce to a bloodbath a ritual that can otherwise work out in exchanging face and political symbols for human life." p. 142.

14. Maurice J. Cullinane, "Terrorism—A New Era of Criminality," *Terrorism: An International Journal* 1, no. 2 (1978): 119.

15. Moorehead, *Hostage to Fortune*, pp. 212-14.

16. Abraham H. Miller, *Terrorism and Hostage Negotiations* (Boulder, Colo.: Westview Press, 1979), pp. 44-45.

17. Moorehead, *Hostage to Fortune*, pp. 5-6.

18. For an absorbing account of terrorist victimization, see Frank Ochberg, "The Victims of Terrorism: Psychiatric Considerations," *Terrorism: An International Journal* 2, no. 2 (1978): 147-68.

19. E. Patrick McGuire, "International Terrorism and Business Security," *The Conference Board-Information Bulletin* 65 (1979): 9.

20. Ibid., p. 12. According to this study, a kidnap and ransom insurance policy will usually contain the following conditions:

(1) The company will make all reasonable efforts to ensure that the existence of the insurance has not been disclosed outside corporate headquarters.

(2) In the event of a kidnapping incident, the company will make a determined effort to confirm that the insured person(s) have in fact been kidnapped.

(3) The company will notify the FBI, or other appropriate local law enforcement agencies, of demands for ransom prior to any ransom payments; and it will comply with the recommendations and instructions of law enforcement specialists.

(4) The company will provide immediate notification of ransom demands.

(5) The company will record the serial numbers of any currency paid in order to secure a victim's release.

(6) The company will make certain that an investigation is mounted to confirm that there is no collusion or fraud on the parts of employees said to be kidnapped.

(7) The company will agree to prosecute all those persons responsible for the kidnapping.

21. McClure, "Hostage Survival," pp. 32-33.

22. A behavioral understanding of attitudinal structuring tactics is found in Richard E. Walton and Robert B. McKersie, *A Behavioral Theory of Labor Negotiations* (New York: McGraw Hill Book Co., 1965), pp. 222-280.

23. Moorehead, *Hostage to Fortune*, pp. 126-129. See also Sir Geoffrey Jackson, *Surviving the Long Night* (New York: Vanguard Press, 1973).

24. Robert Kupperman and Darrell Trent, "The Past is Prologue," in Kupperman and Trent, eds., *Terrorism: Threat, Reality and Response*, p. 39.

25. Ibid.

26. Richard Rescorla, "Managing The Unmanageable," *Terrorism, Violence, Insurgency Journal* 2, no. 2 (March 1981): 10-17. As Rescorla accurately stated, "Public Relations people are hired to get publicity that is favorable. News reporters who are willing to take a hand-out from the PR people in normal times will distrust them in the crunch—when there is a probability that unfavorable facts may be lurking in the story. The media want a chance at someone in the know, someone they have a chance to trip up. There is always a lingering suspicion that no matter the facts, the PR people are putting a coat of the brightest paint on the story and handing it out." p. 12.

8

Effects of Terrorism on Business Operations

ELEANOR S. WAINSTEIN AND
SUSANNA W. PURNELL

Until the decade of the 1970s, American corporate management had little reason to concentrate either resources or planning efforts on the problem of terrorism either at home or abroad. Political upheavals and crime added anxieties and caused losses in certain unstable countries, but the terrorist targeting of businessmen or business facilities was negligible. In the last twelve years, however, terrorists have turned to private enterprise and have found it both vulnerable and lucrative. The number of terrorist attacks directed at businesses has risen significantly, especially against overseas operations. As a consequence, businessmen have had to alter both their management practices and their way of life in order to operate in the changed environment. This chapter identifies the most significant adjustments of the business community.

A number of factors influence research on the business response. First, individual experiences with terrorism vary so widely that it is difficult to generalize the lessons learned. The combination of such factors as the country situation, the terrorists' goals and target, the type of business, and the reactions of the government and company make each incident unique. Second, corporate officials hesitate to talk in detail about their experiences with terrorism or the preventive measures and strategies their companies enact. Businessmen fear that public discussion of their experience increases their vulnerability to terrorists and their criminal imitators. They are also wary of releasing information that might be useful to their competition or embarrass the firm.

As a result of these limitations, we have tailored our research to identify the most likely concerns businesses have when operating in a high-risk environment. We do not, for example, examine specific security measures but we do address the effect the institution of these measures may have on the functioning of the company and the lives of the employees. Our findings are divided into two sections. The first addresses the effects of terrorism on the business itself in terms of legal responsibilities, organized response, budget costs, and productivity. The second section deals with the effects on the lives and working environment of the employees.

Effects of Terrorism on the Firm

RESPONSIBILITY FOR HANDLING THE THREAT

A major consequence of the growing terrorism against business is the latter's responsibility to protect its personnel from the threat. The firm's policymakers cite moral obligations when they indicate the company is unwilling to ask employees to risk their lives for the sake of the firm. They also admit there are practical considerations. Companies would have difficulty hiring employees for high-risk posts if the firm did not provide some assurances of company support against terrorist acts. Moreover, any business would have problems handling the adverse public perception that the firm valued profits over human life. Finally, from a legal standpoint, U.S. courts have made U.S. firms accountable for their employees overseas.

The legal guidelines for the firm's responsibility remain a grey area. Several civil suits against firms have been filed in the U.S. courts that raise the issue of corporate responsibilities toward an employee before and during kidnapping. None of these reached the stage where a judgement was handed down. For example, while William Niehous, manager of Owens-Illinois' Venezuelan subsidiary, was being held by terrorists for three and one-half years, his family sued the corporation, charging that they mishandled attempts to obtain Niehous's release. After the hostage's release, the family continued to press the suit and only dropped it when Niehous was elevated to the position of corporate vice president.[1]

In another case Gustavo Curtis, manager of a Beatrice Foods Corporation subsidiary in Colombia, charged that the parent firm had failed to take sufficient action to warn him beforehand and to effect his timely release after he was kidnapped by Colombian terrorists in 1976. The U.S. corporation hired a security firm affiliated with the corporation's insurance company to conduct the negotiations with the kidnappers. After eight months of bargaining, Beatrice Foods paid a ransom much lower than the terrorists' original demand in exchange for Curtis's freedom. The New York judge dismissed the suit, observing that despite Curtis's harrowing experience the company had acted fairly. The judge also noted that Curtis was employed by an autonomous subsidiary whose separate identity was scrupulously maintained by Beatrice Foods.[2]

As the Curtis case implies, the willingness of a business to take on this responsibility is influenced by the relationship between the parent firm and the employee or affiliate at risk. Corporations have consistently assumed responsibility for handling the kidnapping of an executive or corporate officer, whether employed by the firm in the United States or assigned abroad to run a subsidiary. The degree of involvement diminishes, however, as the relationship becomes more distant from the parent firm, such as in the case of local franchises or distributors.

The acceptance of responsibility for the safety of employees and operations may necessitate some organizational changes. Many international firms have created corporate security officers to implement and oversee the provision of protection. In some corporations, security experts serve the entire organization with members at country, regional, and headquarters level. In others, the subsidiaries take responsibility for their own protective provisions.

Assessments of the terrorist threat may vary significantly between the home office and the local operation, reflecting differing perceptions and concerns. As the local environment deteriorates, managers at the scene may feel the home office has unrealistic expectations concerning the local operation and the terrorist threat. On the other hand, local employees do not always appreciate the concerns of U.S. headquarters. Certainly, this was true when, at the request of President Reagan, several U.S. oil companies ordered their U.S. employees to leave Libya. A number of these employees publicly disagreed with the idea that they could be in danger.[3]

COSTS

Since businesses are profitmaking enterprises, the high costs of terrorism can constitute a major concern to management and sometimes even cause the firm to operate at a temporary loss. To protect personnel and facilities, management will have to make decisions on the many types of security measures available. Electronic warning devices and barriers, armored vehicles, facility and residential guards, and bodyguards are expensive. Armored cars with bullet-proof glass and other safety features cost approximately $40,000 a vehicle, and round-the-clock bodyguard protection can amount to over $100,000 per year. In some countries the cost of prevention may take the form of protection money demanded by terrorists to ensure that businesses will not be targeted.

Many firms weigh these costs for warning and protection against the much higher costs of actual involvement in a terrorist incident, such as damage to the facility, loss of productive work time, loss of the market, and ransom payments in the millions of dollars. Whether the firm can afford to run the risk of such extraordinary expenditures depends upon its profits, the current and projected market situation, the firm's ability to absorb present losses in expectation of future gain, and, to some extent, the company's size and structure. Small companies or companies whose only facility is in the affected area are more vulnerable to the extraordinary expenses terrorist acts impose than are branches of large multinational firms. The latter very likely have resources to sustain such expenses for a limited time while continuing to operate.

The firm can buy insurance against multimillion dollar ransoms, but the premiums themselves can constitute a sizable budget item, depending on the environment of the country in which the business is operating. Coverage may include only key personnel, or extend to all employees. For an additional sum the firm can also insure against damages to the facility or other losses resulting from terrorist acts. In some cases high insurance rates alone have discouraged prospective investors from risking their capital in terrorist-prone countries of the world.

OPERATIONS

The most publicized effects of terrorism are the security measures invoked to protect life and property from such threats. However, the greatest costs to a firm often are the indirect effects such threats have on day-to-day operations. The following are examples of the problems experienced by overseas operations.[4]

Management: Because an expatriate American manager is usually the most vulnerable and the most threatened employee in overseas subsidiaries, corporations typically remove him or her from the area at the earliest date possible and replace the manager with a country national, either on a permanent basis or until the situation improves. If the personnel change is made suddenly in response to a specific threat, the replacement may not be fully prepared and on-the-job training is necessary. This can temporarily penalize the efficiency of the operation.

Technical Assistance: In a high-risk situation, the parent firm or even the Department of State may embargo travel by U.S. nationals to the country in which an operation is located. If technical experts cannot visit foreign plants to repair machinery, install updated production lines, and train the labor force, the plant becomes relatively inefficient. Machines may sit idle or operate inefficiently for long periods of time. A breakdown formerly requiring a matter of days may require weeks to repair. Similarly, producers become reluctant to risk sending in new machinery to update production lines, causing the operation to lag behind competitors elsewhere. The production facility becomes "technology-bound," and thus less able to compete with the updated facilities elsewhere.

Quality Control: Travel restrictions also hinder the ability of company representatives to visit the local plants or make quality control checks on the product sold by local distributors. Corporations facing such eventualities may suffer a declining market for their products if the quality erodes in the face of competition.

Company Goals: A foreign operation of a U.S. firm is only one part of a large and intricate corporate system, all of which is managed to some degree by the home office. Production lines, costs, and marketing factors for plants located around the world are formulated into the overall corporate goals. If production lines become obsolescent due to the high-risk environment, as has happened in some plants in El Salvador, it becomes more difficult to integrate the subsidiary into overall corporate production goals. If the situation persists, the corporation may establish the needed line in another country and phase out the obsolescent plant.

We insert a caveat here, however, because all terrorist situations do not necessarily hinder corporate operations. For the most part, businesses continue to function despite the seeming chaos. For example, an analyst for Eaton Corporation commented on the environment in Italy where his firm has nine plants. He was optimistic about the corporate interests there, characterizing the area as stable despite a contrary view from corporate headquarters in Cleveland. "What's normal for Italy would cause apoplexy here," he commented.[5]

LOCAL GOVERNMENT RELATIONS

One consequence of terrorist threats against overseas operations is that the firm's handling of the crisis may exacerbate relations between the company and the local government. Essentially, the conflict arises because the government and businesses often pursue divergent goals during a crisis situation. The firm's goal is to maintain a viable business operation and protect its employees. The local government, on the other hand, may give first priority to capturing the terrorists. From the government point of view, accommodating terrorist demands by paying ransom or extortion and publishing manifestos only provides the terrorists with the means to continue their attacks.

Many governments prohibit or discourage payment of ransom or negotiation with terrorists on the grounds that such practices encourage future terrorist acts. Some have even prohibited publications of manifestos in the national media, a demand frequently made by terrorists for the release of a kidnapped executive. Since businesses are usually willing to negotiate with terrorists as the best way to effect the safe release of the employee, the corporate negotiators must often circumvent the local authorities.

For example, in Argentina where laws prohibit payment of ransom, corporations experiencing a kidnapping in the early 1970s went to great lengths to keep news of the matter from the authorities for fear that their interference would put the hostage at risk. Such ploys do not always work. When millionaire businessman Baron Empain was kidnapped in France in 1978, the government not only prevented private payment of ransom but stepped in and took over, setting up a phony ransom drop and ambushing the kidnappers.[6]

The struggle between business and government became a fast-paced drama in Ireland recently when an IRA group kidnapped a prominent Dublin businessman, Ben Dunne, Jr., and held him for six days. Even though the Republic of Ireland has no law prohibiting payment of ransom, government policy discourages the practice and recommends sitting out a hostage situation, as they did successfully when Dutch businessman Tiede Herrema was taken in 1975. Dunne's family and associates attempted to ransom him immediately. From the time of Dunne's abduction, however, surveillance of the Dunne family and firm members was constant, and police even tapped their telephones around the clock, as ordered by the minister of justice. As a result, three attempts by employees and friends to pay ransom were intercepted. After Dunne was released unharmed, the Provisional IRA claimed they received a large sum of money, although the Dunne family denied adamantly that any money changed hands.[7]

The willingness of companies to negotiate with the terrorists can also reflect a lack of confidence in the ability of local government authorities to handle the situation. Frank Devine, U.S. ambassador to El Salvador from 1977 to 1980, describes the corporate reaction to the terrorists' kidnapping campaign against foreign businessmen.

> In all cases, the kidnappers warned against turning to the Salvadoran authorities and said that this would endanger the lives of the victims. This warning was taken very seriously, and, since the security services of El Salvador were judged to have a very low level of competence or capability, the companies and families of the captives not only avoided calling them in but pleaded with them to keep their distance.[8]

In at least one instance the conflict of interests between a U.S. company and the local government had long-range consequences for the firm. The ultimate in government confrontations with business is expropriation. This action was threatened in Venezuela in 1976 when Owens-Illinois, in compliance with one of the terrorists' demands to secure release of their kidnapped manager, published a statement by the terrorist group in foreign newspapers in spite of government policy to the contrary. The Venezuelan government started proceedings to buy out the company because it had "violated Venezuela's legal constitutional norms." The government position was that it alone should deal with kidnappers, and it could not tolerate interference with its domestic policy.[9]

Effects of Terrorism on Employees

In addition to its impact on the operation of a firm, terrorism can also affect the employees' life-style and job performance. If the threat is extreme, managers and employees may make significant readjustments at the workplace and at home. However, coping with a high-risk environment also may affect morale and strain relations within the firm.

PROTECTION OF KEY PERSONNEL

Managers often must deal with threats against their personal well-being. Terrorists frequently target executives for their extortionist value. An attack on one executive may intimidate the other leaders of the corporation, making them feel vulnerable and disrupting operations. Terrorists may also attack managers for their symbolic value as high-profile representatives of the corporation. For example, terrorists garner much publicity when they attack American or other expatriate managers of foreign subsidiaries for the crime of "exploitation" of the local labor force. Terrorists can sometimes be quite selective in targeting specific executives, such as, for example, the personnel director of a firm that has just laid off workers.

Although executives worry about the safety of their spouses and children, such threats rarely extend to the family. Terrorists may kidnap executives for the crime of exploitation, but the group's public image would suffer if they tried to justify the targeting of families. There are exceptions. One of the few politically motivated kidnappings in the United States was that of Patty Hearst, captured by the SLA because her father is a rich and well-known publisher. For the most part, such kidnappings are perpetrated by criminals seeking ransom payments—not by terrorists.

Businessmen have responded to the threats to their safety by instituting a number of protective measures. Corporations increasingly provide training and executive protection to key personnel, especially those working in high-risk locations. Such programs encourage the executive to substitute a set of behavior patterns which makes him or her less conspicuous and daily activities less predictable. By making it difficult for terrorists to target the executive, security advisors hope to reduce the probability that a given executive will be attacked. However, encouraging a change in life-style can have significant consequences for that executive. The necessity to keep a low profile and stay out of the society columns may actually negate some of the rewards of the position. Moreover, advocacy of restrictions on the executive's activities may run contrary to that person's personality, often leading to friction between the executive and those responsible for security.

In a high-risk environment, the necessity to employ more stringent protective strategies makes it difficult for executives to perform their jobs. For example, in order to vary established routines, managers keep erratic hours at the office. The effort to restrict information concerning the executives' movements makes it harder to schedule appointments and meetings. The very need for secrecy may promote distrust between executives and their employees.

In effect, under high-risk conditions, executives protect themselves by gradually removing themselves from the workplace and increasingly running the operation from a distance, an arrangement that can penalize the operation as a whole. If the executive discovers he or she has been targeted, the individual usually leaves the country until the danger has passed or moves to another country and runs the operation by telephone calls and unannounced trips back to the office. If the executive chooses to remain in such an environment, security becomes a twenty-four hour concern—a preoccupation that can affect his or her ability to concentrate on the job.

Again, Ambassador Devine describes the reactions of foreign businessmen to terrorist threats in El Salvador.

> Foreigners' morale declined, some companies pulled out their foreign executives, others entered into serious evasive tactics and even operated their businesses from neighboring countries, home offices in the United States sent down security officers and other experts to assess the problem, and to an ever-increasing extent business meetings and even social conversations came to be dominated by the subject of security.[10]

Living in a high-risk environment also has consequences for the executive's home life. Spouses and children worry about his or her safety. The family may have to move from the suburbs to the anonymity of the city or to a safer house with guards, high walls, limited public access, and an array of security devices. The family's social life is curtailed as there are fewer safe public places for the family to go. If the danger persists there is an exodus of expatriate executives and their families. In 1975, after three years of terrorist attacks on foreign companies, the number of American businessmen living in Argentina declined from approximately 1,270 to only 100.[11]

Terrorists may wage campaigns against specific companies. For example, in Argentina the Montoneros threatened, attacked, and murdered executives of several American automobile manufacturers in Argentina. Under these circumstances executives may resign or request transfers. Managers who are going to be able to function in such an environment really have to be volunteers. Such executives usually have a commitment to the local operation and often have to be ordered out of the country when threatened.

THE EMPLOYEE AS HOSTAGE

In a high-risk environment, businessmen also must deal with the possibility of surviving a kidnapping. Employees at risk are often advised to make some preparations for the ordeal. If a hostage has a general idea of what to expect in the way of living conditions, possible interrogation, and probable length of captivity, such information can help him or her cope with many uncertainties of the situation.

Families must also be prepared for the ordeal. A chief concern of hostages is how their families are dealing with the situation emotionally and financially. Plans should be made beforehand concerning what the family will do in the event of a kidnapping. Hostages gain some peace of mind if they know where their families are and what they are doing. Hostages are also relieved of worry if they have their financial affairs in order. Despite such preparation, businesses usually take a number of actions to aid the family. Most companies establish a liaison with the family to keep them informed of the progress. They also provide logistic and financial assistance if necessary.

While the family usually turns over the handling of a kidnapping to the company, some friction may develop between the firm and family. This is especially true if the negotiations drag on or there is a reversal, such as a failed ransom pickup or loss of contact with the kidnappers. Anxious family members may try to establish their own bargaining channels or bring in third parties to participate in negotiations. One firm considers this such a problem that they require the spouse of the hostage to sign a letter delegating the running of the response to the corporation but also absolving the company of responsibility should the kidnappers fail to release the hostage safely.[12]

An example of the strain that can develop between the family and the firm is the experience of Owens-Illinois Glass Co. during the three and one-half-year captivity of William Niehous, vice president of the company's Venezuelan subsidiary. During her husband's lengthy captivity, when there was little or no communication with the terrorists, Mrs. Niehous used the good offices of columnist Jack Anderson to make separate entreaties to the kidnappers. Also believing it possible that her husband was dead, Mrs. Niehous filed a $4 million lawsuit against her husband's employer, charging culpability in Niehous's death and negligence in his kidnapping and ransom.

The effects of the hostage experience vary, depending on the individual and conditions of captivity. All have some reaction whether immediate or delayed. For example, ex-hostages usually report nightmares and over-reaction to loud noises for several months after the experience. However, the consequences of being placed in a life-threatening situation can have much more serious mental and physical manifestations, and companies should be prepared to provide the appropriate medical or psychological help.

During the course of their captivity, many hostages review their lives including their family and career. This often leads to a reassessment of the importance of their career relative to other goals. After his release, William Niehous said he had time during his captivity to assess his life. He regretted moving his family to another country because it meant a promotion, and not having spent more time with his children. "And now I may consider doing the same thing again but I don't think so. I think I'll think more of family situations than personal gain."[13]

A well-publicized example[14] of a change in life-style and priorities after being kidnapped is that of Baron Edouard-Jean Empain, chairman of the Empain-Schneider group, France's major manufacturer of nuclear reactors. Held for sixty-three days and threatened with death, Empain lost the tip of one finger when his kidnappers cut it off and sent it to his family as proof of his identity. By the end of his ordeal, the Baron had lost twenty pounds and was barely able to walk as a result of a muscular condition related to his captivity. After his release, the Baron temporarily stepped down from the chairmanship and took a long vacation. At the time he thought he would never return to France and that his business really did not matter to him. He abandoned a conservative life-style and embarked on a playboy tour of the United States. He described his new outlook: "The thing I regretted during my captivity was not having taken sufficient advantage of life, not having seen enough places, known enough girls."[15] After seven months, the Baron returned to France, shed some of his newly acquired flamboyance, and announced he wanted to resume his position as chairman.

Ex-hostages' attitudes about their captors can be puzzling to the corporate leadership. The victims often express sympathy for their captors. Baron Empain, for example, said of his kidnappers: "Sure they cut off the end of my finger, but from their point of view it wasn't atrocious. For them it was logical; the ransom hadn't been paid."[16] Some hostages may experience the Stockholm Syndrome; having been placed in a position of dependency on the kidnappers for all the necessities of life—indeed, for life itself—they identify with their captors. Other hostages may be so thankful to be released unharmed that they may actually congratulate their captors for treating them so well.

At the other extreme, ex-hostages may continue to feel threatened by the terrorists even after their release. Their families may share such forebodings. As a result, they may not want to tell about their experience or testify in court because their captors threatened retribution. Indeed, many hostages in overseas posts leave the country almost immediately, and often never return.

LABOR RELATIONS

Well-organized terrorists have tried to contest the loyalty of a workforce, especially in the manufacturing industries. Experiences in Argentina during the mid-1970s, particularly in the auto industry, illustrate this tactic. Small, organized groups within the workforce set up shadow labor union committees in an effort to command the support of workers in the plants. Opposition to this attempt often led to violence. For example, one labor union delegate in a Mercedes-Benz truck plant protested the activities of these committees and was machine-gunned at his home a few days later.[17]

Terrorists also try to extend their popular support by demanding better wages and working conditions for labor. In El Salvador, leftist terrorists instigated lock-ins, a tactic by which radical labor groups held management and workers hostage in the plant until the company agreed to increase the wages and benefits of the workforce.

Terrorists may also attempt to infiltrate companies to gain access to information about the business and its executives. Companies often respond to such a threat by instituting more extensive screening of job applicants. A firm in Argentina hired only older women to work in their offices because they were less likely to have terrorist connections.

In high-risk environments, firms often have to reexamine their relations with the workforce. Management may try to improve the situation by establishing more channels for the communication of grievances in an effort to detect any problem in its early stages. Companies also promote the sense that the workers have a stake in the survival of the company. Ironically, then, one consequence of terrorism against a firm is that relations between management and labor may actually improve.

Notes

1. *New York Times*, April 18, 1979, II, p. 5; September 16, 1979, p. 16.
2. *New York Times*, January 5, 1980, p. 42.
3. *Washington Post*, December 13, 1981.
4. See Susanna W. Purnell and Eleanor S. Wainstein, *The Problems of U.S. Businesses Operating Abroad in Terrorist Environments* (Washington, D.C.: The Rand Corporation, R-2842, November 1981), for a more detailed discussion of this topic.
5. Louis Kraar, "The Multinationals Get Smarter about Political Risks," *Fortune*, March 24, 1980, p. 92.
6. *Time*, April 10, 1978, p. 40.
7. *Irish Independent*, October 17-23, 1981.
8. Frank J. Devine, *El Salvador: Embassy Under Attack* (New York: Vantage Press, 1981), p. 66.
9. *New York Times*, April 8, 1976, p. 55.
10. Devine, *El Salvador: Embassy Under Attack*, p. 66.
11. A description of how businessmen lived during this time in Argentina can be found in Ernest McCrary, "Letter from Buenos Aires: Coping with Terrorism in Argentina," *Business Week*, March 9, 1974, pp. 40-41.
12. Purnell and Wainstein, *Problems of U.S. Businesses*, p. 14.
13. William Niehous, interview on *20/20*, July 5, 1979.
14. See, for example: "Empain's Ordeal," *Time*, April 10, 1978, p. 40; "The Kidnapped Baron," *Newsweek*, October 16, 1978, p. 24; and Don Holt, "Kidnapped Baron Regains Corporate Power," *Fortune*, November 6, 1978, pp. 6, 49.
15. Don Holt, "Kidnapped Baron Regains Corporate Power," p. 47.
16. "The Kidnapped Baron," *Newsweek*, p. 24.
17. "Businessmen Under the Gun in Argentina," *New York Times*, February 22, 1976.

9

Organizations Serving the Executive Protection Field

*PATRICK J. MONTANA AND
STACEY M. KRINSKY*

Terrorism is real, it is persistent, and it has very much become a thorn in the functioning activities of society. The decade of the seventies showed terrorist venom being injected into the mainstream of multinational corporations with much success. The deviation from the usual terrorist attacks for political causes to economic reasons is largely a result of the lucrative gains to be achieved from those corporations whose executives wield power, money, and vulnerability.

"Terrorism is the systematic use of violent means by a party or faction to induce a state of intense fear or apprehension."[1] The alarmingly high degree of attacks using violence for effect has brought an open awareness to those who control an organization and, therefore, are susceptible targets of these offensive threats. Since this kind of terrorism is likely to increase throughout the eighties, executives look for an answer, a solution to a force that restricts, immobilizes, and threatens their corporate environment and personal lives.

Executive protection is difficult to define since safeguarding against executive terrorism involves much more than protection and security; bodyguards, and armored cars. "The key objective to executive protection is awareness and prevention planning,"[2] according to Anthony Purbrick of Pinkerton's, Inc. The main objective applied at Scotti School of Defensive Driving is to train people to develop an understanding of security and increase their level of security awareness. The precautionary measures for executive protection at Cappucci Associates is credited to extensive analysis, planning, and implementation of preventive and awareness programs. Understanding the possible threats and causes of violent action are prerequisites to any preventive and protective program. Pinkerton's, Inc., Scotti School of Defensive Driving, and Cappucci Associates, Inc., are but three companies among many in the security field that offer protective services to the executive.

With the vast amount of new technology that exists today, the extent of protection furnished by any one or number of these organizations must relate to the present threat and/or potentiality of violent attacks of terrorism against person or property. "The purpose of executive protection may be described as providing a security for personnel, information, and physical facilities, and preventing influences which are undesirable, unauthorized, or detrimental to the goals of the particular organization being secured."[3] Protection with the right preventive measures may not eliminate terrorist attacks, but it will offer increased security to a person aware of its dangers.

Dimensions of an Executive Protection Program

OBJECTIVES OF A PREVENTIVE PROGRAM

Global terrorism is a strategy employing violence to accomplish two goals: the coercion of an organization (a government, a corporation, or some authority) into altering their policies and meeting certain demands, and the provocation of an emotional response (usually fear and respect) from the general public.[4]

International corporate executives have become targets of vicious attacks because of the valuable asset they represent to the terrorist. The possible threats these companies, executives, and their families face have forced many to reevaluate their corporate and personal security strategy in an attempt to implement necessary programs to safeguard against terrorism. "Loss of life, injury, holding for ransom or political advantage are extremely serious outcomes because of ineffective or nonexistent security measures. The damage, loss of privacy to the corporation or government far outweigh the costs associated with sound protective programs."[5]

Management's acceptance of the need for a preventive protection program is the first step in deterring terrorist attacks. To be effective, management's planning and organization must set the guidelines for direction, authority, responsibility, and performance of preventive programs.

"The purpose of security may be described as providing protection of materials, equipment, information, personnel, physical facilities, and preventing influences which are undesirable, unauthorized, or detrimental to the goals of the particular organization being secured."[6] These functions may sometimes exceed the authority and capability of a corporation's security department, so the management's responsibility for developing an adequate defensive strategy is transferred to third-party protective service resources. Protective service resources include both public and private use of "personnel, devices, techniques, procedures, design features, materials, and educational programs utilized to construct a protection program."[7]

Among the third-party organizations are government agencies, nonprofit security organizations, and privately owned protective services.

Government programs are those provided within each state, local, and federal agency relating to law enforcement, crime prevention, loss control, and property protection aspects of public safety.[8]

Nonprofit security organizations are specifically designed for security professionals whose responsibility may include developing, and managing programs aimed at preventing unlawful acts against person or property. Membership enables support of security functions through publication, seminars, conferences and forums.

Privately owned protective services are additional measures of security on a commercial basis by individuals or organizations who focus on prevention and protection. These services are sold to clients by security companies on a profit-making basis.[9]

Privately owned protective services can further be divided into total protection services and limited protection services. The total protection services will provide countermeasures to deter terrorist activity and alert executives, employees, and their families to actions to be taken in the event of an attack. The framework of this security program is executive protection, crisis management, and consultation. The limited protection services are resources added to the entire executive protection program. These may include insurance, defensive driving, armoring vehicles, bodyguards, and research data.

It is the combination of these preventive protection services that are vital to the organization, for no one protective service will provide the needed defense for eliminating terrorism. "To organize the protective service resources into effective responsive protective services requires appropriate program design, administration and management. The wording, direction, supervision, inspection and development of resources to provide programs is critical to program effectiveness."[10]

METHOD OF APPROACH

Executive Protection "Desire + Ability + Opportunity = Criminal Attack"[11]

Three components of a successful criminal attack and the executive is the victim. Take away an element, the opportunity, and you foil the possible chances of success. Executives, their companies, and their families are taking more precautions to prevent terrorist attacks. These preventive measures range from common sense precautions to highly technical means of prevention. The prerequisite to any program is understanding the threat and the motive behind such attacks. Lower the vulnerability and increase your chances of survival.

Similar to any major organizational strategy planning, defining one's needs is crucial to an executive protection program. The goals, objectives, and an estimate of the risks must be determined. Techniques and processes must be developed under a plan of preparation so that effective control and coordination of the implementation can be achieved. The objective of an executive protection program is to provide a secure environment for the corporation, executive, and his or her family and provide an awareness of the possible threats. An effective executive protection program countermeasures will be defined, shaped, and implemented to meet the needs, problems, and interests of an individual corporation.

The methodology used in creating the most effective protection plan can be broken down into phases.

> Phase I: *Threat and vulnerability analysis*—Definition of problem relating to security needs can be analyzed through data collection of company security surveys, country analysis, and individual vulnerability. This will not only locate weaknesses, but recommend means to reduce risk. After threat evaluation, a detailed framework of response is developed. The threat will be measured and specific vulnerabilities identified, compiled, and prioritized.

> Phase II: *Safeguard planning*—Alternative means of protection is reviewed for a follow-up system to assure system operation, proper response, and success. Each plan is measured for cost-effectiveness and reliability.

> Phase III: *Program implementation*—Communicate guidelines of program to all designated personnel including families of vulnerable executives. The actual crisis and protection training will include protection for on the job, at home, and in transit in the event of terrorist occurrence and post-event responsibilities.

> Phase IV: *Assessment and review*—Safeguarding a system is imperative to achieve the ultimate effectiveness. An assessment will point out weak spots and those changes needed to upgrade security or plans. Frequent review or updates are necessary for a corporation whose needs change over a period of time.

An executive protection program will include not only protection for the executive but an awareness for all associated personnel (chauffeurs, bodyguards, office personnel, domestic help), and family. Terrorists may choose to exert pressure on a corporation by an attack on a person other than an executive. Some primary information needs to be kept on all high-risk people. A dossier will be compiled with vital facts: medical history, photograph, addresses and telephone numbers, frequented places, and vehicle description. During any attempt or actual occurrence, the law enforcement agencies needed must be notified. This will allow for more efficient and collective efforts.

Executive terrorism is desirable because of the money that can be realized. Terrorists have the ability to terrorize because of a network of information that provides transportation, communication, weaponry, and anonymity. The executive provides an attractive opportunity for the criminal attack to be successful. Therefore, executives should be alert and prepared in order to reduce the chances for such attacks.

Crisis Management

> Crisis Management is a unique process that develops strategic responses in crisis situations through pre-selected and trained managers (the Crisis Management Team) using existing skills plus specialized processes to minimize loss of organizational assets.[12]

The crisis management process is the missing ingredient in most corporate assets protection programs and provides the weak link in which terrorists are able to penetrate.

Terrorism can affect the foundation of a corporation and its support systems, and therefore, can trigger the immediate involvement of senior management. In formulating a defense against such terrorist attacks, top management must not only advocate a crisis management team (CMT), but participate in its functions. The CMT should possess the personnel and skilled experts who have ability and authority to control and minimize loss from a potential threat.

Eight basic functions should be performed by the CMT to handle effectively terrorist threats.

1. Leadership: involving a key policymaking executive (though not necessarily the chairman or chief executive officer) to input direction and guidance.

2. Security: "kingpin" of team providing information on the necessary security systems of company and knowledge of adversary weaponry.

3. Legal:	officer familiar with delicate laws involving possible negotiations and strategies.
4. Financial:	key officer in charge of monetary base for CMT and any transactions for ransom or negotiation payments.
5. Human Resources:	specialist experienced in dealing with victims, employees, and families. Will also have access to personnel files for related information. This person may also employ the use of medical and psychological experts as consultants.
6. Public Relations:	skilled professional to handle all media in a positive and controlled manner.
7. Adversary Communications:	exchanges information with terrorist directly or through third party.
8. Crisis Counsel:	advisors on terrorist groups, activities, and techniques. This will consist of internal support (insurance, medical) and external support (analysts and consultants). CMT is sometimes viewed through eyes of terrorist for possible weak links in organization.

All crisis management teams should involve the law enforcement agencies necessary to provide action through joint, collective efforts.

A crisis mangement team must be covered by a corporation charter stating the exact structure, authorizing those involved to act on matters, and releasing members of team from personal liability. Decisions made by a CMT frequently go beyond the boundaries of the normal organizational judgments. A response to a terrorist threat requires individual policies, resources, analysis, and communications to be blended, rather than relying on intuition or emotional response to terrorist attacks.

A multidisciplinary team of high-level executives to minimize losses of all corporate assets in crisis situations will gather information, analyze threats, make decisions, communicate information and decisions, implement decisions, evaluate, and develop alternative strategies. "An organization's total assets protection program should include both preventive and responsive strategies. The Crisis Management System is only part of the total assets protection program and is a responsive strategy designed to be implemented in the event of a crisis."[13]

A crisis management team is an on-going process of commitment to the safety of employees, facilities, and the organization.

Insurance To assure monetary security after death, one buys life insurance. To assure aid during an illness, one buys health insurance. It is not a general practice for the average individual to buy insurance for the protection from kidnapping, but this has become a general practice of executives and corporations who are prime targets for kidnapping, extortion, and ransom demands.

Because of the growth of terrorism, some insurance companies have made provisions to insure the lives and property of directors, executives, employees, and family members of corporations located both in the United States and abroad. This insurance measure relieves the financial burdens of management and enables them to do whatever is necessary for the safe return of person or property.

A kidnap and ransom insurance policy will spell out specific provisions necessary to be met by the insured in the event of an actual terrorist attack. The main condition of the policy is strict confidentiality of the purchase, contents, and the insured. This is to assure that a threat is not executed just because money can be realized by the attack. The insured company must also make all attempts to notify law enforcement agencies of the threat and will further prosecute all persons responsible for the actual act of terrorism.

The insured must comply with all clauses of the contract to be totally effective. The policy is, therefore, individually structured to meet the needs of the insured person or corporation.

Defensive Driving It has already been established that the threat of terrorism is undeniably present and the only possible recourse is the awareness of effective security measures at home, at the office, and most importantly, between home and office. One most frequently takes for granted the vulnerability of a vehicle for potential terrorist threats. Defensive driving techniques are designed to limit the possible attacks by teaching reflex and vehicle capabilities.

The major impetus of a driver training program is placed on the safety, ability, and confidence the driver must possess in handling everyday driving situations in order to minimize risk to the employer. These techniques are designed for accident avoidance, ambush, or any attack in which a vehicle would have to maintain control and the driver exercise precision in smoothness of vehicle operation.

Although the outcome of a defensive driving program should be skill and confidence, a protective driving instruction should also entail offensive driving. "Offensive driving is the violent use of a car and is against everything a driver has ever been taught. . . . Knowing when to use the basic maneuvers in offensive driving is far more important than knowing how to do these maneuvers,"[14] says Anthony Scotti, director of a defensive driving school.

Classroom techniques provide the important information on safety, visibility, control, and skill needed in a crisis situation. The philosophy is to make a driver aware of situations and be able to enforce the methods learned from the driving instruction.

Driving functions frequently taught in a defensive driving awareness program include:

Serpentine maneuver: awareness of the relationship between moving and fixed objects.

Evasive maneuvering: capability of control in emergency situations avoiding panic braking.

Controlled braking: retaining steering ability while controlling brake stop.

Backing: skill in reverse maneuverability and proper use of head checks for visibility.

Double-lane change: emphasis here is on signal, visibility, and maintaining position and speed.

Skid control: designed to provide driving techniques of control and behavior while in a skid.

Off road recovery: will give the necessary skills for returning to a highway or road.

The principle of these strategic driving techniques is placed on everyday application. The offensive (violent) maneuvers, of ramming and bootleg turns, strategically provide the element of surprise for the terrorist and also reverse the command of the situation. Learning these racetrack offensive techniques may be good for dramatizing a potential situation or for utilization under similar road conditions, but streets and highways lend themselves to unexpected actions of innocent motorists. To compensate, a good defensive driving program should emphasize safety and maneuverability. The program should present the necessary knowledge and skill to cope with normal and/or emergency driving situations that can be faced day to day.

With safety as the key issue—who should take a defensive driving program? Anyone responsible for the safe transport of an employer should enroll in a defensive driving program. However, there are protective driving programs for executives who may drive their own vehicles.

Aside from evasive maneuvers, protective driving programs offer practical guidelines to be implemented by both the driver and the passenger. Some suggestions on how to break the potential terrorist threat while in transport:

Be unpredictable: do not establish a set time pattern or route to and from the office or activity.

Vary mode of transportation

Keep low profile: do not have vanity plates or names labeling your belongings, and do not advertise travelling itinerary.

Know the neighborhood: be alert to new and suspicious construction.

Prearrange signal with driver: be alerted to or alert of possible danger.

Never leave car unattended: never park in marked parking space.

Keep doors locked: also keep windows up and do not drive near a curb.

Keep up with car maintenance: gas tank is to be full, brakes and tires checked.

Be ALERT: to internal car environment and external car alterations.

Armored Vehicles "Between 85-90% of all terrorist kidnappings, ambushes and assassinations of political and especially industrial leaders have occurred in or around the automobile."[15] The most vulnerable time, of course, is when the executive is either entering or leaving the car. Transportation has thus become the vulnerable point in the security environment.

Aside from defensive driving techniques, an executive can further establish a degree of protection by purchasing an armored car suitably designed to meet his or her needs. The use of an armored car acts as a deterrent to a terrorist threat, but should never create a false sense of security for the executive. There are still many factors an executive should be aware of before purchasing an armored car.

This guide will furnish some points for those persons in the market for an armored vehicle.

Evaluate a need for an armored vehicle before a potential threat to one's person, family member, associate, or competitor forces the decision for personal safety.

Determine the level of threat since the degree of armoring will depend on potential terrorist activity or protection needed.

Research and obtain information on companies claiming to be armorers.

Draw up a contract with the vehicle builder specifying exact requirements, completion dates, costs, and testing dates.

Choose a type of car commonly used and that will blend in with other cars in the environment, so as not to attract unusual attention. Best key to how well a car is armored is not being able to tell a car is armored.

Observe, if possible, how the armor is attached by looking for any exposed hardware allowing for potential shrapnel, and check performance in different climatic conditions.

Study information on ballistic levels of protection by using the rating of bullet-resisting materials established by Underwriters Laboratory as a guide. For foreign use of a vehicle, Level III is commonly used for protection against kidnapping and assassination attempts by a weapon of similar power to a .44 magnum. Level IV is most frequently used for protection from 30-06 rifle penetration. In the United States, protection in an armored vehicle can start at Level II (handgun power). *NOTE:* Not all armorers adhere to the Underwriters Laboratory ratings, but have their own high standards.

Inspect for driveability since armoring can be a very heavy addition to the car. Test vehicle for acceleration, stopping, maneuverability, weight, and distribution of armoring.

Common sense should tell you there is no such thing as completely terrorist-proof. Follow the standards you and an expert have analyzed as best for meeting your needs.

Manufacturers of armored vehicles generally agree on the commonly found options included in their cars. These include:

> power steering, automatic transmission, high performance engine, four doors, multi-shot capacity transparent armor (glass), automatic locking, nonexploding gas tank, protection from bullet splash, air conditioner, special bolts that will not become missiles if hit by a bullet, and strengthening of chassis, suspension and brakes. . . . Extras can include: two-way public address system, sirens, radio equipment, tampering detection devices, run-on devices, gunports, tear gas ejectors, and any James Bond-type device.[16]

With the standard features and extras, armoring a vehicle can cost anywhere from $20,000 and up, including the price of the car. The length of time to armor a vehicle varies with the specifications. Manufacturers agree a car should be measured by degree of protection. Some executives are even trading their chauffeured limousines for a large armored sedan just to maintain a low profile. Although a small compact car can be armored, the best suited are the medium-sized cars. The bigger cars are even better, lending themselves to armoring and inside comfort.

The future of business is always measured by the terrorist activities prevalent and the growing awareness of individuals in need of additional protection. The last five years proved a tremendous increase in this industry and the prediction is for further expansion. No matter how large this industry becomes, one must remember you will be entrusting your life to someone else's services. Be careful, therefore, in choosing an armorer. Other than armoring a vehicle, confidentiality of clients is a major objective to be respected by the armorer.

Organizations Serving the Executive Protection Field

The following list of companies that serve the executive protection field and the brief descriptions that follow are based on materials researched or received by request of the writers. For easier reference, the list is subdivided into government agencies, nonprofit security organizations, total security services—privately owned, and limited security services. The descriptions will include as much pertinent material as possible provided by the information obtained. Because of the confidentiality of services and clients, several companies requested only a brief synopsis of services provided. An asterisk is provided to show that additional information was unavailable to us but may be obtained by company letter to particular organizations.

The writers do acknowledge the existence of several organizations and companies, whose services provide methods of protection, but because there is no previous recorded literature or the company chose not to send pertinent information because of confidentiality of services or clients, these organizations are not included among this public list of major organizations serving the executive protection field.

GOVERNMENT AGENCIES:

F.B.I.
Law Enforcement Assistance Administration (LEAA)
State and Local Police

NONPROFIT SECURITY ORGANIZATIONS:

American Society for Industrial Security (ASIS) (Washington, D.C.)
International Association of Chiefs of Police (Maryland)

TOTAL SECURITY SERVICES, Privately Owned:

Burns International Security Services (New York)
Cappucci Associates, Inc. (Washington, D.C.)
Control Risks Ltd. (England)
IMAR Corporation (Washington, D.C.)
Magnum Security Management, Inc. (Texas)
Pinkerton's, Inc. (New York)
Rayne International, Inc. (Florida)
Royal-Schutt International, Inc. (New York)
Wackenhut Corporation (Florida)

LIMITED SECURITY SERVICES

INSURANCE: American International Group Inc. (New York)
Chubb Group of Insurance Companies (New Jersey)
INA Corporation (Pennsylvania)
Lloyds of London (England)

DEFENSIVE DRIVING:	Scotti School of Defensive Driving (Massachusetts)
ARMORED VEHICLES:	Armored Vehicle Builders, Inc. (Massachusetts)
	BSR Counter-Terrorism Driving School (Virginia)
	Hess & Eisenhardt (Ohio)
	Odin International Ltd. (Virginia)
	Tetradyne Corporation (Texas)
RESEARCH SERVICES:	Business International Corporation (New York)
	The Merritt Comapny (California)
	Motorola Teleprograms, Inc. (Illinois)
	Risks International, Inc. (Virginia)

GOVERNMENT AGENCIES

FEDERAL BUREAU OF INVESTIGATIONS (FBI)

The J. Edgar Hoover Building
10th and Pennsylvania Avenues
Washington, D.C. 20535
(202) 324-3000

The FBI is responsible for gathering intelligence on the activities of subversive organizations within the United States and investigates federal crimes such as kidnapping. It is the principal security agency in the U.S. government.

LAW ENFORCEMENT ASSISTANCE ADMINISTRATION (LEAA)

Division of the U.S. Department of Justice
633 Indiana Avenue N.W.
Washington, D.C. 20531
(202) 633-2000

The LEAA assists state and local governments in all aspects of law, enforcement and criminal justice.
Services Provided:
1) Development of public protection devices
2) Public Education
3) Recruiting and training of law enforcement personnel
4) Organizing and training of special units to combat crime

Publications:
   Private Security Advisory Council, LEAA, U.S. Dept. of Justice, "Executive Protection Manual" (Washington, D.C.: Government Printing Office).

STATE AND LOCAL POLICE

When instituting a crisis management program or any other countermeasure that is intended to minimize terrorist acts, notification of local law enforcement agencies is essential for swift assistance and cooperation.

NONPROFIT SECURITY ORGANIZATIONS

AMERICAN SOCIETY FOR INDUSTRIAL SECURITY (ASIS)

2000 K Street N.W., Suite 651
Washington, D.C. 20006
(202) 331-7887
Mr. E. J. Crisuoli Jr., Executive Director

ASIS constitutes the largest body of security professionals in the world and encompasses all facets of loss prevention. Most of their services are for security members. However, there are available to nonmembers some published literature, workshops, seminars, and institute programs.
Objectives of ASIS:
   According to its bylaws, the ASIS serves as a clearinghouse for its members on issues related to security and performs a working function by publishing relevant materials and holding conferences for members.
Publication:
   American Society for Industrial Security, "Reducing the Risks of Terrorism," and "Crisis Management," *Security Management Magazine*, (Washington, D.C.: ASIS Publications).

INTERNATIONAL ASSOCIATION OF CHIEFS OF POLICE

Gaithersburg, Maryland

Services Provided:
   Workshops, seminars, and conferences on security and protection.

TOTAL SECURITY SERVICES—Privately Owned

BURNS INTERNATIONAL SECURITY SERVICES, INC.

320 Old Briarcliff Road
Briarcliff Manor, New York 10510
(914) 762-1000
Mr. Joseph A. Malley, Manager, Management Services Division

Countermeasures Provided:
  1) Executive Protection—to provide a secure environment for executive
     personnel and their families*
     a) Threat Analysis
     b) Analysis of Data
     c) Formulation of Recommendations
     d) Program Implementation
  2) Crisis Management—development of a contingency plan for individu-
     al companies which includes procedures to follow in the event of a
     successful threat
  3) Bodyguards
  4) Security Consulting—for both corporate and residential security sys-
     tems
Program Implementation:
  An executive protection program generally takes three months to develop
  from start to finish with a follow-up consultation six months to one year
  after program is put into effect.
Professionals:
  Executive protection programs designed by security engineer consultants,
  and the protection is implemented by former investigative professionals
  from the police and federal law enforcement agencies.
Rate:
  Based on per/day services provided, plus expenses.
Burns global network currently includes more than 160 locations throughout the United States and Canada, Colombia, United Kingdom, Spain, and
the Philippines

JOSEPH J. CAPPUCCI ASSOCIATES, INC.

1333 New Hampshire Avenue N.W., Suite 910
Washington, D.C. 20036
(202) 466-6055
Mr. Joseph J. Cappucci, Chairman of the Board
Mr. Joseph J. Liebling, President

Executive Protection Handbook available by mail from corporate office.

Countermeasures Provided:
1) Executive Protection—program is designed to protect client and minimize interference with lifestyle
   a) Threat and Vulnerability Analysis
   b) Safeguard Planning
   c) Implementation of the Safeguard Program
   d) Reliability Assessment and Design Review
2) Crisis Management—involving training for contingency planning*
3) Hostage Negotiations
4) Defensive Driving
5) Physical Security Systems—to prevent acts of terrorism, sabotage, espionage, and crime
6) Security Consulting

Cappucci specializes in design, planning, and implementing total security systems and can be located internationally as well as domestically.

CONTROL RISKS LTD.

9/13 Crutched Friars
London EC3N 2JS
United Kingdom
(01) 709-0575
Mr. Julian Radcliff, Founder

Countermeasures provided:
1) Executive Training
2) Crisis Management Systems
3) Security Analysis
4) Preventive Programs
5) Country Analysis
6) Post-event/Hostage Negotiations

THE IMAR CORPORATION

(International Management Analysis and Resources)
National Press Building, Suite 1120
Washington, D.C. 20045
(202) 342-0045
Mr. Brooks McClure, Director of Operations

Countermeasures Provided:
1) Analysis of Threat and Vulnerability Studies
2) Country Surveys of Economic/Political/Social Conditions

Crisis Management Handbook available by mail through corporate office.

3) Development of Worldwide Security Strategies and Services
4) Formulation of Crisis Management and Crisis Response Systems
5) Counterterrorist Training—of all corporate echelons including executive assistants, chauffeurs, and corporate aircrew
6) Briefings of High-risk Executives on Kidnap-Evasion and Hostage Survival
7) Preparation of Evacuation Plans and Other Contingency Measures in Politically Volatile Countries

Professionals:
Specialists are chosen after a job analysis of management requirements is completed permitting a better latitude in selecting the person most qualified. Former foreign service and intelligence officers are among the expert staff.

Rate:
Based on per job basis or a retainer fee.

IMAR can provide prompt coverage of all countries and of regional development anywhere in the world.

MAGNUM SECURITY MANAGEMENT, INC.

2550 Electronic Lane
Dallas, Texas 75220
(214) 353-9666
Mr. William Reddick, President
Mr. Ben Rosson, Director of Executive Protection

Countermeasures Provided:
1) Executive Protection
    a) Threat Analysis
    b) Program Implementation
    c) Kidnapping Negotiations
    d) Evasive Driving
    e) Follow-up and Re-evaluation of Methods
2) Crisis Management
3) Security Consulting
    a) Bomb Threats
    b) Extortion
    c) Home Security
    d) First Aid
4) Guard Service
5) Investigations

Program Implementation:
Magnum trains executives in kidnap care and prevention planning. Course is generally three to five days with a follow-up analysis.

PINKERTON'S, INC.

100 Church Street
New York, New York 10007
(212) 285-4845
Mr. Anthony Purbrick, Assistant Director, Department of Investigations

Countermeasures Provided:
1) Executive Protection—program must touch all bases but emphasis is on prevention
    a) Fact-Finding Survey—from everyone connected to particular executive
    b) Examination and Determination of Program
    c) Program of Prevention and Awareness
2) Crisis Management—important part of executive protection plan that allows for a network of communication, authority, and responsibility
3) Bodyguards
4) Security Consulting

Program Implementation:
Program development takes a few weeks to several months depending on security provisions, and also has an upgrade program effective after a period of time.

Professionals:
Executive protection program professionals include former police, military, and federal agents and those that complete the Pinkerton's school program.

Rate:
Based on per/day program charge, plus expenses

Pinkerton's Inc. is the oldest investigation and security service company in the world and can be found in more than 116 offices throughout the United States and Canada.

RAYNE INTERNATIONAL, INC.

1111 South Bayshore Drive
Miami, Florida 33158
(305) 358-9999
Mr. Fred Rayne, President

Countermeasures Provided:
1) Executive Training
2) Crisis Management
3) Security Consultants
4) Bodyguards
5) Hostage Negotiations

ROYAL-SCHUTT INTERNATIONAL, INC.

342 Madison Avenue, Suite 210
New York, New York 10017
(212) 687-6076
Mr. Robert F. Royal, President

Countermeasures Provided:
  1) Executive Training
  2) Crisis Management
  3) Security Consultants

THE WACKENHUT CORPORATION

3280 Ponce de Leon Boulevard
Coral Gables, Florida 33134
(305) 445-1481
Mr. John C. Evans, Director of Executive Protection Division

Countermeasures Provided:
  1) Executive Protection—preventive programs for individuals, families
       and corporations
     a) Environmental Survey
     b) Threat Analysis
     c) Recommendations to Reduce Vulnerability
     d) Implementation
  2) Crisis Management—assistance for developing programs for organi-
       zation, policies, procedures, and plans prior to a crisis incident
  3) Bodyguards
  4) Security Consulting
Program Implementation:
  The systems approach to executive protection is individually planned with
  updates to review program status and allow for adjustment of lifestyle.
Professionals:
  Programs for executive protection include former military, federal, and
  state agents specially trained for protection.
Rate:
  Based on per/day services, plus expenses.

The Wackenhut Corporation includes ninety domestic branches and over
forty international offices providing coordinated services.

LIMITED SECURITY SERVICES

Insurance

AMERICAN INTERNATIONAL INSURANCE GROUP, INC. (AIG)

70 Pine Street
New York, New York 10005
(212) 770-6557

Services Provided:
  Kidnap and Ransom Insurance

CHUBB GROUP OF INSURANCE COMPANIES

51 John F. Kennedy Parkway
Short Hills, New Jersey 07078
(201) 467-6000
Mr. George T. Van Gilder, Assistant Vice-President

Chubb is currently the largest United States writers of executive protection coverage providing kidnap, ransom, and extortion insurance which can be purchased in commercial or personal form.

Coverage Includes:
  1) A ransom payment as the result of the actual or alleged kidnapping of any insured person
  2) An extortion payment as a result of a threat to do bodily harm, abduct, or detain any insured person or damage to any insured property
  3) Fees and expenses of any independent negotiators or consultants with prior approval.
  4) Interest costs for any loan taken to pay ransom or extortion demands
  5) Reward paid to informant for information not otherwise available which leads to the arrest and conviction of persons responsible for terrorist demands[17]

Because of the extreme detail of an executive protection policy and the importance of confidentiality, additional and more explicit information may be obtained from Chubb.

Rate:
The coverage is normally written on a worldwide basis and the costs of such policies are related to the relative vulnerability to loss as seen through a consultant's analysis.

INA CORPORATION

(Insurance Company of North America)
1600 Arch Street
Philadelphia, Pennsylvania 19101
(215) 241-3671

INA and its affiliated companies offer a unique combination of products and services to businesses and industries around the world. Among these services are kidnap and ransom coverage and counsel to business.

The purchase of appropriate insurance helps management relieve some of the financial burdens in case of a terrorist attack. Because of the confidentiality of such insurance coverage, additional information can be received through INA corporate headquarters.

LLOYDS OF LONDON (A. A. Cassidy Syndicate)

9/13 Crutched Friars
London EC3N 2JS
United Kingdom

Services Provided:
  Kidnap and Ransom Insurance

Defensive Driving

SCOTTI SCHOOL OF DEFENSIVE DRIVING

P.O. Box 59
Somerville, Massachusetts 02144
(617) 776-8590
Mr. Tony J. Scotti, President

Countermeasures Provided:
  1)Anti-Terrorist Driving School—trains students to develop an under-
      standing of transportation security and increase their level of securi-
      ty awareness
      Course Content: a) The Driving Problem
                      b) Car Feel
                      c) Evasive Maneuvers
                      d) Tire Selection
                      e) Countersurveillance Techniques
                      f) General Travel Security
                      g) Consumerism

2) Executive Driving Program—to develop an understanding of transportation security for executives and managers who drive their own vehicles

Course Content: a) Theory of Vehicle Ambush
-recognize potential situation
b) Survival Driving
-defensive driving technique
-offensive driving technique
c) Countersurveillance Awareness and Techniques
-warning system
-survival countermeasures
-countermeasure driving techniques
d) Transportation Security
-vehicle security
-travel security

Program Implementation:

Antiterrorist driving school program is a four-day course with a certificate of completion to the student and a subjective and objective written evaluation forwarded to the student's supervisor.

Executive driving program is a one and one-half-day program (twelve hours) using classroom and environmental performance training.

Professionals:

Instructors include police officers and race car drivers. The student-to-instructor ratio is kept low to ensure the best possible learning environment.

Rate:

Includes course instruction, any training manuals, and newsletters of changes affecting the security function.

Scotti School of Defensive Driving offers private classes as well as courses available in foreign languages at an additional cost. The school is conducted in approximately eight locations in the United States and around the world. The Mobile Training Unit (MTU) is equipped to bring the driving program to a locale convenient to the client.

Armored Vehicles

ARMORED VEHICLES BUILDERS, INC.

343 Pecks Road
Pittsfield, Massachusetts 01202
(413) 445-4541
Mr. Michael T. Dan, President

BSR COUNTER-TERRORISM DRIVING SCHOOL

1420 Spring Hill Road
McLean, Virginia 22100
(703) 893-0215
Mr. William H. Scott, President

Armored cars and counter-terrorist driving

HESS & EISENHARDT CO.

8959 Blue Ash Avenue
Rossmoyne, Ohio 45242
(513) 791-8888
Mr. George L. Strike, President

Oldest company in the world specializing in high-quality armored cars for heads of states.

OLDIN INTERNATIONAL LTD.

Sales agent for Advanced Materials Inc.
Alexandria, Virginia
Mr. Thomas Nelson, President

TETRADYNE CORPORATION

2305 Beltline
Carrolton, Texas 75006
(214) 242-1512
Mr. Reg. A. Anderson, President

Manufactures armored cars as well as security electronics.

Research Services

BUSINESS INTERNATIONAL CORPORATION

One Dag Hammarskjold Plaza
New York, New York 10017
(212) 750-6300
Ms. Ruth Karen, Vice-President, Corporate Public Policy Division

Services Provided:
Business International Corporation is an independent organization providing a comprehensive system of business information to corporations

doing business internationally . . . including an extensive, fully integrated system of executive advisory, consulting, research and publishing services.[18]

Publication:

Ruth Karen, *Terrorism and International Business* (New York: Business International) focuses on key policy questions companies need to address; options and cost/benefit relationship.

THE MERRITT COMPANY

Customer Service Department
P.O. Box 955
Santa Monica, California 90406
(213) 450-7234

The Merritt Company publishes a series of security manuals that focuses on management-oriented functions.

The Protection of Assets Manual—provides an in-depth look at all forms of preventive security including guard operation, kidnapping, extortion, terrorism, bomb threats, and hostage survival.

Protection of Assets Bulletin—a monthly service bulletin of updates on preventive security.

Annual Subscription to Manual and Service

MOTOROLA TELEPROGRAMS, INC.

4825 North Scott Street
Schiller Park, Illinois 60176
(312) 671-1565
Mr. Lloyd Singer, President

Services Provided:

1) Audiovisual Materials on Crisis Management and Executive Protection
2) Customized Training Programs

RISKS INTERNATIONAL, INC.

120 South Royal Street
P.O. Box 115
Alexandria, Virginia 22313
(703) 836-6126
Mr. Charles A. Russell, Founder

Risks International is a consulting firm specializing in statistical information on the worldwide terrorist problem and its direct impact on the operations of both domestic and international corporations.

Services Provided Including Publications:

1) *Inquiry Service*—providing a statistical data report on a specific incident tailored to the specific needs of the client
2) *Executive Risk Assessment*—a monthly publication providing data on worldwide terrorist activity involving kidnapping, bombing, assassination, and attacks on business, commercial, and industrial facilities
3) *Quarterly Risk Assessment*—is an extensive publication including the previous month's *Executive Risk Assessment*; a statistical presentation of terrorist activities occurring within the past calendar quarter; and an analysis of the significant terrorist activities, organizations, and trends

Conclusions

COST-EFFECTIVENESS

The key to a successful and cost-effective security and protection training program is the acceptance by an individual or a corporation that security is a personal responsibility.

An executive protection educational program must be accepted by top management; they must analyze present protection needs, plan goals, and implement training programs that are designed and established to coordinate with the needs of the corporation.

Important to any corporate plan is communication of the program's functions to those whose vulnerability or maintenance of the objectives would lead to its success or failure. "The measurement of the cost of adequate protection versus the risk of the abduction confrontation is essentially defined in terms of corporate exposure. The greater the exposure, the more substantial the investment."[19]

Keeping a low profile will not necessarily eradicate terrorism, nor will society be completely protected. Even with cost-effective measures of protection programs, terrorism cannot be defeated. A 1975 study by the Rand Corporation showed the cost-effective probabilities for the terrorist:

100%	probability of gaining publicity.
87%	probability of seizing hostages.
79%	probability that all members of a terrorist team could escape punishment or death whether they seized hostages or not.
69%	probability that all or part of the terrorist demand beyond exit or safe passage would be met.
67%	probability that even if no concessions were obtained through the action, virtually all of the terrorist team could escape by "going

underground'' or accepting safe passage in lieu of demands or surrendering to a sympathetic government.[20]

With such high percentages for terrorist success, the only defense an executive has is the protection and awareness of what these threats can actually produce. Again, the key to a cost-effective security program is acceptance and responsibility. With that in mind, can an executive or a corporation actually place a price on one's life, the disruption to daily activities, inconvenience, freedom of choice, and diversion of resources?

TREND FOR THE 1980s

Terrorism knows no bounds. Each small success will trigger another attempt. "It will increase primarily because, in the short term it seems to pay, for political blackmail gets results, convicted terrorists are released, huge ransoms are paid, and publicity, on a scale unimaginable before the television age, is acquired free."[21]

Furthermore, better transportation and better communication allow the flow of plans through the information network to advance ideology. The fear and intimidation achieved by capturing the affluent and industrial society have made targets more attractive and cooperative.

Improvements in security is projected to deter potential attacks. The past five years showed a fivefold increase in the amount of worldwide terrorist incidents, and this growing threat has resulted in major security developments for both governments and industrial corporations. To compensate for this tremendous increase in terrorism, "governments have established new anti-terrorist intelligence and police organizations, machinery to manage terrorist created crises, and specifically trained tactical units to deal with hostage situations."[22]

The private security industry picks up where the government cannot provide total protection. The greater number of terrorist attacks now aimed at business facilities and executives has led to the proliferation of physical security precautions. Such measures as armored cars, defensive driving tactics, bodyguards, security-patrolled areas, and insurance policies have made a corporate executive return to an environment described as a medieval city of walls or a city of fear. All these physical measures are virtually meaningless without executives being psychologically aware of themselves and their environment. Fear accomplishes little, but confidence in knowing you know what to do and not to do in a possible threat situation can allow you to plan a relatively normal life. There is at least a chance to reduce terrorism. Do take every precaution to remain in control of this situation, because very much like a weed nipped only at the bud, terrorism will grow again if given the opportunity.

Notes

1. *Webster's Third New International Dictionary* (Springfield, Mass.: G. & G. Merriam Co., 1971), p. 2361.

2. Personally communicated by Anthony Purbrick, assistant director, Department of Investigations, Pinkerton's, Inc., February 1981.

3. R. Post and A. Kingsbury, *Security Administration: An Introduction* (Springfield, Ill.: Charles C. Thomas, 1970), p. 9.

4. L. W. Singer and John Reber, "A Crisis Management System," *Security Management*, ASIS rpt. no. 6 (August 1979): 7.

5. Post and Kingsbury, *Security Administration*, p. 867.

6. Ibid., p. 9.

7. Ibid., p. 474.

8. Ibid., p. 6.

9. Ibid., p. 7.

10. Ibid., p. 474.

11. Ibid., p. 476.

12. Singer and Reber, "Crisis Management System," p. 9.

13. Ibid., p. 13.

14. A. Scotti, "Protective Driving," *Security Management*, ASIS reprint no. 6 (1979): 45.

15. Ibid., p. 45.

16. P. Tucker, "Determining the Need for an Armored Vehicle," *Security Management*, ASIS rpt. no. 6 (1979): 37.

17. *Comprehensive Extortion Policy* (Short Hills, N.J.: Chubb Group of Insurance Companies), p. 2.

18. *Business International Corporation* (New York: Business International, 1980), p. ii.

19. Richard B. Cole, *Executive Security* (New York: John Wiley & Sons, 1980), preface.

20. W. Siatt, "Protecting the Human Asset," *Security World*, 1980, p. 22.

21. Richard Clutterbuck, *Living with Terrorism* (New York: Arlington House, 1975), p. 141.

22. Brian M. Jenkins, "Terrorism Outlook for the '80's," *Security Management*, 1981, p. 19.

Selected Bibliography

ABC-TV World News Tonight. Mike Lee reporting. "The PLO." September 9, 1981.

Adler, J. H., and Segre, D. V. "The Ecology of Terrorism." *Encounter* 40, no. 2 (February 1973).

Ardreski, Stanislav. *Prospects of a Revolution in the U.S.A.*. New York and Toronto: Harper Colophon Books, 1974.

Aristotle. *The Politics.* Ed. and trans. T. A. Sinclair. Harmondsworth: Penguin Books, 1976.

Alexander, Yonah. "Terrorism and the Media: Some Considerations." In *Terrorism: Theory and Practice.* Ed. Yonah Alexander, David Carlton, and Paul Wilkerson. Boulder, Colo.: Westview Press, 1979.

Bartholomew, Allen A.; Campbell, Andrew; O'Hearn, Dennis J.; and Milte, Kerry L. "Terrorism: Political and Psychological Considerations." *ANZ Journal of Criminology* 9 (March 1976).

Barzini, Luigi. "Governing Italian Style." *Policy Review* 12 (Spring 1980).

Baumann, Bommi. *Terror or Love? The Personal Account of a West German Guerrilla.* Trans. Gilbert Shelton. London: John Calder, 1979.

Beatty, Jack. "A Death in the Family." *The New Republic* (October 7, 1981).

Bell, J. Bowyer. *A Time of Terror: How Democratic Societies Respond to Revolutionary Violence.* New York: Basic Books, 1978.

Bishop, Joseph W. "Law in the Control of Terrorism and Insurrection: The British Laboratory Experience." *Law and Contemporary Problems* 42, no. 2 (Spring 1978).

Blade. Toledo, October 4, 1981, Sec. A, p.1, col.2.

Bolz, Frank and Hershey, Edward. *Hostage Cop: The Story of the New York City Police Hostage Negotiating Team and the Man Who Leads It.* New York: Rawson Wade Publishers, Inc., 1979.

Brigate Rosse: Rizoluzione della Direzione Strategica. 1978.

Buffa, Pier Vittorio. "Quanto Pesa Cirillo? Centomila Vani." *L'Espresso,* May 17, 1981, pp. 28-31.

Burns International Consulting Services. *Objectives from a Detailed Executive Program.* Briarcliff Manor, N.Y.

Business International Corporation. New York: Business International, 1980.

"Businessmen under the Gun in Argentina." *New York Times,* February 22, 1976.

"Business Targeting: The Ideological Basis." *Regional Risk Assessment: Europe.* Alexandria, Va.: Risks International, 1979.

Camus, Albert. *The Rebel: An Essay on Man in Revolt.* Rev. and trans. Anthony Bower. New York: Vintage Books, 1956.

CBS-TV Evening News. The White House, March 12, 1981.

Clutterbuck, Richard. *Living with Terrorism.* New York: Arlington House, 1975.

_____. *Guerrillas and Terrorists.* London: Faber and Faber Ltd., 1977.

_____. *Kidnap and Ransom: The Response.* London and Boston: Faber and Faber, 1978.

Cole, Richard B. *Executive Security.* New York: John Wiley & Sons, 1980.

Comprehensive Extortion Policy. Short Hills, N.J.: Chubb Group of Insurance Companies.

Cooper, H. H. Anthony. "The Terrorist and the Victim." *Victimology: An International Journal* 1, no. 2 (Summer 1976).

Crenshaw, Martha; Midlarsky, Manus I.; and Yoshida, Fumihiko. "Why Violence Spreads: The Contagion of International Terrorism." *International Studies Quarterly* 24, no. 2 (June 1980).

Crozier, Brian A. *A Theory of Conflict.* New York: Charles Scribner's Sons, 1974.

Cullinane, Maurice J. "Terrorism—A New Era of Criminality." *Terrorism: An International Journal* 1, no. 2 (1978).

Debray, Régis. *Strategy for Revolution.* Ed. Robin Blackburn. New York and London: Monthly Review Press, 1970.

Deutsch, Morton. *The Resolution of Conflict: Constructive and Destructive Processes.* New Haven: Yale University Press, 1973.

Devine, Frank J. *El Salvador: Embassy Under Attack.* New York: Vantage Press, 1981.

Dinges, John, and Landau, Saul. *Assassination on Embassy Row.* New York and London: Pantheon Books, 1980.

Dinstein, Yoram. "The New Geneva Protocols: A Step Forward or Backward?" *The Yearbook of World Affairs* 33 (1979): 265-83.

"A Drive against Terrorism." *The Boston Globe,* May 19, 1981, p. 35.

EFE. Spanish news agency. "Roban en Santander 8 Mil Kilos del Explosivo Goma 2," July 26, 1980.

_____. "Ofrecen Recompensa a Quien Aporte Datos sobre el Robo de Explosivos en Satander," July 28, 1980.

_____. "Se Responsabiliza ETA con el Robo de los Explosivos," July 31, 1980.

_____. "Se Encuentra Secuestrado el Ciudadano que Declaró más Ingresos a la Hacienda Española," Valencia, January 15, 1981.

_____. "Pide ETA $2 Millones y Medio para Librar al Millonario Industrial Luis Sunyer Sanchis," Alicante, January 17, 1981.

_____. "Provoca Unánime Repulsa el Secuestro de Ingeniero de la Central Nuclear de Lemoniz," Bilbao, January 31, 1981.

_____. "Condenan Partidos Políticos el Asesinato de un Ingeniero," Madrid, February 7, 1981.

_____. "Vuelan Planta Eléctrica de Iberduero cerca de Bilbao," May 1, 1981.

_____. "Cazan a los Terroristas que Desataron una Ola de Atentados en Chile

Anoche." *Diario las Américas*, Miami, November 14, 1980.

_____. "Culpan a Comandos Terroristas por los Atentados Dinamiteros." *Diario las Américas*, Miami, November 15, 1980.

_____. "Vuela la Guerrilla por Segunda Vez un Importante Oleoducto." *Diario las Américas*, Miami, May 2, 1981.

_____. "Un Millón sin Electricidad por Obra de Terroristas." *Diario las Américas*, Miami, May 6, 1981.

_____. "Azota a Lima una Ola de Atentados." *Diario las Américas*, Miami, May 7, 1981.

_____. "Atentado en Guatemala contra un Oleoducto." *Diario las Américas*, Miami, May 10, 1981.

_____. "Aumenta el Terrorismo en Lima." *Diario las Américas*, Miami, May 14, 1981.

_____. "Destruyen Oleoducto en Atentado Terrorista." *Diario las Américas*, Miami, June 29, 1981.

Flynn, Joe B. *The Design of Executive Protection System*. Springfield, Ill.: Charles C. Thomas, 1979.

Frank, Gerold. *The Deed*. New York: Simon and Schuster, 1963.

"Frederick J. Hacker Interview." *Penthouse* (November 1977): 138-40.

Freedman, Lawrence Z. "In His Own Work." *People Weekly* (June 5, 1978).

Freud, Sigmund. *Civilization and Its Discontents*. Trans. James Strachey. New York: W.W. Norton, 1961.

Friedlander, Robert A. "Terrorism and International Law: What is Being Done?" *Rutgers–Camden Law Journal* 8 (Spring 1977): 383-92.

_____. "Banishing Fear from the Skies: A Statutory Proposal." *Duquesne Law Review* 16, no. 3 (1977-1978): 283-86.

_____. *Terrorism: Documents of International and Local Control*. Dobbs Ferry, N.Y.: Oceana, 1978.

_____. "The Origins of International Terrorism: A Micro Legal-Historical Perspective." *Israel Yearbook on Human Rights, 6*, 1978.

_____. "Reflections on Terrorist Havens." *Naval War College Review* 32 (March-April 1979): 59-67.

_____. "Coping with Terrorism: What Is to Be Done?" In *Terrorism: Theory and Practice*. Ed. Yonah Alexander, David Carlton, and Paul Wilkinson. Boulder, Colo.: Westview, 1979.

_____. *Terrorism: Documents of Local Control*, vol. I. Dobbs Ferry, N.Y.: Oceana, 1979.

_____. *Terrorism: Documents of International and Local Control*, vol. II. Dobbs Ferry, N.Y.: Oceana, 1979.

_____. *Terrorism: Documents of International and Local Control—From the Terror Decade of the 1970's to the Dangerous Decade of the 1980's*, vol. III. Dobbs Ferry, N.Y.: Oceana, 1981.

_____. "Terrorism and National Liberation Movements: Can Rights Derive from Wrongs?" *Case Western Journal of International Law* 13, no. 2 (Spring 1981).

_____. *Terrorism and the Media: A Contemporary Assessment*. Gaithersburg, Md.: International Association of Chiefs of Police, 1981.

Fromm, Erich. *The Sane Society*. Greenwich, Conn.: Fawcett Publications, 1955.

_____. *The Anatomy of Human Destructiveness.* New York, Chicago and San Francisco: Holt, Rinehart and Winston, 1973.

Goren, Roberta. *Soviet Attitude and Policy to International Terrorism, 1967-1977.* Ph.D. diss., University of London.

Gorney, Cynthia. "Voices from a Bogota Jail." *The Washington Post,* June 7, 1981, p. D5, col. 1.

Greenburg, Martin H., and Norton, Augustus R. *International Terrorism: An Annotated Bibliography and Research Guide.* Boulder, Colo.: Westview Press, 1980.

Gurr, Ted Robert. *Why Men Rebel.* Princeton, N.J.: Princeton University Press, 1971.

Hacker, Frederick J. *Aggression: violence dans le monde moderne.* Trans. Rémi Laureillard and Hélène Bellour. Paris: Calmann-Levy, 1972.

Hayes, Thomas. "Ransom Costs are on the Rise for US Businesses." *New York Times,* November 19, 1979, p. D6, sec. 4.

Hazelton, Lesley. "Respectable Terrorism: When Its Victims Become Violent." *Harper's* (October 1980).

Heyman, Edward, and Mickolus, Edward. "Observations on 'Why Violence Spreads' " *International Studies Quarterly* 24, no. 2 (June 1980): 299-305.

_____. "Imitation by Terrorist." Quantitative Approaches to the Study of the Diffusion of Terrorism." In *Behavioral Approaches to the Study of Terrorism.* Ed. John Gleason and Yonah Alexander. New Haven: Yale University, 1981.

Hoffer, Eric. "Beware the Intellectual." Edison Electric Institute, *Symposium: Science, Technology and the Human Prospect.* Washington, D.C.: The Association of Electric Companies, 1979.

Hoge, James W. "The Media and Terrorism." In *Terrorism, the Media, and the Law.* Ed. Abraham H. Miller. Dobbs Ferry, N.Y.: Transnational Publishers, 1982.

Holt, Don. "Kidnapped Baron Regains Corporate Power." *Fortune* (November 6, 1978).

Horowitz, Irving Louis. "Political Terrorism and State Power." *Journal of Political and Military Sociology* 1 (Spring 1973).

Howe, Irving. "The Return of Terror." *Dissent* 22, no. 3 (Summer 1975).

Hoyt, W. "Driving in the Age of Fear." *New York* (May 1, 1978).

Irish Independent. October 17-23, 1981.

Jackson, Geoffrey. *Surviving the Long Night.* New York: Vanguard Press, 1973.

Jackson, George. "Bringing the Country to Its Knees." In *Social Justice and its Enemies.* Ed. Thomas Ford Hoult. New York: Halstead Press, 1975.

Jenkins, Brian M. *International Terrorism: A New Mode Of Conflict.* Research Paper no. 48. California Seminar on Arms Control and Foreign Policy. Los Angeles: Crescent Publications, 1975.

_____. "Terrorism Outlook for the '80's." *Security Management.* 1981.

Jenkins, Brian; Johnson, Janera; and Ronfeldt, David. "Numbered Lives: Some Statistical Observations from 77 International Hostage Episodes." *Conflict: An International Journal for Conflict and Policy Studies* 1, nos. 1 & 2 (1978).

Kane, George. "Traveler's Diarist." *The New Republic* (March 14, 1981).

Karkashian, John E. "Terrorism and the Overseas Executive." *New York Times,* May 18, 1980, p. 16 F.

"The Kidnapped Baron." *Newsweek* (October 16, 1978).

Kraar, Louis. "The Multinationals Get Smarter about Political Risks." *Fortune* (March 24, 1980).

Kuhne, R. J., and Schmitt, R. F. "The Terrorist Threat to Corporate Executives." *Business Horizons* 22 (December 1977): 77-82.

Levy, Bernard-Henri. "The War Against All: Every Man His Own State." *The New Republic* (February 11, 1978).

Lowenthal, Richard. "The West's Intellectual Crisis: Reorienting Thinking Toward an Era of Rapid Change." *Atlas World Press Review* (February 1978).

Malraux, André. *Man's Fate*. Trans. Haakon M. Chevalier. New York: The Modern Library, 1934.

Marcuse, Herbert. *Counter-Revolution and Revolt*. Boston: Beacon Press, 1972.

May, Rollo. *Man's Search for Himself*. New York: Delta, 1953.

_____. *Power and Innocence: A Search for the Sources of Violence*. New York: Delta, 1976.

May, William F. "Terrorism as Strategy and Ecstasy." *Social Research* 41 (Summer 1974).

Mazé, Jules. *Sous la terreur*. Paris: Librarie Hachette, 1947.

McClure, Brooks. "Hostage Survival." *Conflict: An International Journal for Conflict and Policy Studies* 1, nos. 1 & 2 (1978).

McCrary, Ernest. "Letter from Buenos Aires: Coping with Terrorism in Argentina." *Business Week* (March 9, 1974).

McGuire, E. Patrick. "International Terrorism and Business Security." *The Conference Board—Information Bulletin* 65 (1979).

McKnight, Gerald. *The Terrorist Mind*. Indianapolis and New York: Bobbs-Merrill Co., 1974.

Miami Herald. September 30, 1981, p. 12A.

Mickolus, Edward. "Multilateral Legal Efforts to Combat Terrorism: Diagnosis and Prognosis." *Ohio Northern University Law Review* 6, no. 1 (1979): 13-51.

_____. *The Literature of Terrorism: A Selectively Annotated Bibliography*. Westport, Conn.: Greenwood, 1980.

Miller, Abraham H. "Negotiations for Hostages: Implications from the Police Experience." *Terrorism: An International Journal* 1, no. 2 (1978): 125-45.

_____. *Terrorism and Hostage Negotiations*. Boulder, Colo.: Westview Press, 1979.

_____. ed. *Terrorism, the Media, and the Law*. Dobbs Ferry, N.Y.: Transnational Publishers, 1982.

Moorehead, Caroline. *Hostage to Fortune: A Study of Kidnapping in the World Today*. New York: Atheneum, 1980.

Morgan, Tom. Book Review. *Psychology Today* (August 1977).

Murphy, Patrick V. "The Police Perspective." In *The Media and Terrorism: A Seminar Sponsored by the Chicago Sun-Times and Chicago Daily News*. Chicago, Field Enterprises, 1977.

National Advisory Committee on Criminal Justice Standards and Goals. *Disorders and Terrorism: Report of the Task Force on Disorders and Terrorism*. Washington, D.C.: LEAA, 1976.

New York Times. March 6, 1979, p. A8, col. 4.; April 18, 1979, II, p. 5.; September 16, 1979, p. 16.; September 30, 1979, Sec. 1, p. 28.; January 5, 1980, p. 42.

Ochberg, Frank. "The Victims of Terrorism: Psychiatric Considerations." *Terrorism: An International Journal* 2, no. 2 (1978).

Parry, Albert. *Terrorism: From Robespierre to Arafat.* New York: Vanguard Press, 1976.

Pisano, Vittorfranco S. "Spain Fades the Extremists: Cannons to the Left and Cannons to the Right." *Terrorism, Violence, Insurgency Journal* 2, no. 6 (July 1981).

Post, R., and Kingsbury, A. *Security Administration: An Introduction.* Springfield, Ill.: Charles C. Thomas, 1970.

Purnell, Susanna W., and Wainstein, Eleanor S. *The Problems of U.S. Businesses Operating Abroad in Terrorist Environments.* Washington, D.C.: The Rand Corporation, R-2842, November 1981.

Rabe, Robert L. "The Journalist and the Hostage: How Their Rights Can Be Balanced." In *Terrorism, The Media, and the Law.* Ed. Abraham H. Miller. Dobbs Ferry, N.Y.: Transnational Publishers, 1982.

Rapoport, David C. *Assassination & Terrorism.* Toronto: CBC Learning Systems, 1971.

Rayne, Fred. "A Plan of Action for Top Management." *Security Management.* ASIS rpt. no. 6 (August 1979).

Reber, J., and Singer, L. "A Crisis Management System." *Security Management.* ASIS rpt. no. 6 (1979).

Reducing the Risks of Terrorism. Washington, D.C.: ASIS Publication, 1978.

Regional Risk Assessment: Latin America. Alexandria, Va.: Risks International, 1979.

Roucek, Joseph S. "Violence and Terror." In *Social Control.* Ed. Joseph S. Roucek. Toronto, New York and London: D. Van Nostrand Company, 1974.

Sabine, George H. *A History of Political Theory*, 3rd ed. New York: Holt, Rinehart and Winston, 1961.

Sartre, Jean Paul. "Preface." In *The Wretched of the Earth.* Ed. Frantz Fanon, trans. Constance Farrington. New York: Grove Press, 1968.

Schafer, Stephen. *The Political Criminal: The Problem of Morality and Crime.* New York: The Free Press, 1974.

Schumer, F. "One Man's Bomb—Another Man's Business." *Forbes* (August 6, 1979).

Scotti, A. "Protective Driving." *Security Management.* ASIS rpt. no. 6, (August 1979).

———. "How to Purchase an Armored Vehicle." *Assets Protection* 6 (January/February 1981).

Sheehan, Thomas, "Italy: Terror on the Right." *The New York Review of Books* (January 22, 1981): 23–26.

Siatt, W. "Protecting the Human Asset." *Security World.* (1980).

Singer, L. W. and Reber, John. "A Crisis Management System," *Security Management*, ASIS rpt. no. 6 (August 6, 1979): 7-13.

Sloan, Stephen. *Simulating Terrorism.* Norman, Ok.: University of Oklahoma Press, 1981.

Sommer, Heidi, and Sommer, Michael. "The Project on Media Coverage of Terrorism: A Summary of National Surveys and other Investigations, 1977-1979."

In *Terrorism, the Media, and the Law.* Ed. Abraham H. Miller. Dobbs Ferry, N.Y.: Transnational Publishers, 1982.

Sorel, Georges. *Reflections on Violence.* Trans. T. E. Hulme and J. Roth. New York: Collier Macmillan Publisher, 1961.

Stephens, Maynard M. "The Oil and Natural Gas Industries: A Potential Target of Terrorists." In *Terrorism: Threat, Reality, Response.* Ed. Robert Kupperman and Darrel Trent. Stanford, Calif.: Hoover Institution Press, 1979.

Stephens, Maynard M., and Miller, Bowman J. "Terrorism and the Corporate Target." In *Political Terrorism and Business: The Threat and Response.* Ed. Yonah Alexander and Robert H. Kilmarx. New York: Praeger, 1979.

Sterling, Claire. *The Terror Network.* New York: Holt, Rinehart, 1981.

Time. April 8, 1976, p. 55; April 10, 1978, p. 40; May 4, 1981, p. 34; September 14, 1981, p. 48.

"Terrorism: An Overview 1970-1978." *Executive Risk Assessment* 1, no. 2 (December 1978).

"Terrorist Operational Patterns." *Executive Risk Assessment* 3, no. 1 (January 1981).

Tinnin, David B. "Terror, Inc." *Playboy* (May 1977).

Tucker, P. "Determining the Need for an Armored Vehicle." *Security Management.* ASIS rpt. no. 6 (1979).

U.S. Central Intelligence Agency, National Foreign Assessment Center. *International Terrorism in 1979.* Washington, D.C., 1980.

_____. *Patterns of International Terrorism in 1980.* Washington D.C., PA81-10163U, April 1981.

U.S. Congress, House, Committee on Internal Security. Terrorism Hearings, Part 3. 93rd Cong., 2nd sess., 1975, pp. 4025-28.

U.S. News & World Report (September 14, 1981).

Venturi, Franco. *Roots of Revolution: A History of the Populist and Socialist Movements in Nineteenth Century Russia.* Trans. Francis Haskell. New York: Grosset & Dunlap, 1966.

Walton, Richard E., and McKersie, Robert B. *A Behavioral Theory of Labor Negotiations.* New York: McGraw-Hill Book Co., 1965.

Walzer, Michael. "The New Terrorists: Random Murder." *The New Republic* (August 30, 1975).

_____. "The New Terrorists." *Corriere della Sera.* Milan, January 4, 1981, p. 1.

Washington Post. September 29, 1981, p. A1; December 13, 1981.

Weichmann, Louis J. *A True History of the Assassination of Abraham Lincoln and of the Conspiracy of 1865.* Ed. Floyd E. Risvold. New York: Vintage Books, 1977.

West, Rebecca. *Black Lamb and Grey Falcon: A Journey through Yugoslavia.* New York: The Viking Press, 1943.

"Where Kidnapping is Business." *New York Times,* December 29, 1979, D1.

Wilkinson, Paul. "Still Working 'for the Extinction of Mankind': An Assessment of the Significance of the Resurgence of Fascist Terrorism in Europe." *Across the Board* 18, no. 1 (January 1981): 27-30.

Wilson, James Q. "Thinking about Terrorism." *Commentary* (July 1981).

Zoll, Donald Atwell. *Reason and Rebellion: An Informal History of Political Ideas.* Englewood Cliffs, N.J.: Prentice-Hall, 1963.

Index

About the Contributors

Robert A. Friedlander received his B.A. (1955), M.A. (1957), and Ph.D. (1963) from Northwestern University in the fields of European and American history. He obtained his J.D. from the De Paul University College of Law (1973). He is the author of fifty articles and review essays dealing with law and politics both domestic and international, in addition to a three-volume study of international terrorism, and co-editor of a volume on self-determination. He has written extensively in the fields of terrorism, human rights, and American foreign policy. He is a Life Member of Delta Tau Kappa (International Social Science Honor Society), a Life Fellow of the Institute for International Sociological Research (Cologne, West Germany), member of the Editorial Board, *TVI Journal*, member of the Advisory Board, *Denver Journal of International Law & Policy*, a Program Director of the Institute for International Analysis, Washington, D.C., and a former Assistant Project Director of the Chicago Council on Foreign Relations. He is currently Professor of Law, at the Ohio Northern University College of Law.

Phillip A. Karber is Vice President for National Security Programs at The BDM Corporation of McLean, Virginia. For the last twelve years, the focus of his professional activity has been in assessing the European military balance in both conventional and nuclear forces and examining its relationship to the U.S. strategic posture. Starting in 1974 he served for four years on loan to the Office of the Secretary of Defense as Director of National Security Study Memorandum 186, conducting a Net Assessment of NATO and Warsaw Pact trends in military capability.

Over the past two and one-half years he has made numerous visits to European countries for discussions on the current state of NATO's defenses at the request of either European or U.S. governments. His most recent trip in April 1979 was an invitation from the Netherlands to brief its Parliamentary Defense and Foreign Affairs committees on the European military balance.

He has testified before committees and subcommittees of the U.S. Congress on issues dealing with new weapons development, European security and the U.S.-Soviet comparative conventional military postures. Most recently, he testified before the Senate Foreign Relations Committee on SALT II.

He has authored numerous articles and contributed to seven books dealing with defense issues. He is a member of the U.S. Army Science board and the European American Arms Control Workshop.

Stacey M. Krinsky received her B.S. in Education from Buffalo State College (1976) and her M.B.A. in Management from Hofstra University (1981). She is currently a management consultant.

Joseph A. Malley is manager of Burns International Consulting Service. He has developed security and loss prevention programs for NASA's External Tank Assembly Facility, major U.S. corporations, and an independent oil company.

Previously, he was a manager of management consulting services for Peat, Marwick, Mitchell & Co., providing general management consulting services to governments, institutions, insurance companies, and various businesses.

Mr. Malley is a graduate of Dartmouth College and a senior member of the American Institute of Industrial Engineers. He is a Certified Management Consultant and a Certified Management Accountant.

R. William Mengel, President, EAI Corporation has been involved in research and lectured and written on the subject of terrorism for over fifteen years. He has directed and contributed to a number of programs that assessed the threat and consequences of terrorist acts to the U.S. government and businesses within the United States and abroad. Mr. Mengel has pioneered efforts in the evaluation of relative risk and attractiveness, deterrence, and behavioral factors related to terrorism.

Edward F. Mickolus received his Ph.D. in Political Science from Yale University, following his undergraduate work at Georgetown University. He is presently an analyst in the Office of Global Issues, U.S. Central Intelligence Agency. His articles have appeared in the *International Studies Quarterly, American Political Science Review, Journal of Irreproducible Results, Orbis*, and many other journals and books. He is the author of *Transnational Terrorism: A Chronology of Events, 1968-1979* and *The Literature of Terrorism: A Selectively Annotated Bibliography*.

Abraham H. Miller is Professor of Political Science at the University of Cincinnati. He is author of *Terrorism and Hostage Negotiations* (Boulder, Colo., Westview Press, 1980); editor of *Terrorism, the Media, and the Law* (Dobbs Ferry, N.Y., Transnational Publishers, 1982), and co-editor of *Black Power and Student Rebellion* (Belmont, Calif., Wadsworth Publishers, 1969). A specialist on political violence, his research on the black urban riots won the 1976 Pi Sigma Alpha Award of the Western Political Science Association. Dr. Miller has lectured both here and abroad on the subject of political terrorism. He has lectured to the Anglo-American Ditchley Foundation, Oxford, England; the International Red Cross, Geneva, Switzerland; and the Hebrew University, Jerusalem. His research has appeared in such scholarly journals as the *American Political Science Review*; the *Public Administration Review*; the *Western Political Quarterly*; *Ethnicity*; *Terrorism*; and *Politics and Society*, among others.

Professor Miller received his Ph.D. from the University of Michigan (1968) and has taught at the University of Illinois and the University of California, Davis. In 1976-1977, he was a Visiting Fellow with the National Institute of Justice where he did research on terrorism and hostage negotiations.

Patrick J. Montana has been associated with International Management Advisors, Inc., in New York since March 1980 after founding his own human resources consulting firm a few months earlier. For the past six years he served as President of the Professional Institute and the National Center for Career Life Planning of the American Management Associations. Previously he was Director of Planning and Manpower Development for the Sperry and Hutchinson Co., and he continues to serve as Professor of Management at Hofstra University's School of Business.

During 1973, he served as a Presidential Interchange Executive with the U.S. Department of Labor in Washington, D.C. He received the Secretary of Labor's award for "Outstanding Work in Executive Development and Pioneering Work in Executive Counseling." An expert in second career planning, Dr. Montana serves also as Corporate Consultant to *50 PLUS Magazine*, a publication of Whitney Communications Corporation.

He received a M.B.A. from the University of Cincinnati and earned his Ph.D. from the Graduate School of Business at N.Y.U. He is the author of eight books and numerous articles, and is listed in *Who's Who in America*.

Susanna W. Purnell is an associate researcher with the Rand Corporation. In addition to several classified case studies concerning diplomatic kidnappings, she is an author of the following Rand Corporation publications: *The Problems of U.S. Businesses Operating Abroad in Terrorist Environments*, *Long Range Developmental Planning in the Air Force*, *Review of Federal Programs to Alleviate Rural Deprivation*, and *The Connection Between Migration and Welfare Dependency in the Chicago Metropolitan Area*.

George S. Roukis received his Ph.D. degree in History and Russian Area Studies from New York University. He is an Associate Professor of Management and Industrial Relations at the Hofstra University School of Business and a professional labor arbitrator. He formerly served as U.S. Deputy Assistant Secretary of Labor (1973-1975) and presently serves as a neutral referee on the National Railroad Adjustment Board and numerous Public Law Boards in the railroad industry.

He has recently edited a comprehensive research study, entitled, "The Industrial Relations Regulatory Environment: Problems and Prospects" and published several articles on collective bargaining and industrial relations in the *Journal of Collective Negotiations in the Public Sector* and *Labor Law Journal*.

He has settled over 1,000 labor disputes and is a member of the National Academy of Arbitrators.

Charles A. Russell is an associate of Risks International, Alexandria, Virginia. Dr. Russell has lectured extensively on the subject of terrorism and appeared as an expert witness before Congressional Committees investigating terrorism. In collaboration with Mr. Bowman Miller of the Department of State he has written several articles including "Profile of a Terrorist," "Out Inventing the Terrorist," "Transnational Terrorism: Terrorist Tactics and Techniques," "The Evolution of Revolutionary Warfare: From Mao to Marighella and Meinhof," and "Terrorism and the Corporate Target."

Dr. Russell is a member of the Bar of the U.S. Court of Appeals and the U.S.

Court of Military Appeals and holds advanced degrees from Georgetown University (J.D.) and American University (Ph.D.).

Eleanor S. Wainstein is a staff member of the Rand Corporation in Washington, D.C. Her work in the field of terrorism includes the recent Rand Report *The Problems of Businesses Operating Abroad in Terrorist Environments*, various case studies of diplomatic kidnappings, and studies of potential nuclear-related targets. Ms. Wainstein has a B.A. degree from Mount Holyoke College and a M.A. from Stanford University.